Applied Linguistics and Language Study

General Editor: C. N. Candlin

Second Language Grammar: Learning and Teaching

William E. Rutherford

London and New York

Addison Wesley Longman Limited
Edinburgh Gate, Harlow,
Essex CM20 2JE, England
and Associated Companies throughout the world.

Published in the United States of America by
Longman Inc., New York

First published 1987
Sixth impression 1996

BRITISH LIBRARY CATALOGUING IN PUBLICATION DATA
Rutherford, William E.
  Second language grammar: learning and
  teaching. – (Applied linguistics and
  language study)
  1. English language – Grammar – Study and
  teaching 2. English language – Study and
  teaching – Foreign speakers
  I. Title   II. Series
  428.2′4   PE1112

LIBRARY OF CONGRESS CATALOGING IN PUBLICATION DATA
Rutherford, William E.
  Second language grammar.
  (Applied linguistics and language study)
  Bibliography: p.
  Includes index.
  1. Language and languages – Study and teaching.
  2. Grammar, Comparative and general – Study and teaching.
  3. English language – Grammar – Study and teaching.
  I. Title   II. Series
  P53.R87 1987   418′.007   86–18563

ISBN 0-582-55375-X

Set in 10/12pt Linotron 202 Erhardt
Produced by Longman Singapore Publishers (Pte) Ltd.
Printed in Singapore

Contents

30,79

92917

Preface

If we can define applied linguistics as a discipline which seeks to
explain how language can be acquired and used in the practices of
social life, this latest contribution to the *Applied Linguistics and
Language Study* series by William Rutherford ought to stand close to
the centre of our concerns. It does so, I believe, because it makes
a bold and controversial stand in an attempt to provide a governing
metaphor which will harmonize the various defining concerns of the
discipline: the concern with language data, the concern with the procedures governing their acquisition and use, the concern with the
conditions which give rise to and constrain the data we observe and
seek to explain. This metaphor is that of language as an organism,
a system in process, as it were, whose fuzzy edges present in their
apparent amorphousness a considerable challenge to those who would
see systematicity only describable in the static constructs of a struc-
turalist paradigm. What Dr Rutherford does in this book, therefore,
is more than provide a unifying perspective on interlanguage, learning
and pedagogy; he requires applied linguists to take a considered look
at the theoretical bases of their work. Especially, to ask those
concerned with language teaching and learning if they are able to
maintain that their approach to interlanguage data is in harmony with
what we know about the organizational principles of language and
what learners actually produce, whether their view of such data is
in accord with our understanding of how language is learned,
whether their pedagogical practices support or run counter to what
they hold to be the governing characteristics of acquisition. The
results of such an uncomfortable look, however explicable in terms
of research fashion or practical constraint, do not encourage. For all
manner of good reason, we see attempts to understand what the
author tellingly calls the 'movement' of language acquisition in terms
of static constructs; we see the enumeration of discrete target-
language forms as being synonymous with the accounting of learning;
we see syntactic data collected and tabulated outside and away from
the discoursal and social contexts of their production; we see too little

relationship being drawn between the acquisition of particular languages and the general organizing principles of human language. Pedagogically, the picture is even more bleak, though Dr Rutherford spares us too harrowing an account. Syntax seems either to have been forgotten in current curricula, obsessed with static definitions of so-called speech acts, or treated as a fundamentally uncommunicative sideshow to the games that teachers play, or worse, since more deceptively, packaged in problem-solving tasks whose focus is still the isolated forms of structuralism, insensitive to the organic and principled growth of grammatical capacity in the learner.

How then does this book offer a harmonious alternative? It does so, firstly, by arguing that the development of interlanguage syntax is constrained by three factors: general organizing principles common to all language, the selective and focusing influences of mother tongue and target language, and the exploratory processes of learners' cognition, themselves both general and individualistic in nature. If grammar acts as the bridge between concepts and context (in Widdowson's phrase) then the growing syntacticization of the learner's interlanguage is a tribute to his increasing enfranchisement from the bonds of context. Through grammar the learner can make words effective and become master of his own communicative environment. Seeing grammar thus as a social device compels an inter-dependence of form and function; grammar is to be understood in relation to semantics and pragmatics, firmly set in the contexts of language use. The developmental characteristics of grammar implicit in such a view not only suggest parallels between the ontologies of first and second languages but, crucially, provide the motivation for linking the growth of grammar to the cognitive processes and learning activities of the learner. Through an understanding of hypothesis formation and testing, we can explain how interlanguage syntax takes the forms and courses that it does, how learners gradually determine boundaries and form rules, how they tolerate fuzziness and apparent irregularity and how they make use of packaged routines in advance, as it were, of their capacities to analyse them into constituent units. Grammar, in this definition then, does not only offer a way of under-standing semantic relationships or the demands of discourse, it also offers insights into the charting of the processes of language learning. Gradual and variable grammaticization is a datum for understanding learner differentiation. Note, however, that this depends on our focus being not on the accumulation of entities (in Dr Rutherford's phrase) but on the exploration of processes, of how the learner adapts his language to the specific conditions and contexts of learning, constrained in this by particular typological pressures and the quality of the input and his interaction with it.

There is, however, a second dimension to the alternative perspective of this volume, one entirely consistent with the view of grammar in respect of language and acquisition outlined above. This is the status of the book as a contribution to pedagogic grammar. Here we need to make an immediate disclaimer, one echoed by Dr Rutherford in his Foreword. This volume is not an array of techniques for packaging grammar for some pedagogic programme. It is not a set of exercises or a bank of tasks. What it does is to offer a principled way for treating the teaching and learning of second language grammar, with profound implications for the design of curricula and the organizing of classroom procedures.

At the centre of these implications is the concept of *consciousness-raising* (C-R) and its place in pedagogy. Specifically, the role of C-R in relation to the central place accorded to grammar in the curriculum. The concept itself is entirely in harmony with central principles of a communicatively-oriented curriculum: it presupposes drawing upon the contributions of the learner and it explicitly advocates the refinement of the learner's metacommunicative and metacognitive awareness. It accords to the teacher principles for both the selection and the presentation of data, all of which harmonize, as we say, with established communicative practice. Where it principally differs is in its object of focus. Its concern is with developing the learner's powers of judgement and discrimination in respect of the semantic and discoursal demands on the grammatical structures of the target language, emphasizing in this reflective mode how well the learner understands the relationships between form and meaning. In productive mode its concern is with enabling learners to adjust their grammar to reflect the location of their utterances in discourse, to extend their grammatical means for expounding particular logical and semantic relationships, and gradually to convert their prefabricated routines into analysed language.

What is striking about the final part (Part Five) of this book is how well it reflects current pedagogic concern for learner-centredness and the centrality of learner-training in the curriculum. Grammar is not only seen as central to language but interpreted as grammaticization is implicative of learning. It will be for the readership to determine the extent to which the case is made: revise the concept of grammar and it occupies its central place in the language curriculum, not discrepant but in harmony with educational and personal aspirations. What cannot be denied is the way in which the author has put his concept of interdependence into effect, not least in the constant connections drawn between theory and practice in this classic contribution to *Applied Linguistics and Language Study.*

Christopher N. Candlin
General Editor

Lancaster
May 1986

Foreword

One should assume that the title of this book, as I suppose with most books, is an indication of what the book is about. For the intended readership then, this could suggest ways in which one might perceive the grammatical organization of the non-native language to be learned and the learner's own interim grammar of such a language, ways in which one might reason that the learner unconsciously goes about the task of learning these things, and ways in which that task may be pedagogically facilitated. In a work of this sort, however, mention of the words 'grammar' and 'pedagogical' often gives rise to other kinds of expectation on the part of the reader. Perhaps not out of place then would be a word or two concerning what this book is *not* about.

Second Language Grammar, although largely devoted to a look at the learning of English grammar from an adult-learner viewpoint, is not a pedagogical treatise on how to form grammatical constructions in English. Nor is the book to be considered a manual of instruction on how one goes about the actual teaching of grammar. One will also not find here a book-length effort to justify the pedagogical attention to language form, though some discussion of this issue has been woven in. What I have attempted to do, rather, is to sketch out some general principles; perspectives on the nature of grammar, of learning, and of teaching that represent something of a departure from what has traditionally been referred to as 'pedagogical grammar' – perspectives that derive to a large extent from the results of more recent research in these three disciplines. To all this has been added a pinch of metaphysics and several dashes of speculation. I can only hope that at least some of the pleasures of writing such a book may rub off in the reading of it.

I have, of course, benefited a great deal in this endeavour from the work of my colleagues around the world, many of whose names are to be found in the list of references at the back of the book. For their extended discussion of various portions of the manuscript, I should like particularly to thank Larry Selinker, Jacquelyn Schachter,

Stephen Krashen, and Suzanne Flynn — and for other valuable commentary, Lydia White, Mike Sharwood Smith, Manfred Tienemann and Edward Finegan, none of whom are to be blamed for what I have done (or sometimes not done) with their contributions. A special debt of gratitude is owed to the general editor of this series, Christopher Candlin, who extended the original invitation to write this work for Longman and whose many insightful commentaries and exemplary patience with my various delays have helped to ensure that a necessarily complex task turned out nevertheless to be an eminently rewarding and enjoyable one.

William Rutherford

Professor of Linguistics
University of Southern California
1986

Part One
On language, learning, and consciousness

I do not believe in things; I believe only in their relationship.

Georges Braque

When we try to pick out anything by itself, we find it hitched to
everything else in the universe.

John Muir

The learning and the teaching of someone else's mother tongue are
endeavours that have been carried on, in some recognizable form,
probably for as long as humans have been able to take note of and
record such activity. We may catch glimpses of it through the literature of the ages from the *De grammatica* of St Augustine to the antics
of Hyman Kaplan, from the obstinacy of Shakespeare's Caliban to
the ingenuousness of *My Fair Lady*. In more recent generations, and
coincident with the spread of middle-class mass education, we have
seen language-learning/teaching activities coalesce into particular
methods and approaches. And of course by only a few decades ago
modern foreign-language teaching had finally emerged as a full-blown
academic profession, with its own rapidly proliferating professional
societies, tenured faculty, serious research, academic journals, and
contending theories. The present book then is a product, at one and
the same time, of modern language theory and of the centuries-long
tradition of language pedagogy.

Although discussion about the teaching of languages has been
going on for centuries, perhaps even millennia, only relatively recently
on this vast time scale have we given any serious thought at all to the
question of how languages are learned. What has now made it
reasonable for us even to ask this question has a lot to do with
modern developments in a number of different fields of research –
to some degree, communication theory, education, and sociology – but
above all in linguistics and psychology, and their amalgamation:
psycholinguistics. To the extent that the 'how' and 'why' questions
of language learning lead us to probe the nature of the structure and

functions of the human brain, psycholinguistics can be considered one of the cognitive sciences. Current linguistic theory in fact takes language itself to be one of the 'windows', so to speak, into the workings of the mind.

Speculation on the use of language as one of the clues about how the mind works may at first seem a bit removed from the business of teaching languages. After all, aren't there already enough classroom factors to contend with that we can actually observe (e.g. differences in age, maturation, proficiency, motivation, intelligence, aptitude, native language, etc.) without having to worry as well about something as arcane as mental processes? The answer to this of course is that what happens inside one's head, as concepts are formed and transmitted in what we know as language, is an absolutely crucial concern for any educational discipline that takes the nature of language itself as its point of departure. And language teaching is such a discipline. The sort of cognitive change that language teaching is intended to bring about – namely, the learning of a language – is one that is ultimately explainable only by recourse to the kinds of theoretical abstraction that are needed for research in general into how the mind actually works.

Learning and teaching, then, are inextricably bound together – on the face of it, certainly not a particularly startling observation. If nothing else, the learning/teaching symbiosis would seem to indicate that for anything having to do with language, the 'teachability' of that phenomenon would depend crucially upon its 'learnability'. Yet we may have legitimate cause to wonder how much of what passes today for 'formal' language instruction is an actual realization of this learning/teaching relationship. How much of what is taught as second-language 'grammar', for example, represents a choice determined rather by what we think can be linguistically analysed as a piece of target-language structure than by what it is possible in the classroom to learn or assimilate of such structure? How often, for that matter, does what we know of the very organization of language itself lead us to question the often different language-organization assumptions that underlie the treatment of grammar in language pedagogy? The implication here of course is that in actual practice the language-learning/teaching relationship – at least with respect to second-language grammar – is a far from perfect one. For a glimpse at some of the aspects of this imperfection, we will turn our attention to theoretical findings in a discipline closely allied with psycholinguistics and one of our newest fields of research: second-language acquisition.

1 The learning of grammar

It is natural that in language-learning research we should not lose sight of the learner's goal in the task at hand – namely, the mastery of the target language. It is an objective that has remained fairly constant throughout the many centuries of documented language teaching (see Kelly 1969), notwithstanding the varied utilization of that mastery (from, for example, rhetorical prowess in the Middle Ages to travel abroad in the present). In addition to the goal of language learning, however, other fundamental questions have also begun to interest language-learning researchers. One of these is the matter of description – namely, of the path that the learner traverses in attempting to reach that goal. Others are matters of explanation, e.g. the question of to what extent the biological endowment for language acquisition that shaped the development of our languages in child-hood also plays a role in language acquisition during adulthood. Still another question of crucial concern would be the lack of full success characterizing the overwhelming number of second-language learning experiences. We will begin our discussion through attention to how language acquisition has often been viewed in the recent past.

1 A conventional view of language acquisition

The progress that the second-language learner makes can be considered from a number of different perspectives. The kind of progress that is perhaps most familiar to language-teaching professionals is the kind that can be measured by means of some sort of test, the most common example being one that tests, usually in discrete-point fashion, the learner's 'knowledge' of certain target-language structures. Structural knowledge that can be measured in this way played an important role in the early days of second-language acquisition research – research whose findings purported to demon-strate that mastery of English morphemes like past tense *-ed*, plural *-(e)s*, progressive *-ing*, tense-carrier *do*, etc., occurred not only in a relatively fixed order but also in an order that held constant for the

L2 learning of both adults and children.[1] Mastery was assumed to have occurred when learners produced the morphemes in 'obligatory' formal contexts about 85 per cent of the time. The focus of interest upon language production at the morphemic level and the belief that 'mastery' of language form could be measured quantitatively and cited as percentages went hand in hand, as it were. And statistical procedures that had served the evaluation task in discrete-point testing of classroom learning sufficed just as well for tabulation of language items for research purposes. Implicit in this kind of research, then, is a view of language learning wherein learner progress is tantamount to an increasing accumulation of language constructs that have been 'mastered'.

For the sake of convenience, we might call the view of language learning just sketched out one of 'accumulated entities'. That is, a person begins his task of learning a second language from point zero and, through the steady accumulation of the mastered entities of the target language (e.g. sounds, morphemes, vocabulary, grammatical constructions, discourse units, etc.), eventually amasses them in quantities sufficient to constitute a particular level of proficiency. That this view is fairly widely held among language-teaching professionals is substantiated by the bulk of available commercially produced foreign-language textbooks. Characteristic of the overwhelming majority of these products is the discovery of a target language whose structure has been analysed into its putative constituent parts, the separate parts thus serving as units of pedagogical content, focus, practice, and eventual mastery. The 'parts', it is important to remember, are not necessarily only units of grammatical structure, but 'functions' and 'notions' as well.[2]

This characterization of language pedagogy is meant to apply of course to those aspects of it in which learner attention is drawn to features of the target language itself. That which is drawn attention to, however, and the manner in which the attention-drawing is accomplished are usually mute testimony to a belief among language-teaching professionals – whether stated or not – as to how language is organized and how the learning of that organization proceeds. Language learning then, so the conventional view would have it, entails the successive mastery of steadily accumulating structural entities, and language teaching brings the entities to the learner's attention. (We must assume that all teaching attempts at the very least to expose the learner to structural features of the target language, whether or not conscious attention is drawn to them.) If this brief description of one aspect of language learning is valid, then the relationship here between (perceived) learning and teaching is a close one. We must in fact question, however, whether language learning thus described has this validity.

2 The problem with 'accumulated entities'

The conception of increasing language proficiency as a development reflected in the steady accumulation of more and more complex language entities is a difficult one to maintain once one looks a little more closely at what language learners actually do in the course of their learning. We might begin this kind of scrutiny here by asking the following question: if language knowledge develops primarily in terms of accumulated structural entities, then what kinds of learner production would we expect to see along the way?

For one thing, we would expect that well-formed target-language structures would, one after another, emerge 'full blown', so to speak, on the learner's path towards eventual mastery of the language. To take one example, a relative clause like *who smoke* (as in *There are many people* **who smoke**) would appear as such at some point in the learner's development and be added to his 'repertoire' of already existing structures. And if the learner went on to master the language, we could in principle tabulate the expansion of his repertoire up to the point where all of the well-formed structures of the target language had been accounted for.

We would also expect that two structures fulfilling similar semantic roles would, for learning purposes, be in 'competition' with each other, as it were. But since in the early stages the learner doesn't really need two forms for the same semantic role, the more 'complex' of these two structures would temporarily be 'avoided' and the less complex of the two would serve the semantic function of both. After more learning had occurred, the more complex (avoided) structure would finally emerge to take its rightful place in the learner's pantheon of already mastered entities. Two such structures might, for example, be relative clause (people *who smoke*) and noun complement (the need *to smoke*), both of which serve in a general sense as modifiers of their head nouns (namely, *people* and *need*). Since some learners produce, along with *the need to smoke*, also *people to smoke* (meaning, presumably, 'people who smoke'), it would appear that for purposes of noun-phrase modification they are letting the 'less complex' noun complement construction temporarily 'stand in' for the 'more complex' relative clause. Two otherwise semantically equivalent structures have thus 'vied' for supremacy at one point in the learner's developing grammar, and the easier of the two would appear for the moment to have 'won out', or so the reasoning would go.

If language knowledge develops structure by structure, learner production would meet still another expectation for us. We would look for emerging full-blown structures to carry the range of semantic interpretation known to obtain for such structures in native-speaker competence. For instance, at the point when the English 'present perfect' verb construction appeared, we would expect to see, in addition to its core meaning of 'present relevance of a prior event', the peripheral senses of 'result/state' (The government *has changed* hands), 'recentness' (The government *has* just *fallen*), 'persistent situation' (The government *has been* about to fall for three years), and 'experiential' (The government *has* never *changed* hands).[3] Language structures, in other words, do not exist independent of the 'meanings' they are meant to carry. When well-formed grammatical constructions surface in learner language, we should therefore expect that the same array of meanings is in principle attributable to the forms in question – again, so the reasoning would have it.

Finally, a structure-by-structure concept of language-learning progress would presuppose final mastery of a given target structure once it had surfaced 'error-free' in learner language – with no subsequent fluctuation in well-formedness through 'reanalysis' and reworking with other features of the target language.[4] It would also presuppose that what amounts to only partial attainment of target-language criteria for the overwhelming majority of L2 learners[5] can be assessed in terms of a finite quantity of still 'missing' (i.e. unlearned) items.

We said a short while ago that progress in second-language learning can be considered from several different perspectives and we have just explored some of the dimensions of one such perspective – namely, the concept of language learning that entails the successive mastery of steadily accumulating and increasingly complex language entities, or learning by a kind of formal 'agglutination'.[6] In the remainder of this chapter we will outline an alternative perspective for looking at how some of the formal properties of language are learned and we will accomplish this through consideration, as we said earlier, of what we think learners actually do in the course of their learning. The chapter will conclude with a brief discussion of the relationship between these observations and the concept of universals of language and of language acquisition.

3 What language learners do

What kinds of language then *do* language learners produce? What can we observe about the various routes that they traverse from ignorance of the target language to outcomes ranging from partial knowledge of the target language to near mastery of it? What kind of influence does the mother tongue exert? What characteristics of the learning process apply to *all* learners, irrespective of mother tongue? What does learner language – or, to adopt the more general term, **interlanguage**[7] – reveal at any time about the extent of the learner's linguistic competence?

In beginning to address these questions, consider first the general nature of the language learner's task. He is about to gain entry into a new, unfamiliar, perhaps even forbidding cognitive system – that is, the target language. It is a system that invariably will differ from the one he already knows (i.e. his mother tongue) in ways that are perhaps striking and often even quite spectacular. These differences are such that he will constantly confront the need to express familiar or routine thoughts by means of an initially alien code and, in turn, to interpret and understand that same code used to express the (unpredictable) thoughts of the person with whom he is trying to communicate. Given the fact that 'code' is a deceptively facile term for an unfathomably complex labyrinth of intertwining, overlaying, and convoluted phonological, syntactic, semantic, and pragmatic relationships, we may well wonder how the learner of another language manages to make any headway at all. How does he begin to make use, even in the most rudimentary sense, of new language machinery whose very abstruseness defies even the most advanced computerization? It is probably safe to say that if the learner had successfully to negotiate the entire linguistic labyrinth before starting to function in his new language, then indeed no headway *would* be made.

Very little would be accomplished either, notwithstanding the inevitable differences between native and target language, if the beginning learner had nothing to build his new language upon or nothing to fall back on, so to speak. In other words, the learner does not embark upon his second-language learning experience as a *tabula rasa* or in total ignorance of everything concerning language and what we use it for. What he does bring to this initial language-learning task is a kind of prior knowledge of two different sorts. One sort we might describe as 'knowledge that' – an unconscious 'foreknowledge' or innate 'inkling' of what shapes the organization of the target language can assume – and the capacity, given a little start in the new language, to make good guesses about what he *doesn't* know. The other sort we will call 'knowledge how' – the ability temporarily to bend the new language into forms that will, with maximal efficiency, serve the initial desire for rudimentary communication, an ability that the learner retains from the similar experience of having acquired his mother tongue.[8] Both of these cognitive capacities are crucial, for without them no language learning would be possible at all. Thus, the task of learning another language may be a formidable one, but what the learner already 'knows' about language in general, and also about how to use a language for any of its various social and cognitive functions, renders it an eminently *possible* one.

Everyone who has acquired a native language, then, unconsciously 'knows' something about how to acquire any other language. That being so, we might therefore expect that this prior 'knowledge' will manifest itself in some way through what the learner attempts to produce (i.e. say and write) in his new language at the earliest stages of learning. That is, we should not be surprised to find early on in learner production evidence of regularity suggesting that certain general 'processes' are at work. What then can we actually glimpse of this production that might plausibly be attributable to these language-learning processes – processes that transcend their particular manifestations in individual learner languages?

There is one pervasive characteristic of early interlanguage that is designed perhaps to render the target language optimally learnable. It is the tendency to let the relationship between form and meaning be as direct as possible. This tendency translates to learner production wherein, contrary to normal language expression, *all* meaning finds direct and unambiguous grammatical realization. The immediate reflexes of this in the production itself are that

1. the target-language syntax is made to serve a need for keeping pieces of propositional content separate from each other to whatever extent possible;
2. elements that bear a close semantic/syntactic relationship to each other occur adjacent to each other;
3. structural redundancy persists.

All of this is the result, one might say, of efforts on the part of the learner to make the links between syntax and semantics as tight as possible. And this 'effort' is in reality, of course, nothing more than the simple consequence of the learner's need to make early communication in the new language intelligible to him, and perhaps to mould the target language into a form that is amenable to some kind of rudimentary parsing (see Chapter 9.6). It would be useful at this point to cite a few examples of these grammatical reflexes of the learner's natural early tendencies to create and maintain a tight 'fit' between syntax and semantics in the language he or she is learning.

One of the most common activities in a foreign-language class is that wherein the learners are asked to write a 'composition' on a familiar topic. Let us suppose, for example, that the language being learned is English, that the learners are adults with a variety of mother tongues, and that they have not yet progressed very far. The assigned topic for a written paragraph is, let's say, 'My Home Town'. A not untypical sample of a 'paragraph' produced in such a setting might go like this:

> [1]My home town Lamgur. [2]Have not much people. [3]Some people they was very rich people to have big house. [4]Always we notice expensive car which they have it in garage. [5]Maybe soon Lamgur have better condition for people and people of Lamgur too poor. [6]I hope so.

Putting aside the matter of problems in subject-verb agreement, article usage, choice of vocabulary, organization, etc., let us consider the question of semantic-syntactic relationship. Notice first that there is a fairly direct syntactic representation for semantic elements that are closely related. In sentence 4, for example, where *have* and *car* 'go together', we find the relative pronoun *it* holding the semantic place of *car* in the relative clause from which *car* has been (in target-language parlance) 'extracted' (see Chapter 9.4.1).

Notice further that the learner has a tendency to maintain a kind of separation between bits of propositional content. Thus, in sentence 4 *always* occurs outside the clause rather than inside – likewise *soon* in sentence 5; and again in sentence 5 *maybe* in clause-external position is the equivalent in early interlanguage of the clause-internal modal *may* in native English. In sentence 5 there is still another instance of propositional separation – namely, the use of conjoined sentences rather than an 'integration' of the second into the first by means of subordination (e.g. with a relative clause like *who are too poor*).

Notice too the places where redundancy is eliminated – and also where it is built in. That the subject of *have* in sentence 2 (interpreted as the adjacent *Lamgur*) is 'missing', for example, does not render the sentence any harder to understand and shortens it by one word. In sentence 4, however, whereas the structure of native English *requires* a 'missing' object of *have* (from which position it would have been extracted in the making of the relative clause), this learner chooses to *put* something in object position (namely, the pronoun *it*), so as to render the sentence·easier to understand. It is easier, or clearer, by virtue of the fact that the close verb-object (*have-car*) semantic relationship is reflected in a syntax wherein (a) both verb (*have*) and object (*car/it*) receive surface realizations; and (b) the realizations occur adjacent to one another.

In discussing the characteristics of the 'My Home Town' passage it is well to remind ourselves that our sample is a picture of learner competence that is 'frozen' in time, as it were. Detection of other kinds of things that learners do – for example, the progressive **reanalysis** of grammatical phenomena – requires that we observe the development of individual learners over *elapsed* time. Characteristics of language-learner development that emerge with the passage of time will be touched on in later chapters.

The illustration of interlanguage to which we have had recourse is an approximation of native English. As it turns out, the choice of English here as the target vehicle for semantic/syntactic alignment is one that is quite apt, for some researchers (see, for example, Hawkins 1985) believe that English allows a looser linear relationship between meaning and grammatical form than do most other languages. Thus, the learning of English by speakers of mother tongues with organizational principles that are fundamentally different in these respects affords us the valuable opportunity to observe how one aspect of language learning develops – namely, the relationship of form to meaning.

4 Language universals

Learner attempts to bend the target-language forms to the more direct service of intended meaning are an example of one of the two kinds of knowledge the learner brings to the task of acquiring a second language – 'knowledge how', as we said earlier. Since all learners manifest such a need for ongoing, although temporary, target-language adjustment, we can properly assign the term 'universal' to this aspect of learner language. What we are witnessing, then, with these form-to-meaning relationships is an example of 'universal **processes**' at work in language learning.

We have also called attention, however, to the learner's prior 'knowledge that' the language he is learning possesses certain properties – that is, properties that all languages share and that the learner therefore 'knows' simply by virtue of the fact that he has the language capacity of a human being. What kinds of property, then, are we talking about?

Consider again the sort of language typified in the earlier learner-produced sample called 'My Home Town'. By any current standards of correctness, the kind of English displayed in that passage would be deemed far from acceptable. What we have in the passage is of course an example of early learner-language – language that is full of those inevitable characteristics that we customarily identify as 'errors'. And they are errors of many different kinds, as we have already seen. It is important to note, however, that although the characteristics that we called attention to are errors in English, they wouldn't necessarily be errors in many of the thousands of other languages in the world. For example, the equivalent of the missing *is* in *My home town Lamgur* would not be required in Vietnamese; the 'double subject', as it were, in *Some people they . . .* is common in Chinese; the missing subject in *Have not much people* is a feature of Spanish or Italian; the superfluous *it* in *. . . expensive car which they have it in garage* would be required in Arabic. We could cite many, many more such examples. The point we wish to emphasize here, however, is that the kinds of error we have been talking about are errors with respect to the grammatical system of one language – English. They are instances where what has been violated is a grammatical rule that applies to one language but not by any means to all languages. Grammatical violations of this kind we will call **language-specific**.

What kind of phenomenon would constitute a grammatical violation in *any* language? Or, to turn this around, what grammatical principles apply without exception to *all* languages? Reflect for a moment on how we go about forming a simple yes-no question – something like *Is the boy apt to stay?* It is very helpful to think of such a question as 'derived' in some sense from its corresponding declarative sentence, *The boy is apt to stay.* Essentially, all we have done then, in order to form the interrogative from the declarative, is move the word *is* to the front of the sentence. Now, obviously, not all sentences contain the word *is*, so for another sentence it would of course be some other verb form that we move to the front. How might one describe the operation we have just performed in the most general terms? Since sentences can certainly contain more than one verb, perhaps one would want to say that to change declaratives to interrogatives you take the first verb in the sentence and move it to the front. So far so good.

Let us test this general rule on a modified version of our original sentence. Since we've already acknowledged that sentences can contain more than one verb, we'll adopt a version of our example that also adds a few more words, including another verb. We'll say something like *The boy that's the nuisance is apt to stay*, where we now have two occurrences of *is*. If we apply our general rule, we take the first verb in the sentence and move it to the front. Since there are now two verbs in the sentence (both of them *is*), we move the first *is* to the front, yielding the question *Is the boy that the nuisance is apt to stay?* But this of course produces nonsense. The correct formation of the interrogative from our longer declarative requires that we move to the front of the sentence not the first *is* but the second, giving us *Is the boy that's the nuisance apt to stay?*

What, then, is wrong with our 'general rule'? Maybe it should specify that we move the *last* verb to the front. Although the rule restated in this way would derive the correct interrogatives for the two samples given so far, notice that all we have to do to invalidate our revised rule is devise a declarative sentence with even more verbs in it – say, *The boy that's the nuisance is apt to stay if he's allowed to*. The simple test of forming the interrogative by moving the last *is* to the front will again produce gibberish, as anyone can readily see. And of course in this instance it is the second *is* that must be moved in order to form the question correctly.

If we've had to reject all of the explanations offered so far for yes-no question formation, what is the correct generalization for this? It isn't hard to see that the verb element (i.e. *is*) to be moved forward in each case is the verb in what we would call the main clause, not the verb in the relative clause (*that's the nuisance*) or the verb in the *if* clause (*if he's allowed to*). The correct generalization is therefore one that makes reference not to the sequence or the number of verbs in the sentence (i.e. first, second, last, etc.), but to the **structure** in which the verb appears. The structure that we've needed to refer to for the formation of yes-no questions in all three of the previous examples is the **main clause**.

The point of this extended exercise is to demonstrate that rules of language cannot be stated independently of the structure of whatever the rule is intended to apply to. In other words, language rules are **structure dependent**. Although we have provided examples of this in English, it is important to realize that the principle applies to all other languages as well. There is no language known to us, for instance, that forms questions in the arbitrary way that we attempted earlier, nor would we ever expect to find such a language. What we have revealed here then is a principle – namely, **structure dependency** – that is valid for the grammatical rules of any human language that one might encounter. A principle of this kind we can therefore properly call **language universal**.

There are a number of other language-universal principles that we could have mentioned here as well – principles, like structure-dependency, that serve to place limits on the almost infinite arbitrary ways in which language might be conceived[9] (see Chapter 10). These constraints are absolutely necessary to the very existence of human language itself, for without them language variation would be limitless, and grammatical operations would be far beyond the capacity of the human mind to compute for learning purposes.

Universal principles apply without exception to human language as a whole. There is compelling evidence[10] that such principles cannot ever have been 'learned' by human-language users, that the principles must instead be 'innate' or part of the genetic endowment of humans for the fundamental activity of acquiring language. It follows, then, that universal principles are never 'violated' by the language learner, whether it is the mother tongue or some other language that is being learned. That is, the language learner may make all kinds of errors in the course of learning, but we will never find him violating, for example, the principle of structure-dependency by producing in any language the kinds of ungrammatical yes-no questions discussed previously. Ironically, such violations occur only when we exemplify them in a book like this!

We have already drawn a distinction between two kinds of knowledge that the language learner comes endowed with – 'knowledge how' and 'knowledge that' – and we have identified 'knowledge how' as the learner's ability to adapt the new language to his specific learning conditions, or to exploit his knowledge of language-universal **processes**. It is obvious, then, that the learner's innate knowledge of language-universal **principles** is what we mean by 'knowledge that'. Earlier we raised the question of what traces these two kinds of 'universal' leave upon the form of interlanguage itself, and we cited examples of universal processes at work with regard to the 'My Home Town' paragraph. What examples do we have in interlanguage of universal principles at work? The only kind of example there could really be is the endless, exceptionless *application* of these principles in whatever language product we choose to examine. In other words, any learner-language product is an example of universal principles in operation simply by virtue of that product's being intelligible language. Thus, existence of the two kinds of knowledge we have been discussing is supported by two kinds of evidence. Evidence that the learner 'knows *how*' the language being learned can be brought into the service of communication – evidence that universal processes are in play – comes in the form of grammatical-rule violations that are specific to that language. Evidence that the learner 'knows *that*' the language being learned is a possible human language – evidence that universal principles are in force – comes with the *absence* of violation of any grammatical precepts that can be generalized to apply to all languages. These two kinds of (unconscious) 'knowledge' are the essence of what the learner himself automatically contributes to the task of learning a language. But it is only when the learner, always possessed of this knowledge, is exposed to intelligible data from the new language that the language learning actually takes place – an interaction of the universal with the specific, so to speak. In the next chapter we will consider the possible relationship between such knowledge and the matter of grammatical consciousness-raising in language pedagogy.

Activities

1. It has been noted that the appearance in English interlanguage of phrases like *people to smoke*, meaning probably 'people who smoke', are possible candidates for misanalysis by language researchers, since from the perspective of target English they look like noun-complement constructions. What other interlanguage data that you have encountered in the course of your experience might also be prone to this kind of misanalysis?

2. Select some writing produced by a second-language learner of low proficiency and note whether it manifests any of the characteristics observed in connection with the 'My Home Town' example on page 9. Where the characteristics differ, what factors might be contributing?

3. We noted that language obeys a principle of **structure dependency** whereby grammatical rules have to be stated in terms of syntactic categories (e.g. main clause), and not, for example, in terms of numerical sequence or random appearance. What then of pairs of sentences where the negative *not* seems to attach equally well to more than one verb, e.g. *I think he doesn't know the answer/I don't think he knows the answer*. Would this be an exception to the structure-dependency principle? Why not?

Notes

1. See, for example, Dulay and Burt (1974), Bailey, Madden and Krashen (1974).
2. Wilkins (1984, p. 81) offers a similar observation: 'The types of syllabus that we have discussed so far are all concerned with specifying and arranging the "things" to be learned. Inevitably the items to be learned will occur in a linear sequence and it must be supposed that these approaches are based on a theory of learning which holds that material to be learned can be mastered or accumulated piece-by-piece.'

    Lightbown (1985) also criticizes this view of language learning – her term for the items is 'grammatical building blocks'.
3. See Comrie (1976), Flynn (1985). See also Slobin (1983) for similar observations with regard to tense/aspect development in child L1 and language history.
4. See Kellerman (1985) and Bialystok (1982).
5. See Davies (1984) for a useful discussion of the 'partial outcome' phenomenon. See also Rutherford (1986).
6. The notion of structural entities accumulating in the learner's mind is not unlike the observation of Slobin's (1979, p. 65) that,

    in the domain of mental experience, we seem to think of the mind as a container filled with ideas and emotions as objects – objects which themselves can have physical characteristics: *filled with grief, full of ideas, grasp an idea, a thorny problem, a hairy theory*. Abstract ideas can also be treated as objects of manipulation: *the plan slipped through my fingers; she held onto that hope*. Or mental contents themselves become animate subjects: *That idea really grabs me*.
7. The term 'interlanguage' is the contribution of Selinker (1972).
8. The distinction between 'knowledge that' and 'knowledge how' comes from Ryle (1949). It is similar, I believe, to what Widdowson (1983) calls 'competence' and 'capacity'.
9. For a readable discussion of language universals that presupposes a minimum of background knowledge, see Comrie (1981).
10. For a useful summary of this, see Chomsky (1975).

2 Consciousness-raising

There is general consensus among learning theorists, educational psychologists, and language-teaching professionals that the learning of *anything* does not occur in a vacuum. That is, successful learning of whatever kind comes about only when what is to be learned can be meaningfully related to something that is already known. Learning, in other words, must take place within some kind of familiar context or framework – an extension of the familiar to the *un*familiar, if you will.[1] The natural question to raise, then, is what such 'frameworks' – and ones familiar to the learner – we might identify for the learning of second-language grammar. If we interpret 'familiar to the learner' in the broadest possible sense, then certainly we must include here what every language learner knows unconsciously – namely, the language universals that we just finished discussing: universal principles and universal processes. The most general learning framework we can conceive of then – indeed, the set of absolute prerequisites for language learning to take place at all – is one in which these universals, or the learner's unconscious knowledge *that* and knowledge *how*, come into contact with the mass of data constituting the language to be learned.

1 Grammatical consciousness-raising

In what way, we are entitled to ask, would grammatical consciousness-raising (C-R) fit into this roughly drawn, very general picture of language learning? Satisfactory answers to a question like this really require that we first narrow the scope of inquiry a bit by asking exactly what it is that grammatical C-R is expected to accomplish. The unstated assumption of many language-teaching professionals, past and present, has long been that an essential part of language teaching is 'the teaching of grammar' (included in what we here refer to in more general terms as 'grammatical consciousness-raising'). A look at what has been written over the years on the subject tells us that this assumption usually has two parts to it:

1. a belief that language is built up out of sets of discrete entities and that language learning consists of the steady accumulation of such entities by the learner, as we discussed in Chapter 1;
2. a belief that the essential characteristics of the entities (e.g. the 'rules' for their formation) can be directly imparted to the learner through teaching.

Grammar teaching then, for those who hold these beliefs, is looked upon as a sort of conduit for direct passage to the learner's competence of discrete formal entities (and the simplified 'rules' that make these up) in the language he is trying to learn.

The fundamental problem with all this should by now be becoming familiar. The above *belief 1*, with all that we have come to know about language and language learning, simply does not hold up. And with the invalidity of *belief 1*, *belief 2* must collapse as well. If even more proof is needed, a little further reflection upon the real meaning of *belief 2* alone ought to reveal one other essential defect: if, for even as well analysed a language as English, the most brilliant linguists can as yet come nowhere near knowing fully what constitute the proper generalizations and the correct formulations of the rules of English syntax, then how can anything of this sort, in whatever 'simplified' form, be profitably 'taught' by any teacher or 'learned' by any learner? An attempt at grammatical C-R of this kind in pedagogy is at best inconsistent with everything that we think we do know about how language is organized, how it develops, and how it is learned. What kind of grammatical C-R *can* we properly conceive of then?

1.1 *C-R as an aid to learning*

First of all, it would be well for us to divest ourselves of the notion, not altogether uncommon, that the shortcomings of any grammar-teaching approach we might care to identify can be attributed to the deficiencies of whatever particular theoretical description happened to be 'borrowed' for the occasion. Theories of grammar, though highly important to language pedagogy for other reasons, are not theories of language acquisition, and it is acquisition, after all, that grammatical C-R must be made to serve. Once we become accustomed to seeing grammatical theory in this light, then light is shed as well on the sensible role of grammatical C-R in pedagogy. The objects of grammatical focus and attention are there, as one well-known researcher, S. P. Corder, has put it, 'to help the learner learn whatever it is he learns, but are not necessarily *what* he learns. Pedagogical descriptions are *aids* to learning not the *object* of learning; so long as we keep that firmly in our minds we shall not get confused by the ambiguity of the expression "teaching grammar" . . .' (Corder 1973, p. 331).

The proper function as well as the importance of grammatical C-R thus starts to assume more clarity. Considered as a *facilitator* of language learning, or as the means rather than the end, grammatical C-R is seen to have a number of different roles to play and several different 'modes' of operation. The roles we may speak of can, and should, be conceived as instantiations of the 'familiar-to-unfamiliar' learning progression cited earlier. The modes of operation have to do with the means for attention-getting and degree of explicitness.

1.2 C-R roles and universal principles

What of these 'roles' then? There is at least one characteristic that is common to every *successful* language-learning experience we have ever known, and that is that the learner is exposed one way or another to an adequate amount of the data of the language to be learned.[2] This is obviously the *sine qua non* for learning a language, whether it is one's own mother tongue or someone else's. Yet the circumstances in which we learn a new language are often limited to the extent that, contrary to the experience of acquiring our native language, we have access to considerably *less* than the necessary range of data for making appropriate generalizations. This is especially true in situations where the classroom is the only resource for such data. The role of C-R here is thus seen as one in which data that are crucial for the learner's testing of hypotheses, and for his forming generalizations, are made available to him in somewhat controlled and principled fashion. We say 'somewhat' here because although we may not always fully know the correct generalization to be made, we do know many of the data over which the generalization probably holds. For C-R and the learner's access to necessary data, therefore, the learning progression in terms of 'familiar to unfamiliar' will be manifest in the accretion of new data to old and in the abandonment of old hypotheses for new ones.

Another role for grammatical C-R in the 'familiar-to-unfamiliar' progression – and a role that re-emphasizes the value of C-R for hypothesis testing – can be deduced from the relationship between language-universal principles and language-specific information, as we touched on briefly at the beginning of this section. Take, for example, the fact that all languages have a 'basic word order' containing the universal constituents *subject, object,* and *verb*.[3] The verb constituent, depending upon the particular language, will either precede subject and object (e.g. Hebrew), follow subject and object (e.g. Japanese), or divide subject and object (e.g. English). Languages are alike in that they manifest one of these three basic word orders[4] and that they all may deviate from these orders under certain conditions. They differ in the amount of deviation allowed. Two extreme examples of this are English (almost no deviation) and Russian (the extent of whose permissible deviation is often referred to as 'free word order'). Thus, the existence of what we call 'basic word order' is language-universal; the amount of permitted departure from basic word order is language-specific.[5]

It has often been noted that word order in Spanish is considerably more flexible than in English. The learning of either Spanish or English by native speakers of the other language will very quickly come up against this contrast in degree of departure from basic word order. However, whereas the English-speaking learner of Spanish notices right away that Spanish word order is relatively free, the Spanish-speaking learner of English does *not* at first notice that English word order doesn't have this freedom. (In general, it is easier to notice the presence of something that one expects to be absent than the absence of something that one expects to be present. See Chapter 10.4.2 for a discussion of this with relation to 'universal grammar'.) C-R thus comes into play here only to provide the *negative* data (i.e. that we *can't* freely move the basic word-order constituents of English) that are necessary for guiding the hypothesis formation of the Spanish speaker learning English. Although in this instance the 'familiar' are the universal characteristics of basic word order and the 'unfamiliar' is the degree of language-specific word-order deviation, C-R is invoked to aid the learner's perception of only how such deviation may be *constrained* in the target language. This is a useful example of how four different phenomena – a universal principle, a language-specific departure, a learning precept, and grammatical consciousness-raising – may all be seen to converge in a particular learning experience.

1.3 *C-R roles and universal processes*

We may see a similar convergence for the role of grammatical C-R with regard to universal *processes*. Recall that the learner, having already acquired his mother tongue, therefore knows in general 'how' language serves to carry out a variety of communicative functions, one of which is certainly 'communication'. In other words, what one uses language *for* is familiar to him; what is *un*familiar, or what he *doesn't* yet know, are the ways in which those functions may be syntactically realized in the language he is learning. For an example of this, take the following passage, culled from a piece of writing produced by a Mandarin Chinese speaker learning English:

> All people can choose their mate in their own way. These ways can classify two types.

Most teachers of English will diagnose the second sentence as an abortive attempt by the writer to render the English **passive** construction, something like

> These ways *can be classified* into two types.

Upon performing the extremely important task of checking with the learner himself, however, we in fact find that his intent was to produce not the passive form but rather a Mandarin-like **topic-comment** construction, analysable as something like:

> These ways   [we] can classify [them] (into) two types[6]
> TOPIC   COMMENT

This is evidence of a universal process at work. The learner has already introduced into the discourse the piece of 'new' information represented as *in their own way* at the end of the first sentence. *These ways*, opening the second sentence, is therefore ready to function as a kind of discourse 'anchor' for the rest of the passage. The 'anchor' is felt by the learner, perhaps under the influence of his native language, to have the character of **topic**; hence his attempt in English to forge a topic-comment construction. But English syntax demands that the 'anchor' be realized as **subject**, with its predicate occurring here as a passive construction. Notice now that although the wrong grammatical operations have been utilized by the learner, the major constituents of his two sentences still occur in the naturally correct order for the easiest processing of the discourse. That is, the 'new' information appears earlier in the sentence, the 'old' or 'given' information later (see Chapter 6.1).

Here then we might use C-R to bridge the gap between the learner's prior knowledge of how major constituents may be properly ordered for effective communication (the 'familiar') and the learner's ignorance of the special grammatical devices that English requires for the correct rendering of that order (the 'unfamiliar'). And as learning progresses, grammatical C-R can (at least for some learners) perform the more general task of aiding his gradual (probably unconscious) reanalysis of non-English topic-comment as English subject-predicate, with all of the ancillary grammatical information that this entails. All of these exemplified tasks serve to define the ultimate role of grammatical C-R as a 'facilitator' of language learning, where 'facilitation' is to be understood as nothing less than the illumination of the learner's path from the known to the unknown.

What we have been briefly considering here are possible roles for grammatical C-R as it affects the learning of the most broadly definable formal characteristics of language. We will continue to probe the relationship between C-R and these sweeping grammatical phenomena in some of the chapters to come. Also to come will be an examination of the 'modes of operation' of C-R, which we mentioned earlier but have since said very little about. Since these 'modes' have to do with the 'how', 'how much', and 'how often' aspects of our topic, we properly relegate discussion of them to the more detailed areas of the book. We turn our attention next to the rationale for C-R, and we will conclude this chapter with some observations concerning the history of grammatical C-R in pedagogy.

2 The rationale for consciousness-raising

Not all language-teaching professionals believe that grammatical consciousness-raising of some kind has an important place in the classroom,[7] and some researchers hold that it has almost no place at all. For the sake of convenience in the ensuing commentary, we will collapse these positions under the rubric 'no-C-R'. In all fairness to those who espouse no-C-R, it would be useful here to try briefly to summarize their case for that position before going on to discuss it.

2.1 *A case against C-R*[8]

Proponents of no-C-R believe that C-R is neither a sufficient nor a necessary condition for mastery of another language and cite an extensive collection of research to buttress their claims.[9] They believe that for formal instruction, the only applicable set of conditions – both sufficient *and* necessary – stipulates that the learner be exposed to genuine language that is slightly beyond his present comprehension, that he or she be psychologically and emotionally receptive to this language input, and that a large proportion of learner activity be comprised of classroom exchange identifiable as 'comprehensible' and in which the learner has a personal investment. None of these conditions would of course be anything but compatible with the objectives of consciousness-raising and we must therefore look further to learn why C-R is expressly excluded from this scenario.

A number of theoretical assumptions underlie the imposition of the learning conditions promulgated through no-C-R. Clearly the most important of these has to do with the learner's capacity for engagement of his or her own language faculties in the course of using the target language. There are two such faculties invoked: one of them is that which all of us relied upon exclusively for the childhood development of our mother tongue; the other is that by means of which we may consciously bring meta-linguistic judgements and decisions to bear upon formal aspects of linguistic output. Language assimilation accomplished through the former is termed 'acquisition', and that accomplished through the latter, 'learning'. (We will observe this terminological distinction for the rest of the present discussion.)

Crucial for those who subscribe to the no-C-R position, however, is the *discreteness* of 'learning' *vis-à-vis* 'acquisition'. While many other researchers acknowledge that language competence can represent both what the learner has 'picked up' in a naturalistic sense and what he has been 'taught' through attention to form, the no-C-R position claims that the one cannot absorb the other, i.e. that 'learning' cannot become 'acquisition'. Furthermore, since it is only 'acquisition' that can serve the ultimately authentic function of spontaneous language use in naturalistic settings, 'learning' is relegated to the peripheral role of performing a check upon well-formedness, i.e. 'monitoring', for those learners who are personally more disposed to engage their 'monitors'.

Also called up in support of the no-C-R position are research findings purporting to demonstrate that a small set of English morphemes (e.g. plural -(e)s, past tense -ed, articles, progressive -ing, copula be, etc.) occurring with high frequency in the language of native English speakers emerges in two separate instances of interlanguage – viz. child L2 and adult L2 – always in roughly the same order, pedagogical intervention notwithstanding.[10] From this we are to conclude that acquisition of the target language proceeds in accord with a 'natural order' with regard to its organizational units, and that to attempt to 'teach' those units is unnecessary (since the aforementioned conditions are all that *is* necessary) and possibly even detrimental (where the units are taught out of their natural order).[11]

A final argument against according grammatical C-R any meaningful role in language pedagogy derives from the recognition that we are as yet quite far from understanding the full intrinsic organization of even as well worked-over a language as English, let alone any others. To try to impart to a learner the grammatical rules of a language when knowledge of it is, even among experts, both incomplete and inaccurate is therefore doomed to failure. Thus if C-R has any value for the learner at all, it can only be (a) in the editing of writing embodying samples of a very small subset of complex grammatical features that will have resisted acquisition; and (b) in the satisfaction of learner expectations that C-R should form part of the language-learning experience (i.e. the 'face validity' of C-R). The no-C-R position – as outlined here – obviously calls then for some comment.

2.2 *The language problem in no-C-R*

Behind the no-C-R position lie two sets of assumptions, one set deriving from a body of research that constitutes the theoretical underpinning, the other deriving from beliefs (conscious or unconscious) about the nature of language organization itself and how it comes to be 'acquired by the learner'. Since most of the theoretical assumptions have been the subject of discussion elsewhere in the literature (see, for example, Munsell and Carr 1981), it is the *language* assumptions of no-C-R that bear mentioning here.

If we examine the no-C-R position, the picture of language and of language learning/acquisition that emerges is essentially the one of 'accumulated entities' that we drew for language-teaching professionals in general in Chapter 1.1 (see also Chapter 3). This view is probably most clearly revealed in the importance attached to the aforementioned 'natural order' of acquisition and the implications that have derived from it. From the belief that there is a demonstrable natural order of acquisition for some language items – a claim rooted, as we have noted, in the findings of the morpheme-acquisition studies of the early 1970s – have developed two additional assumptions:
1. that all of language form is itemizable in the manner of the above morphemes;
2. that acquisition of language form is tantamount to steady accumulation of those items in some as yet unidentifiable order.

However, serious discussion of such pan-linguistic acquisition orders among proponents of no-C-R has seldom ventured beyond consideration of the original set of morphemes in question, and indeed it would be difficult to imagine *in what sense morpheme-acquisition research procedures might embrace anything at all in the syntax of the language.*[12]

We can therefore understand how it is also that grammatical

consciousness-raising – narrowly construed here to the 'teaching of grammar' – must be of little value to the learner. Grammar teaching means teaching the 'rules' of grammar, but since such teaching can result only in 'learning', and also since very little of syntax can be 'learned' anyway – and furthermore since what little 'learning' does come about cannot in any case become 'acquisition' (the only mental disposition that can generate meaningful and appropriate use of language) – the whole grammar-teaching enterprise must necessarily constitute an exercise in futility.

It is worth noting in all of this, however, that should the language-organizational concepts assumed by proponents of no-C-R turn out somehow to be valid, then 'grammar-teaching' in the above sense *would* be a futile enterprise – but for reasons that would derive from the nature of language itself and not from any particular theoretical stance on the nature of language acquisition. In other words, no-C-R proponents are right to criticize much of traditional, narrowly defined 'grammar teaching', but they do so for the wrong reasons. We are therefore compelled to question the validity of the no-C-R position on three counts: questionable concepts (1) of language and its organizing principles; (2) of language acquisition; and (3) of grammatical consciousness-raising.[13] If *no*-C-R is not justified then, does it necessarily follow that C-R *is* justified?

2.3 *Justification of C-R*

Let us reiterate that grammatical C-R differs from conventional notions of 'grammar teaching' in fundamental ways, as suggested at the beginning of this chapter and at various other points throughout the book. Clearly the one most important distinction to draw – and one from which follow other differences both qualitative and quantitative – is that C-R is a *means* to attainment of grammatical competence in another language (i.e. necessary but not sufficient, and the learner contributes), whereas 'grammar teaching' typically represents an attempt to *instil* that competence directly (i.e. necessary *and* sufficient, and the learner is a *tabula rasa*). It is probably not unreasonable to assume that a small amount of both these kinds of pedagogical 'focus on grammar' has figured in the available studies purporting to demonstrate the efficacy (or not) of classroom attention to language form, though our ignorance in this area is not often recognized (see below).

Lending support to grammatical C-R, then, are a variety of

research findings in academic areas of inquiry ranging from theoretical linguistics to experimental psychology. Harley and Swain (1984) have shown, for example, that exposure of the learner to meaningful input alone, although necessary, is not a sufficient condition for being able to produce 'a marked formal aspect of the L2 in a classroom setting'.[14] Furthermore, according to Spada (1985), 'learners require opportunities for both form-focused and function-focused practice in the development of particular skill areas, and if one or the other is lacking they do not appear to benefit as much'.[15] This observation is not unrelated to that of several psychologists who write that 'a blending of the two modes of learning [explicit and implicit], interference effects included, is still preferable to the use of only one or the other. In fact, this should not be too surprising for this is the way in which knowledge of most complex environments is acquired' (Reber *et al.* 1980, p. 501).[16] Other evidence points to the utilization of form-focused instruction in productive use of a language (Prokop *et al.* 1982) and where there is no exposure to the language other than in the classroom (Sorace 1985 and van Baalen 1983).[17] Still others have observed differential effects upon learner proficiency stemming from the particular *varieties* of form-centred tasks (Hulstijn and Hulstijn 1984) and the recognition of individual learning dispositions for such task performance (McLaughlin *et al.* 1983). Also, classroom instruction can have a positive effect upon an L2 learner's formation of hypotheses about target-language structure (Pica 1983). Finally, we need to note as well the possible benefits upon learning to be derived from meeting the learners' *preference* for some attention to language form (Wesche 1979; Newmark 1973; Krashen 1982).

The studies just cited, as indeed most research on the effect of classroom instruction, are product-oriented. That is, they assess the state of the language learner's ability/knowledge/competence, etc. by examining his output/judgements, etc. at a particular point in his development – viz. following administration of the research experiment in question. Of equal value to us then are those studies (precious few of them) which seek to explore the effects of instruction upon the changing internal states of the learner's grammatical competence – research findings that are process-oriented. One such study[18] claims to have identified a set of *constraints* upon learnability/teachability for those target-language forms that are interrelated in terms of their amenability to processing by the learner. It has been shown, for example, that in the acquisition of German as a second language the following three rules have to be learned in the sequence given, for the successively heavier processing demands therein require that the earlier rule be learned as a prerequisite to the later.

adverb preposing: *Da kinder spielen*
(*There* children play)
verb separation: *Alle kinder muss die pause machen*
(All children *must* the break *have*)
inversion: *Dann muss alle kinder die pause machen*
(Then *must all children* the break have)

According to the results of this research, instruction will not enable the learner to bypass either of the stages preceding the application of 'inversion' but it *will* improve the learner's acquisition in three distinct ways: learning will be faster; the quantity produced will be greater; and the contexts in which the rule can apply will be extended. The claim here then is that teaching can make a difference, but only where a developmental sequence can be articulated with reference to interdependent and successively heavier processing demands upon the learner. Subsequent research suggests that considerably more language structure might be analysable in this fashion.

As a postscript to accounts of empirical research purporting to validate *whatever* theoretical stance regarding the relationship of formal instruction to language proficiency, it needs to be recognized that the big unknown quantity in all of this is the nature of the instruction itself. Since there are so many possible instructional variables having different potential effects upon the learning experience, one simply cannot assume that such loosely defined events as 'formal instruction', 'attention to language form', 'grammatical consciousness-raising', 'grammar teaching', or whatever, will have any empirical value without seriously looking at what is actually happening in such situations (Sharwood Smith 1981). In the words of one researcher, R. Ellis, 'the nature of "language teaching" cannot be taken for granted, no matter how apparently prescribed the method is. All teaching provides both "instruction" and "exposure". It is necessary, therefore, to examine the actual interactions that take place.' (Ellis 1984, p. 153).[19]

Our assessment then is that C-R is alive and well, even if it is due for a bit of reorientation and rethinking. An apt and rather artful depiction of these expectations was recently provided for us by E. Stevick:

[Consciousness-raising] casts light on the unfamiliar pathways and the arbitrary obstacles through which [the student] must eventually be able to run back and forth with his eyes shut. It can thus save him a certain amount of time, energy, and barked shins. It is for this reason, of course, that the teacher needs to know these same pathways and obstacles – not only to run back and forth in them for herself, but also to see them as they look to a newcomer. On top of this are the skills of knowing when to turn on the spotlight of [consciousness-raising] and when to turn it off, and knowing just how to aim it so that it will help the student instead of blinding him.

Stevick 1980, p. 251

It is instructive to remind ourselves that the need to justify C-R in language pedagogy is a relatively recent one. For most of the 2,500-year history of language teaching, the importance of C-R was simply assumed, and for long stretches of this history C-R (in the narrow version called 'grammar teaching') and language pedagogy were even virtually synonymous. A more comprehensive look at these historical developments would thus not be inappropriate here.

3 Grammatical consciousness-raising in brief historical perspective[20]

The notion that language teaching should have as one of its components (whatever else it may include) the need to raise in some way the learner's consciousness of aspects of the grammatical structure of the language he is learning goes back perhaps several millennia.[21] By contrast, the advancement of language-teaching methods that accord little or no importance to grammatical consciousness-raising are about a hundred years old and thus, in terms of this more sweeping time-scale, relatively recent. It must be realized, moreover, that not only has grammatical focus long been considered a *necessary* part of language instruction; it has also even to this day often been considered a *sufficient* condition for successful language learning. In the words of one researcher, D. Wilkins, 'this is the tradition that we have inherited'. (Wilkins 1984, p. 73).

The importance attributed to a knowledge of language form throughout the history of language pedagogy derives in part from a number of other historical circumstances. One of the most important of these is the early relationship of language study to scholarship in general. In the Middle Ages, for example, our modern concept of a multi-disciplined academia simply did not exist. Academic learning in medieval Europe embraced the three branches of law, theology, and medicine, but even among these the disciplinary boundaries so familiar to us today were considerably blurred. Within the medieval academic world the study of grammar was accorded a prominent place in philosophy, which was in turn a branch of theology. The inclusion within philosophy of grammar, logic, and rhetoric was an inheritance from classical antiquity and serves to underscore the fact that at the time they 'were all thought of as facets of the same reality of language use' (Kelly 1969, p. 301). Since one of these uses – or one of the purposes of language teaching in the Middle Ages – was the development of rhetorical skill, it is not very difficult to understand the close relationship of grammar study to the other medieval disciplines. Parenthetically, the modern notion of hyphenated disciplines and the 'application' of the findings of one discipline to another – as in, for example, 'psycholinguistics' and 'applied psycholinguistics' – can have come about only in an academic world wherein an original holistic universe of knowledge and belief has first been fragmented, the continually subdividing parts eventually entering into our smaller-scale specialized recombinations. Early grammar study was thus not 'applied-' anything, or not 'grafted on to' any of its sister disciplines, but rather fused with them in a general embodiment of prevailing knowledge, which itself was believed in the Middle Ages to be the property of the soul (Kelly 1969, p. 302). In fact, the very word 'grammar' traces back ultimately to the ancient Greek *grammatikos*, pertaining to letters or learning.

Grammatical consciousness-raising in pedagogy carries one indispensable prerequisite, and that is that something be known about the grammatical structure in question. Now during the millennium preceding the sixteenth century the only language whose structure was thought to be known – indeed, the only language in the Western world (other than Greek) whose structure was deemed worth knowing – was Latin. Thus, when we talk about language study a thousand years ago it must be realized that we are referring essentially to the study of Latin, which was the language of theology, of medicine, and of law – in short, the language of the Western world in which most knowledge of the time was encoded and through which it was transmitted. To study Latin was to study its grammar, and until the invention of printing and the first appearance of books in the fifteenth century the actual teaching of Latin was entirely oral, its grammar rules even being presented in verse form.

With the Renaissance came increased interest in the European vernaculars as cultural vehicles and as languages worth studying in their own right. Language learning of the time drew a distinction between the study of grammar and of literature, strived for accuracy over fluency, used Latin (until the eighteenth century) as the language of grammatical explanation, and relied upon an inductive methodology. The induction principle was carried into the seventeenth century, when we find the first promulgation of 'the idea later to become the keystone of nineteenth-century methodology: that languages are to be learned in the same way as one's mother tongue' (Kelly 1969, p. 39).

The rising importance of the vernaculars led to other developments that were to influence significantly the course of future language teaching – the growing belief that the study of another language was best accomplished via knowledge of one's own, and the recognition of Latin grammar as the model for studying the grammar of any language. It was in this climate that emerged the early development at Port-Royale in the seventeenth century of 'general grammar', not unlike, in its assumptions, what the twentieth-century generativists now call 'universal grammar'. And, as 'the only possible analytical scheme to follow was that which had been developed for Latin, so the illusion that all languages shared a basic grammar was complete' (Kelly 1969, p. 55).

From belief in the essential oneness of basic structure across languages it was but a short pedagogical step to propound the teaching of languages by translation between the known language (the mother tongue) and the one being learned i.e. **grammar-translation methodology**. And with the ascendancy of grammar-translation in the eighteenth century came the first language descriptions expressly for language learners, or the first 'pedagogical grammars'. The continued entrenchment of grammar-translation throughout the nineteenth century saw a gradual loosening of the relationship between literary models and grammar study, to the point that by the early twentieth century the study of formal language systems *per se* bore little relation either to literature or to the purposes for which language learning was undertaken. In Kelly's words, 'language skill was equated with ability to conjugate and decline' (p. 53).[22]

The formal excesses of grammar-translation methodology had early on provided the impetus for alternative approaches to language teaching based upon how children were believed to learn their mother tongue. Language learning was thus starting to be regarded as a form of behaviour, rather than just the internalization of sets of abstractions, and the most important exponents of this movement in the nineteenth century were the 'Natural Method' and the 'Direct Method'. Although the two differed sharply in that the Natural Method, unlike the Direct Method, recognized no distinction between the way in which first and second languages are learned, both methods, at least in principle, accorded little or no instructional role to grammatical attention. In a sense, the differential regard for grammatical C-R, as embodied in early twentieth-century grammar-translation *vis-à-vis* direct methodism, has continued to this day, though the names of the methodologies in question keep changing. As for consciousness-raising itself, however, all its proponents throughout history seem always to have assumed that the matter to be raised to consciousness comprised the *combinatorial units* of whatever model of language analysis happened to prevail at the time.

Just as virtually every contemporary 'innovation' in language teaching seems to have an antecedent somewhere back in the 2,500-year history of language pedagogy, so it is perhaps also with grammatical consciousness-raising conceived as a tool of language learning rather than the object of such learning. An apt example of this would be the variety of inductive methodology in vogue during the Renaissance and traceable to St Augustine, wherein the learner was made to play an active role in the discovery of principles of language organization whose subsequent articulation in formal terms could only complete a learning process that had already begun. We have ample reminders, it seems, that the profession of language teaching, like so many other professions, is far more preoccupied with where it imagines it is going than with where it actually has been.

Activities

1. It is often noted that no attempts at grammatical consciousness-raising attend the learning of one's native language and that C-R therefore need not be invoked for the learning of a second language either. What assumptions underlie this position? What arguments could be made both for and against the position?

2. If grammatical C-R has a place in the language curriculum, should this be the case for all learners? That is, are there some learners who might benefit more/less than others? How would you go about determining this?

3. What beliefs or opinions do *learners* have about the usefulness, or otherwise, of grammatical C-R in their course of instruction? Tabulate their responses to this kind of question and compare them with those gathered from other learner populations (e.g. younger versus older adults, university versus high school, oral skills versus reading only, intensive versus few hours per week, etc.).

Notes

1. This notion is by no means just a twentieth-century discovery. It is traceable at least back to classical antiquity. See Kelly (1969).

2. The seeming triviality of this statement can be offset by consideration of the fact that there is *a priori* no reason why this should be so. Given the notion that language is rule-governed behaviour, one might imagine that it should be possible, at least in theory, to learn a language (or some part thereof) by learning only the (generative) rule system and the lexical input to those rules, without exposure to the raw data. That this is *not* possible has to do with more than just the fact that theories of grammar are not theories of acquisition.

   Note that the key word in the passage in the text is 'successful'. As Steve Krashen (personal communication) reminds me, nearly all 'traditional' language-teaching methods do not assume that exposure to the data is necessary but rather that we acquire by (in Krashen's terms) 'learning becoming acquisition' via output practice and error correction.

3. We ignore here, for now, the fact that in basic sentence form for a number of known languages the notion of **subject** is much less important than that of **topic**. The prominence, or not, of subject *vis-à-vis* topic constitutes a typological parameter for the classification of languages, with English providing a prime example of 'subject-prominence', Mandarin Chinese a prime example of 'topic-prominence', and Japanese an example of a language in which both 'topic' and 'subject' are part of basic sentence structure. See Chapter 9.

4. Languages having one of these three word orders make up approximately 98 per cent of the world's known languages. Of the remaining 2 per cent, VOS (e.g. Malagasy) and OVS (e.g. Hixkaryana) are attested; OSV is as yet unknown.

5. Word-order flexibility is a function of a number of other factors. See Hawkins (1985).

6. The bracketed items, where *we* is 'understood' and *them* is co-referential with topic, can be dispensed with in typical topic-comment constructions for languages which have them.

7. Representative of this position (i.e. no significant role for C-R) would be, for example, the work of Krashen (1982, *inter alia*), Newmark (1973), Dulay, Burt and Krashen (1982), etc.

8. The case against C-R being laid out here is essentially the position held by my friend and USC colleague, Steve Krashen.

9. See Krashen (1982) for a useful summary of such research.

10. See Krashen (1982, Chapter II, Section A2) for a review of this research. See Allwright (1984b, p. 209), however, for observations that natural-order data have been obtained largely within instructional settings only: 'What we do not have, it seems, is a comprehensive statement of a "natural order" based exclusively on uninstructed learners.'

11. Krashen (personal communication) says that teaching in accord with the 'natural order' is also detrimental, i.e. it is a form of tampering with 'comprehensible input'.

12. See Rutherford (1984) for a discussion of this problem. White (1985b, p. 13) has this to say: 'The finding of universal morpheme acquisition

orders . . . does not help us to determine aspects of the acquisition of syntax, nor do they seem to fall out from any theory as to what the universals might be.'

13. We will note here also that pervading the articulation of the no-C-R position are the notions of language 'itemization' and of the mind as 'receptacle' for acquisition of such 'items'. This is the sense in which we must comprehend how, 'in the case of the second-language performer who has acquired *nearly all the grammar* of the second language but who still has some *gaps*, the use of the conscious grammar can *fill in* many of the *non-acquired items*' (Krashen 1982, p. 90; emphasis added). Also fitting this image is the metaphorical use of language in speaking of 'portable rules' that the learner may 'carry around in his head' as 'mental baggage'. And we find it as well where the numerical designation in 'i(nput) + 1' (or 2, or 3) refers to the next 'rule' or 'structure' to be added to the learner's cumulative competence. (See also White 1986.)

This item/unit concept of language organization is anything but inconsistent with the 'itemization' of the language faculty itself – namely, the isolation of 'learning' from 'acquisition' and imperviousness of the one to the other. Indeed, if 'learning' is relevant only to 'items' of grammar that can be 'carried around in one's head', then it should come as no surprise, (a) that the learning of nothing more complex than morphemes and low-level syntax ever gets talked about, and (b) that learning does not become acquisition – since very little of consequence could have been 'learned' in this sense in the first place. (See Hurtig 1977) for some useful discussion of syntax and the mental representation of propositional content.)

Criticism of Krashen's position should nevertheless not blind the reader to the important fact that Krashen is one among few in the field of L2 acquisition with a theory that is sufficiently developed to merit serious criticism of any kind. It is also a theory that is articulated with clarity sufficient to allow pedagogical implications to be drawn from it in principled fashion – a substantial contribution to the field.

14. See Harley and Swain (1984, p. 309). The findings here are based on immersion data. See also Swain (1985).

15. See Spada (1985, p. 22). It is useful to include here a larger portion of Spada's text (p. 23):

It is important to emphasize that these findings relate only to the effects of the interaction between contact and instruction on improvement and not to the main effects of instruction on learning. This is a crucial distinction because one might be tempted to interpret these findings as evidence for the need for more grammar-based instruction in the classroom. However, this is clearly not the case because separate analyses carried out to investigate the main effects of instruction on learners' improvement revealed that there were no significant differences among the classes on the two measures in question (i.e. the grammar and writing tests) that could be attributed to instructional variation alone . . . What the results of the combined effects of instruction and contact do imply, however, is that learners who live in what

Krashen (1981) has referred to as 'acquisition-rich' environments and take advantage of such settings to use their communicative skills in the L2, also need opportunities to focus on the structural properties of the language and attend to form.

16. It is worth quoting further here from Reber *et al.* (1980, p. 500):
    Of the various possible combinations of explicit and implicit training procedures, it seems clear that the optimum mode is that in which the subjects begin with explicit information about the structure of the grammar and then observe an extended series of exemplars generated by it. This finding is similar to that reported by Danks and Gans (1975) [J. Danks and D. Gans, Acquisition and utilization of a rule structure. *Journal of Experimental Psychology: Human Learning and Memory*, vol. 1:201–8], who found that the learning of the rule system of a miniature linguistic system (albeit, a relatively simple one compared with that used in our experiments) was optimized by showing subjects the rule matrix early in the training phase. Interestingly, they also reported that merely informing a subject that there were rules but withholding concrete information concerning their nature had no facilitative effect and may even have inhibited performance.

17. Sorace (1985, p. 252) draws attention to 'the difficulty of explaining these results [viz. development of metalinguistic knowledge] in a theoretical framework which denies any productive function to meta-linguistic knowledge. It is hard to justify the growing interaction between the subjects' metalinguistic knowledge and their productive use of the [foreign language] if one is not prepared to admit either that formal knowledge can be applied in production or that it has at least a more central function than limited monitoring.'

18. The study is by Pienemann (1985), who reminds us that the learners of L2 German here were not adults but Italian-speaking children. Pienemann has since replicated his study using adult learners, with similar results.

19. See also Allwright (1984b, p. 206).

20. Much of the material in this section is based on Kelly (1969).

21. This is not to say by any means that the purpose or the manner of consciousness-raising has always been a consistent one. Quite the contrary. Kelly (1969, p. 34) notes that
    since the beginning of language teaching the manner of learning the syntax and flexions of language has been disputed. Accepted methods have ranged from the inductive, by which the pupil himself arrives at rules from examples, to the deductive whereby one proceeds from rules to a knowledge of the language. At all periods of language teaching both have existed, but never on an equal footing. Inductive methods were most fashionable during the late Renaissance and early twentieth century, while deductive approaches reached their greatest development during the late Middle Ages and the eighteenth century.

22. It is well to note, in the words of McArthur (1983, p. 59), that 'those who used and developed classical grammar ... were ... basically concerned with reading and writing; speech was a secondary consider-

ation for people who wanted to train scribes, clerks, and scholars or readers of a revered foreign literature. Those were the primary goals, and for such goals the grammar-translation method worked adequately for centuries'.

Questions to Part One

1. To what extent does the 'accumulated entities' concept describe your own experience and/or beliefs in language learning and teaching?

2. Of what real value to language teaching is knowledge having to do with characteristics of interlanguage development that seem to pertain to language learners in general, irrespective of native language?

3. Why would you imagine a principle like structure dependency would turn out to be a language-universal one?

4. Corder is quoted (pp. 17 and 18) as stating that 'pedagogical descriptions are aids to learning not the object of learning'. What implications would this have for a language-teaching programme?

5. Would an assumption that the learner comes to the language-learning experience as a 'blank slate' or *tabula rasa* have any different bearing on what and how you yourself teach? If so, what would be different?

6. Do you think there is anything to be inferred from the fact that grammatical C-R of some kind figures in the overwhelming mass of documented language-teaching practice for these two millennia, or is this observation of little consequence?

7. Based upon what you know of the history of the language-teaching profession and the state of the profession at the present time, what predictions would you make for the fate of grammatical C-R in the future?

Part Two
On edge in language

Observed patterns of matter are reflections of patterns of mind.

Fritjof Capra

We live in a time, in a space, in a culture that has 'edges'. We frame historical events within rather arbitrary time-spans called *decades*, *centuries*, and *millennia*. And the time-frames themselves each take on a flavour of their own, e.g. the decade of the 'complacent fifties' ushered in the decade of the 'rebellious sixties'. Some of us live within arbitrary political borders, boundaries, even barriers. And we talk of going to the 'ends' of the earth and of the 'limits' of outer space. Our cognitive capacities find expression in the 'frontiers' of knowledge, the 'brink' of discovery, the 'threshold' of new experience, the 'cutting edge' of research. We 'stake out' intellectual 'territory' and then 'break new ground', 'extend our domain', and 'defend our turf'. And we see dividing lines between science and nature, the imaginary and the real, abstract and concrete, the spirit and the letter – 'mind over matter'. Edges, borders, demarcations of every conceivable kind ... these serve to categorize, compartmentalize, and objectify most of what we experience – the means by which we choose to comprehend almost everything around us, or what we refer to as 'reality'. It would be surprising indeed if this 'comprehension' were not also reflected in the way we look at language.

In the next three chapters we will first explore this notion a bit more and then consider some implications for language learning and language teaching that derive from an alternate way of conceptualizing language.

3 Living language

1 Metaphors of language

If our conception of reality is prone to psychological demarcation, our concept of language – what it is, how it is learned, how it is taught – seems to have 'edges' as well. We tend to think of language as somehow 'put together' and that to know something of how it 'works' we have to 'take it apart'. Language professionals therefore find it useful and convenient (perhaps even necessary) to try to understand the nature of language by unravelling it, decomposing it, disassembling it. We analyse it into layers – phonology, morphology, lexicon, syntax, semantics, discourse – and confer upon each its respective unitary designation: phoneme, morpheme, lexeme, tagmeme, sememe, theme/rheme. We break language down in order to build it up, and we call the resultant debris 'building blocks'. We utilize the analytic techniques of segmentation and classification in order to identify 'immediate constituents' and we talk of 'parts of speech', structures, categories, subcategories (and even 'strict subcategories'), components, frameworks, and configurations. We speak of the 'acquisition device' by which language is acquired and of the physical 'mechanisms' by which language is rendered as utterances – speech circuits, hearing mechanisms, articulatory apparatus. The very terminology that we employ in analysing and describing language, in other words, reveals that our general concept, at least to some extent, is one in which language is a complex thing with many edges, with attached and moving parts – that is, a *machine*.

The notion of language as a machine works satisfactorily for us in certain respects – language after all contains systems, and to probe the intricacies of any system is at least to impute to it the components that ostensibly comprise it. Yet there is another side to language that is not very machine-like at all, a side in which the 'edges' become greatly blurred or disappear altogether. Language is constantly in the act of change and growth, whether it is the historical development of a language over a time-span measured in millennia or the 'historical' development of an idiolect from age two to age five. Growth of course is quite unmachine-like, or alien to that which we can conceive of in purely mechanical terms. The apt descriptive term for 'growth' then is not 'mechanic' but 'organic'. Thus, although language has characteristics that lend themselves to the 'machine' metaphor, it has a great deal to it that also suggests very aptly the metaphor of *organism*.

Organism is a better general metaphor than machine for what we know about language as a medium of developing interaction among humans. Machines are constructed, whereas organisms grow. Machines have precision; organisms have plasticity. Machines have linear interconnections; organisms have cyclical interconnections. And, perhaps most important of all, machines are sterile, whereas organisms are fecund.[1] The cellular structure of the human body, for example, will have renewed itself thousands of times during one's lifetime – one's body at age forty-four and at age four will be totally 'different' in terms of actually present and living cells; yet those very bodies, separated as they are by forty years, are the 'same' in terms of the genetic coding of their cells. The nature of language considered as an organism offers striking parallels to these cellular characteristics. Although the English language today, for example, is in a real sense quite different from the English language of four hundred years ago, yet it retains a kind of 'genetic coding' that readily identifies it as successively 'regenerated' English of, say, Shakespeare's time and not regenerated sixteenth-century French or sixteenth-century Arabic. To the great extent then that we may ascribe to language these characteristics of growth, change, plasticity, fecundity, genetics, regeneration, etc. – to this extent we may quite naturally conceive of language as an organism.

Language therefore has a side to it that can properly be called *organic*, as well as a side that one can properly call *mechanic*. In truth, these are really two sides of the same koine, so to speak. Both metaphors are needed, for language has *form* as well as *function*; it has aspects that are *static* and others that are *dynamic*; we look at language *product* in addition to language *process*; we ascribe part of the language complex to *competence*, part of it to *performance*. This dual nature of the language phenomenon – a kind of 'yin and yang' of language, if you will – has been cited by others,[2] although to cite the duality is not necessarily to exploit it for purposes of formal learning. That is certainly more easily said than done. One well-known language-teaching professional, H. Widdowson, has noted this dilemma by calling attention to the difficulty of reconciling the exactness of linguistic analysis with the open-endedness of communication (Widdowson 1979, p. 243), and we will subsequently have more to say about such 'reconciliation' as it relates to grammatical conscious-ness-raising in pedagogy. But we want first to look in more detail at the organic aspects of interlanguage development.

2 The interlanguage organism

Interlanguage, at least in part, seems to be forever becoming some-thing else. It is true, of course, that this sort of quasi-permanent state of change is evident for all language development – a single language over centuries, the spread of dialects, the transition of pidgins to creoles, the learning of one's mother tongue. Although the kinds of change that we observe over the time it takes to learn a second language (L2) have much in common with change in these other language realms, there are some ways in which L2 change is also different. This will become apparent as we start to examine the actual metamorphosis of interlanguage.

One of the most obvious clues to the nature of interlanguage metamorphosis is to be found in what the learners themselves do with a classroom writing assignment which they have ample time to complete and which holds some amount of genuine interest for them. It should be stipulated that the assignment is to be completed with pen, not pencil, so that a clear record is present of many of the learner's editorial emendations. For an example then of the kind of editing we might see, we will use the sample text from Chapter 1.3:

[1]My home town␣Lamgur. is ␣ [2]It has ~~Have~~ not much people. [3]Some people ~~they~~ was very rich people who ~~to~~ have big house. [4]~~Always~~ we always ␣ notice expensive car which they have ~~it~~ in garage. [5]Maybe soon Lamgur have␣ a better condition for people and people of Lamgur too poor. [6]I hope so.

In what ways can we say that the learner's edited text differs from that text before editing? Although in neither version do we have a product that could pass for literary English, what we do have is an informative mini-record of a relationship between the learner's written production at two different phases of the learning experience. The emendations, therefore, offer us clues as to what the learner himself is doing in passing from the earlier phase to the later one. Notice first what has happened in those parts of sentences that represent the major constituents of **subject, object,** and **verb.** The verb missing from the earlier version of sentence 1 (*is*) has been inserted in the later version. Likewise with the subject of sentence 2 (*it*). And in sentence 3 the redundant pronoun subject (*they*) has been eliminated. Also eliminated in sentence 4 is the redundant pronoun object (*it*). The learner has thus restored an absent major constituent in two sentences (1 and 2) and has deleted a redundant major constituent in two others (3 and 4).

What else has he done? Notice that *have* has become singular *has* in sentence 2 in agreement with the singular subject *it* (i.e. *Lamgur*). And the indefinite article *a* has been added in sentence 5 where nothing appeared before. Also, the frequency adverb *always* in sentence 4 has been moved from outside the sentence to its natural place between subject and verb. Finally, the infinitive-like *to have* in sentence 3 has given way to the finite, relative clause-like *who have*. We now need to ask whether all this represents merely random editing or whether there is in fact a relationship to be discerned among the emendations themselves.

The first observation we can make is that the editing, though desirable, does not appear to have rendered the passage any more comprehensible than it was before. Indeed, to another learner with the same general English-language proficiency, it may now be even a little *less* comprehensible, and one is entitled to wonder why that should be. This leads us, then, to our next observation: the very editing that has created a closer approximation of target English has also made the relationships between syntax and semantics less direct than before. The most obvious example of this is in sentence 4 and the now empty space where *it* formerly marked the semantic object position of 'car' and kept the verb-object relationship an overt one. (We will have more to say about this in Chapter 4.3.) The last general observation we will make for the moment is that not all instances of the same textual feature were necessarily emended by the learner. That is, *have* became *has* in sentence 2, but this didn't happen in sentence 5; the necessary **copula** (viz. *is*) was inserted in sentence

1, though not in sentence 5 (*are*); a necessary **determiner** (i.e. *a*) was supplied for *condition* in sentence 5, but this didn't happen for *house* in sentence 3 or *car* in sentence 4; and although morphologically marked 'agreement' was activated for some subject-verb relationships, it was left untouched for **quantifier-noun** in sentence 2 (*much people*).

Before reaching our general conclusions as to what developmental processes may be revealed to us in the learner's emended passage, it would be well to note a characteristic of learner development that is difficult to show in sample texts of this kind. Where one might expect that language learners should progress in steady and ever closer approximation to the target language norm, it often happens that learner progress is in fact unsteady, but where there is a perceived regularity in this very unsteadiness. Learners have been observed apparently to manifest early correct usage of a grammatical form (e.g. the English determiner), to then 'regress' to ungrammaticality at a later stage, only to emerge finally with the grammatically correct usage once again. This can happen, for example, where the learner absorbs and uses correctly an unanalysed 'chunk' of the target language (e.g. modal + verb), then analyses it and perhaps falsely analogizes to infinitivals (i.e. *modal + to + verb*), but ultimately sorts out the complexities for target-like usage once more. The phenomenon has been referred to as a 'U-shaped' learning curve (Kellerman 1985), learner performance at the first stage of which can easily convey a false impression of formal mastery. Early movement to the bottom of the curve then is really to be interpreted as another phase of learner development and not unlike that depicted in the sample text under discussion.

We can now let our three observations add up to one rather complex conclusion concerning the progress of the language learner in question, as revealed in the emended text. This is that a process is at work wherein interlanguage of an earlier phase has become more **grammaticized** in a later phase. In other words, a learner-language mode in which the form-meaning relationship was maximally direct is giving way to later modes, in unsteady but ever closer approximation to target English, wherein the relationships become more and more *in*direct as the compensatory **grammaticization** principle takes hold. It is a gradual process (as is everything else with regard to language learning), and it is a process that does not necessarily apply uniformly to all grammatical features of the same rank, as we have just seen. What we have here then is something akin to the growth of cells in the human body, where the cells are regenerated over time but still carry the same genetic code. With interlanguage, it is the language form that is 'regenerated', i.e. grammaticized, and it is the language function that remains fairly constant. This process of **grammaticization** is perhaps the characteristic of language that most aptly suggests for us the metaphor of language as an organism.

Activities

1. Arrange for some brief, appropriately chosen written work to be done by your students during class but stipulate that they must use (non-erasing) pens and (if this ever needs reaffirming) that they should do all the deleting, inserting, rewriting, etc. that they want. Then examine the products for the kinds of evidence of interlanguage grammaticization that have been discussed. Are any of your observations similar to those noted in connection with the learner sample in section 2?

2. In the nearest library, find a volume containing photographs of an edited manuscript by some well-known writer in English (or use a copy of something written and edited by you) and compare these kinds of emendation with those made by your students. In what ways do they differ?

Notes

1. I owe these observations to F. Capra (1982, pp. 268–73).
2. We are using 'yin and yang' here in a sense somewhat different from that of C. J. Bailey (1982).

4 Psycholinguistic aspects of grammaticization

The broad concept of language – and especially interlanguage – that we have been seriously entertaining here is one in which language is seen as not just successive states of 'being' but also long avenues of 'becoming'. It will be useful, then, to examine in more detail just what it means for aspects of interlanguage to be in this process of 'becoming'. And as we do so we will also begin to consider the possible implications of our concept of language development for grammatical consciousness-raising in pedagogy. Discussion of the fullest implications, however, will be reserved for Part Five.

Interlanguage in the process of 'becoming' is easily witnessed through **grammaticization**,[1] the most visible manifestation of the organic nature of language. Grammaticization, however, embraces a wide range of developmental phenomena, and it is some of these that we now want to bring to the fore.

1 Topic and subject

Our general tendency to want to pull things apart in order to see how they go together is the most common means at our disposal for analysing syntax. Applying the technique to language at the sentence level leads to identification of what we consider to be the major constituents participating in sentence constructions across any random sampling of the vast number of languages known to exist or to have existed. The degree of prominence attributed to these constituents, and their possible ordered combinations, comprise the frameworks that we resort to for gross comparison among languages – their broad classification into types, or language **typology** (see Chapter 9). One such typological framework serves to distinguish languages according to whether sentence structure is plausibly to be analysed as **topic + comment** or **subject + predicate**, or possibly both. A typical topic-comment construction, for languages that have them such as Mandarin or Japanese, might look like this:

Elephant   nose is long
TOPIC   COMMENT

The rendition of this topic-comment into normal English subject-predicate would require (aside from the addition of a determiner: *the*, *a*, *this*, etc.) the introduction of the possessive marker (*'s*):

The elephant's nose   is long
SUBJECT   PREDICATE

The alteration we've just made is an example of grammaticization – where the loose topic-comment relation has been converted to the tighter, syntactic subject-predicate relation by means of extra grammatical 'machinery' – in this particular case, the possessive marker. Although our examples are greatly over-simplified, they are nevertheless representative of similar metamorphoses to be seen in historical language change, in the learning of one's mother tongue, and in the learning of a second language.

It would not be surprising if we should find early on in the language-learning experience evidence of influence or 'transfer' from the learner's mother tongue where the L1 makes heavy use of topic-comment form and the L2 does not. And in fact such influence does occur and has been amply documented.[2] What perhaps is surprising, however, is the incidence of topic-comment in early interlanguage where neither L1 nor L2 manifests this form in their basic sentence construction. Topic-comment as a principle of fundamental language organization has immediate serviceability for the learner, especially where complex L2 grammatical paraphernalia have not yet been learned. Since the relation between topic and comment is not a syntactic but a 'discoursal' one (Li and Thompson 1976), sentence constructions can easily be generated in which the learner does not have to worry about grammatical 'agreement' or what 'goes together' with what of any kind. The connection between topic and comment need only be one in which the topic establishes the realm within which what is being said in the comment holds. Topic-comment therefore represents a form of language organization that one conveniently falls back upon when there is less time for planning what to say or write – that is, less opportunity for grammaticizing – and this applies to all aspects of communication through the medium of language. Our particular interest in topic-comment phenomena here, however, has also to do with the grammaticization process to be observed where the learner gradually (and unconsciously) reanalyses topic-comment as target-language subject-predicate. We will later discuss the contribution that grammatical consciousness-raising can make towards facilitating this reanalysis.

2 Word order

The extent to which any language incorporates the notion **topic** and/or **subject** serves as a framework for typological classification, as we have just seen. Languages for which the category 'subject' is a meaningful one are also classified by means of a typological framework consisting of the possible linear orders that subject (S), object (O), and verb (V) may manifest, as we touched on in Chapter 2.1, and to which we return in more detail in Chapter 9. Of the six mathematically possible permutations of these elements, three account for about 98 per cent of the world's known languages, and in all three we find the subject occurring before the object: VSO, SVO, SOV. Recall that where L1 and L2 have different orders we seldom find the L2 learner resorting to the basic word order of his native language, perhaps because ample evidence for establishing the correct L2-order is available from the very onset of the learning experience for the new language in question.[3] But what we do find in learner language – and again we mentioned this briefly in Chapter 1 – are two important characteristics that are closely bound up with basic word order, both of which have to do with the learning of languages with properties similar to those of English.

The first such characteristic concerns the **modification** of basic word order. Classification of languages according to the natural order of their basic sentence constituents is not meant to imply that there cannot in certain circumstances be deviation from that order. Languages can in fact be further classified according to the amount of deviation from basic order that any particular language allows. As prototypical examples of the applicable range of such a property, Spanish allows fairly wide choice in the reordering of its basic SVO, whereas English allows very little. The English-speaking student of Spanish learns this new word-order freedom right away, whereas the Spanish-speaking student of English has the more difficult task of *un*learning the principle of word-order freedom for his L2 experience. It is often in the unlearning of something from the mother tongue that we find a heavy tendency for the learner to fall short of target-language norms, and indeed one can easily identify disallowed deviations from L2 English basic word order (e.g. *Was very interesting that movie*) in the early production of Spanish-speaking learners (see Chapter 10).

The second of the two characteristics cited above concerns the means at the learner's disposal, other than word-order freedom, for shifting the propositional content within the L2 sentence. The 'means' in question are the grammatical movement possibilities in a language like English, and for speakers of most other languages acquisition of these factors is no simple task. What we may glimpse in the learner production of English, then, is a gradual reanalysis of the function of word order – from freely placing propositional content according to principles of discourse and pragmatics (the simpler function), to fixing the grammatical positions of subject, object, and verb (the more complex function). It is a question, on the one hand, of word order in the service of discoursal relations (e.g. old information first, new information later; see Chapter 6.1) and, on the other hand, word order in the service of grammatical relations (e.g. subject before verb, object after), with all shades of gradation in between. The learner's acquisition of the grammatical 'machinery' necessary for representation of these relations in target English is another instance of the developing grammaticization that we have frequently been calling attention to. Later we will consider the matter of raising-to-consciousness of these language properties in pedagogy.

3 Syntactic-semantic distance

In Chapter 1 we briefly discussed the general tendency for all language learners initially to 'bend' the target language to the extent that form and meaning relationships are rendered as direct as possible. And in a sense the L2 learner's early recourse to topic-comment form and basic word-order deviation is another manifestation of this same tendency. But the need for rapid processing of complex propositional content with limited grammatical means serves to shape human language in such a way that form and meaning become more 'distant' from each other and the relationship between them more attenuated, more so in some languages than in others. It follows then that part of the L2 learning experience is one in which the learner acquires these L2 grammatical means for loosening form-meaning relationships to the extent required in the language being learned. As we saw in Section 2, this 'loosening' – that is, utilizing grammatical devices instead of linear order to maintain the necessary links between form and meaning – is yet another example of the grammaticization process at work.

It is thought by many language researchers that in English the form-meaning relationships are even more indirect than in most other

well-known languages. What do we really mean when we speak of
this 'indirectness'? We will attempt to answer the question by looking
at how a lot of learners first cope with L2 form-meaning indirectness
and then eventually master it.

Probably the most obvious sense in which the match between form
and meaning is indirect, or perhaps even twisted, is where something
'expected' from a semantic viewpoint is simply not realized in the
grammar. L2 learners will early on typically translate this expectation
into reality, by themselves supplying whatever it is that they feel
semantically should be there. For example, take the following pairs
of phrases where one is a version of the other, the first in conventional English and the second in learner-language English:

(1) a. a subject that I am interested in.
    b. a subject that I am interested in *it*.
(2) a. the boy whose bicycle I bought.
    b. the boy *who* I bought *his* bicycle.

In (1a) the close semantic relation between *in* and *a subject* has been
obscured by the grammatical rule that replaces *subject* with the relative
marker (*that*) and moves it to the front of the relative clause, thus
leaving a semantic 'hole' next to the 'stranded' preposition *in* (see
Chapter 9.4). But the learner, in his early struggle to make the target
language optimally learnable, needs to fill in this hole, for he hasn't
yet acquired the ability to process the L2 with semantic gaps of this
kind. He therefore temporarily solves the problem by filling the
semantic hole with a pronominal copy of the noun *subject*, namely *it*,
as we see in (1b). In this fashion, then, the learner himself brings L2
form and meaning into closer alignment and thus renders usable a
complex portion of target-language syntax that would otherwise be
for the time being inaccessible to him. We see much the same phenomenon in (2), where the learner's version (2b) among other things
retains subject, verb, possessive, and object (*I-bought-his-bicycle*) in
their original positions, the whole attached to *boy* through the simple
link of the relative marker (*who*). (We return to this topic in more
detail in Chapter 9.4.1.)

Another effect of tenuous form-meaning relationships can be seen
with L2 learners at higher levels of proficiency, where there is a
wider choice of form for grammatical realization of intended meaning.
Consider the following examples of target English:

(3) a. To imitate his accent is impossible.
    b. It's impossible to imitate his accent.
    c. His accent is impossible to imitate.

Since all three examples express essentially the same propositional content (and irrespective of the discourse context that might accommodate one more easily than another), which of the three would an L2 learner of English be more likely to produce? Example (3a) is unlikely because of its 'heavy' subject (*to imitate his accent*), which makes it more difficult to process and occurs only under special circumstances; (3c) is unlikely because the form-meaning relationship is quite skewed – *imitate* and *accent* (in a verb-object relationship) are at opposite ends of the sentence, and *impossible* seems to be predicated of *his accent* rather than *to imitate his accent*, which is the correct interpretation. That leaves us with (3b), and of course this is what the learner would most likely produce, as we know from the research that bears on this (Kellerman 1979). What 'goes together' semantically in (3) *literally* goes together in the syntax of (3b), where closely related elements occur next to each other (see Chapter 10). The learner's eventual acquisition of L2 language like (3c), as well as (1a) and (2a), would again be evidence that his ability to process loose form-meaning relationships in English is growing – that is, that he is increasingly able to grammaticize.

4 Noun-to-verb ratio

The conventional written form of a language is characterized, among other things, by a much greater incidence of nouns in contrast to verbs. This can easily be verified through casual inspection of any printed matter at hand. Here, for example, is an excerpt from the entry under 'newspaper' from a standard encyclopedia (in which, for our purposes, verbs are *italicized* and nouns are in **bold face**):

(4) **Newspapers** *have* a **distribution** that *is* wider than that of **television news**. Since the **invention** of the **telegraph**, which enormously *facilitated* the rapid **gathering** of **news**, **newspapers** *have bought* their services from the great **news agencies**. **Improvements** in **typesetting** and in **printing** *have made* possible the **publication** of huge **news editions** at great **speed**. Modern **newspapers** *are supported* primarily by the **sale** of **advertising space**, as they *are sold* at only a **fraction** of the **cost** of **production**. In recent **years newspapers** *have wielded* vast **influence** through their controlling **interests** in other **media**, *including* **radio** and **television**.

The New Columbia Encyclopedia, p. 1929

Although what counts as a verb or a noun is occasionally not all that clear, our tabulation for the above passage would be about 29 nouns to 9 verbs, or a ratio of better than three to one.[4]

Let us compare (4) with a passage typically produced, as part of a writing assignment and with ample time for completion, by a learner of English with low proficiency. Again, verbs are *italicized* and nouns are in **bold face**:

(5) My **country** famous **newspaper** *is* 'Times of Mukar'. It *establish* around 1920. It *publish* in three other **city**. **Circulation** *are* 270,000 **copy**. There *are* many **people** *buy* **copy** and *read* all **news** about current **topic, education,** and etc. It *print* much **advertising** and *are* *distribute* all over my **country**.

Our tabulation for the above passage is 13 nouns and 9 verbs, for a ratio for not quite 1.5 to one. (If we also include the repeated pronoun *it*, the noun tabulation goes to 16 but the ratio is still not much more than 1.5 to one.) Notice, then, that (5), though a much shorter passage, has as many verbs – nine – as the longer passage (4), but that the ratio of nouns to verbs in (5) is much lower. These observations therefore allow us to distinguish L2 interlanguage from L2 target language by the fact that learners initially produce far fewer nouns in relation to verbs. Is this simple statistical contrast all that we may note for the moment, or is there more of interest to be said on the subject? In other words, what else is going on in (4) *vis-à-vis* (5) that might have this difference in ratios as one of its consequences?

4.1 *Verb-argument*

There are several factors to be observed in connection with the higher ratio of nouns to verbs in (4) compared to (5). These have to do with the semantics of the verb, the derivation of the noun, and some matters of common usage. First of all, verbs are described linguistically in terms of sets of features and one of these features concerns the number of noun-phrases or **arguments** that are in a close definable semantic relation with a given verb.[5] It is thought that the more such **verb-argument** relations there are, the more 'complex' the verb in question. For example, the verb *admire* (*something, by someone*), with its two arguments, would be less complex than the verb *blame* (*something, on someone, by someone*), which usually has three. L2 interlanguage development is characterized among other things by the use, as learning progresses, of verbs with more arguments and of the increasing presence of noun-phrase arguments where they are required. Thus, almost all the verbs in (5) have no more than two arguments (serving as subject and/or object), the one exception being *distribute*, whose required object is missing. Now contrast (5) with

(4), where there are two verbs with *four* arguments – namely, *buy* (*something, from someone, by someone, for* [*price*]) and *sell* (*something, to someone, by someone, at/for* [*price*]). It is not hard to see that the choice of more complex verbs in the target English of (4) contributes directly to a statistically higher occurrence of nouns.

4.2 *Verbal nouns*

Consider next the derivation of the various nouns in (4) and (5). Single nouns in most languages can be anything from simple and concrete (*bell, water, cat*, etc.) to complex and abstract (*blame, admiration, rudeness*, etc.). The difference in complexity has largely to do with whether or not the noun derives from a verb (or an adjective). 'Concrete' *bell, water, cat* do not come from verbs, whereas 'abstract' *blame, admiration, rudeness* are formed from the verbs *blame* and *admire* and the adjective *rude*. We therefore may properly call these **verbal nouns**. Now since verbs, as we have just seen, are in particular relationships with certain closely associated noun-phrases, so likewise are the verbal nouns that derive from them. We thus have *blame* (*for something, on someone, by someone*), *admiration* (*of/for something/someone, by someone*), *rudeness* (*of someone*), etc. Not only then have we had a cluster of noun-phrases (i.e. arguments) associated with a single verb but we also now have the verb itself appearing as a noun.

Notice the incidence of verbal nouns in the two passages (4) and (5). In (5), the sample of early learner language, we find only two apparent verbal nouns – *circulation* (*circulate*) and *education* (*educate*) – and even these are used more in their concrete, simple-noun sense. In contrast to (5), however, the target-language passage (4) reveals ample instances of verbal nouns, along with their closely associated noun-phrases as well. In (4) we find, for example, *invention* (*of the telegraph*), *sale* (*of advertising space*), *interests* (*of newspapers* [*their*], *in other media*), etc. Furthermore, if we reflect upon the fact that sentences are limited to one (main) verb per clause but are not at all limited in the number of verbal nouns that may occur, then we may easily see how strongly the use of verbal nouns contributes to the statistically higher general occurrence of nouns as opposed to verbs.

4.3 *Effected object*

The third factor contributing to the higher ratio of nouns to verbs in (4) – a considerably weaker factor than the two that we have just cited – is one that has to do with stylistics. Compare the first sentence of (4) with the last sentence of (5). In (4) we find *Newspapers* **have**

a distribution . . . and in (5) *It* [*newspaper*] *are distribute* . . . It is
the difference between the 'straight' verb form *are distribute*[*d*] and
a version sometimes referred to as the **effected object**[6] – *have a distribution* – wherein the original verb has become a verbal noun. Other
examples might be *act* versus *take action; push* versus *give a push;
attempt* versus *make an attempt*, and in all cases we have in the
effected object an often preferable stylistic variant that contains the
verbal noun. The choice of the effected-object construction, then,
will obviously further increase the incidence of nouns over verbs in
the target language. That such constructions occur much less
frequently in early learner language is yet another factor contributing
to the much lower ratio of nouns to verbs at the onset of learning.

4.4 *Nouns, verbs, and learning*

Before we summarize this discussion of the noun-to-verb ratio, it
would be useful to mention what we are able actually to observe in
interlanguage as this ratio widens towards target-language norms.
We will observe then what it is that can happen between the phase
where the learner produces, for example,

(6) The problem is (we) *destroy* nature.

and the phase where he produces

(7) The problem is the *destruction* of nature.

Does the learner progress in such a fashion that (6), at some point
in the learning process, suddenly becomes (7)? In other words, does
the learner's grasp of the grammaticization that turns *destroy* into
destruction happen in such a manner that development of the other
grammatical accoutrements of noun-phrase construction (i.e. *the* N *of*)
proceeds apace?

It is by now perhaps obvious that learning does not progress this
way. It is almost always possible to discover intermediate courses of
development (as well as regression, or 'back-sliding'), and between
the times when (6) and then (7) would have been produced we would
quite likely find something like (8):

(8) The problem is the *destroy* of nature.

What (8) would reveal is that although the learner knows the formal
features of this particular kind of noun-phrase construction (i.e. *the*
N_1 *of* N_2), he has not yet learned the formal features of (at least some)
lexical categories – namely, nouns that are formed from verbs. In brief
then, progression from (6) to (7) requires the learning of both noun-

phrase settings and verbal-noun constructions that the settings will contain; example (8) opens a window for us upon the intermediate course in which at one point the formal setting has been learned but not yet the form of the lexical item that goes into that setting. The learner's use of a verb like *destroy* in a formal context that demands instead the noun *destruction* is sometimes identified as 'major lexical category confusion'. However, such 'confusion' may well be taken as strong evidence, among other things, that grammaticization is at work.

We want now to try to sum up what we have been saying about the noun-to-verb ratio and its relationship to grammaticization. The ratio of nouns to verbs in interlanguage is one that changes as learning progresses. Early interlanguage writing is characterized by a ratio that comes close to being even, whereas target written-language norms are characterized by a noun-to-verb ratio that is roughly three to one. Contributing to the target-language ratio are essentially three factors:

1. the use of verbs that have more noun phrases (i.e. arguments) in close semantic association with them plus the actual appearance of those arguments;
2. the recourse to verbal nouns for compressing more propositional content into single-sentence form;
3. the occasional stylistic choice of the effected-object construction over the single-verb variant.

Constant widening of the learner's noun-to-verb ratio is commensurate with his increasing capacity to integrate these factors into his network of knowledge 'how' – that is, his ability to grammaticize.

5 Coordination and subordination

The last of the developmental phenomena delineated by grammaticization that we will consider here is that of **coordination** and **subordination**. Although these terms denote two kinds of grammatical construction that prevail in natural language, they are not necessarily equally weighted in different languages and they have very different privileges of occurrence in language development, especially in second-language acquisition. In general, interlanguage will reveal a tendency early on to rely more heavily on coordination structure with a gradual shift, as learning progresses, towards the degree of subordination characteristic of the target language.

Take, for example, the learning of the grammatical means for expressing the concept of **concession**. Among the various ways in which concession is realized syntactically in English, we may note the use of coordination with *but* and subordination with *although*, as in (9) and (10):

(9) Prices rise *but* wages stay the same.
(10) *Although* prices rise, wages stay the same.

It is believed that a coordination construction like (9) is easier for the language user to process than a subordination construction like (10), where the user has to, as it were, hold in suspension the initial subordinate clause until he perceives the main clause to come and discerns the proper semantic relation between the two. It should therefore not be surprising if the L2 learner's emerging grammatical competence first embraces the coordination alternative, and indeed we find ample evidence of heavy reliance upon coordinate structure in early written interlanguage – long sequences such as [clause] *and* [clause] *but* [clause] *so* [clause], etc. The relatively later acquisition of the subordination alternative is related to the greater command of grammaticization required of the user of such constructions.

Is the learner's progress in these areas therefore to be characterized by a path that leads directly from acquisition of language like that of (9) to the addition of language like that of (10)? Just as we have noted intermediate courses of development in the acquisition of other syntactic phenomena, so also can we note transitory tendencies with coordination/subordination. Often to be seen then in interlanguage production are sentences like (11):

(11) *Although* prices rise *but* wages stay the same.

It is as if the learner, venturing into the uncharted grammatical territory of concessive adverbial clauses with *although*, still needs the already familiar semantic 'compass' provided by concessive *but* until his new grammatical orientation is more solidly grounded.

Earlier, we examined similar transition phases of interlanguage in connection with relative clause 'subordination', and it is worth briefly calling that once more to our attention. In the discussion of **syntactic-semantic distance** of Section 3 we took note of interlanguage production in the form of examples (1b) and (2b), repeated here as (12) and (13):

(12) a subject that I am interested in *it*.
(13) the boy *who* I bought *his* bicycle.

One way to look at such examples is not so much as malformed English relative clauses as interlanguage 'tacked on' sentences, with *that* and *who* serving as a kind of conjunction. From the learner's standpoint then the simplest way of modifying the nouns *subject* in (12) and *boy* in (13), on the way to acquisition of the more complicated target L2 relative clause, is to tack a full sentence on to the head noun by means of *that* and *who*. We thus have *that* + *I am interested in it* and *who* + *I bought his bicycle*. In conceptual and processing terms, it is less difficult merely to 'attach' B to A (**parataxis**) than it is to 'enmesh' B in A (**syntaxis**) – that is, to grammaticize. We therefore find that initial language learning favours the 'attachment' alternative over, shall we say, 'enmeshment'.

It is time now to look back over all that we have been considering in our exploration of these psycholinguistic aspects of grammaticization.

6 Summary

Grammaticization is perhaps the most prominent manifestation of language conceived as an *organism*. Interesting clues to the actual process of grammaticization at work in the written language of learners are often to be found in the editorial emendations of the learners themselves. What such records (as well as a record of the learner's progress over a length of time) can reveal are aspects of grammaticization that not only range over sizable portions of interlanguage but also interact with each other in important ways. Among these aspects we have noted five in particular:

1. The learner's reanalysis, reinterpretation, and reorganization of early **topic-comment** as later **subject-predicate** (for target languages where **subject** and not **topic** is the point of departure for arrangement of information within the sentence).
2. The learning of the functions of **word order** (in a language like English) as a means for expressing grammatical relations, and the acquisition of the grammatical devices (e.g. movement rules) necessary for maintaining that order.
3. The learner's growing understanding of the special grammatical resources for relating grammatical form to meaning where (in a language like English) there is often no close linear correspondence between the two; i.e. form and meaning are 'distant' from one another.
4. The increasing capacity of the learner to realize grammatically the full set of **arguments** for any given verb and to make use of verbs that have larger sets. The concomitant of this is the learner's growing awareness of the formal distinctions among major lexical

categories and his or her ability to exploit these distinctions (e.g. turn verbs into nouns and clauses into noun-phrases) for the 'compression' of larger amounts of propositional content into smaller sentence space.

5. The learner's progress in abandoning much early **coordinate-structure** arrangements of information for target-language utilization of **subordination** and the major grammatical resources that this requires.

Activities

1. What comments concerning English SVO structure can you make about the following excerpted passage written by a Spanish-speaking native of Venezuela?

> In South America are many interesting place. One of them is Carabobo Camp. Was here, in Carabobo, where the Independent War against Spain was won. Was a crude battle and many Latinoamericans were killed. For any visitor is interesting to know that in this place happened the liberty of Latinoamerica. Was Simon Bolivar the man who conduced the battle and was him who got the liberty for four more countries.

2. What comments concerning form-meaning relationship can you make about the following excerpts from a passage written by a native speaker of Arabic?

   a. I will take my guest to give him the chance that he would see the Egyptian pyramids.

   b. I would like to give him the opportunity that he could see some of the Egyptian people.

3. What factor is it that determines grammaticality among the following questions? Notice that presence of the category **verbal noun** is a sufficient condition but not a necessary one.

1. What time is the game?	6. *What time is the airport?
2. *What time is the clock?	7. What time is class?
3. What time is the interview?	8. *What time is college?
4. *What time is the ticket?	9. *What time is the radio?
5. What time is the flight?	10. What time is the radio programme?

4. Tabulate *all* the verbal nouns in example (4), Section 4.2, and determine first how many individual noun-phrase semantic relationships each has and, second, which such relations are actually realized in the syntax of the passage.

Notes

1. The term 'grammaticization', as it is used throughout these chapters, will be unavoidably ambiguous at times. That is, grammaticization denotes a developmental phenomenon that can be found in a number of different language realms: language history, dialectology, pidgin→creole, L1 acquisition, and of course L2 acquisition. The ambiguity that is unavoidable in these discussions arises in those instances where grammaticization may be understood as a development either in the history of the English language (*that man his hat → that man's hat*) or in the metamorphosis of L2 interlanguage (*that man hat → that man's hat*). On occasion the two developments may coincide.

   The ensuing elaboration of 'grammaticization' owes a great deal to ideas developed in Givón (1979).
2. See, for example, Schachter and Rutherford (1979) and Rutherford (1983). Topic-comment transfer may be more apparent in written than in spoken interlanguage, as suggested by Fuller and Gundel (1985).
3. See Chapter 9, Section 6, for a related explanation in terms of the learner's parsing abilities.
4. High ratio of nouns to verbs is a general characteristic of 'planned' language (e.g. formal writing). 'Unplanned' language (e.g. ordinary speech) reveals a ratio of nouns to verbs that is much lower.
5. In linguistic terms, this is referred to as 'predicate-argument relationship'. See Chapter 9.3.
6. This term comes from Quirk *et al.* (1972). In Quirk *et al.* (1985) these examples would be identified as 'eventive object'.

5 Consciousness-raising and the language organism

More than once so far throughout these pages we have made reference to commonly held beliefs about what the nature of grammatical consciousness-raising in the classroom should be. When something *about* the language to be learned is brought to the attention of the learner, we can often assume that it will turn out to be a language *construct* or *entity* of some kind – the passive, relative clauses, the present perfect, for example, all come easily to mind here. And in those classroom situations where a premium is placed on overt reference to language form, it is not very hard to understand why it should be to *units* of this kind that the learner's attention is drawn. Indeed, if any explicit mention is to be made of target-language information, then one may well wonder how it could really, in all practicality, be done otherwise. For purposes of 'teaching' language form, it would seem, one has to 'get a handle' on something, and the most natural kind of thing to try to 'grasp' in this way is a solid, stable, fixed piece of the total language product – something with edges to it . . . in other words, a language *construct*.

1 Attention to the grammatical product

Our association here of language *construct* with language *product* is not exactly accidental. A language-learner product – in the sense that we speak of 'learner production' – is what the great majority of language-teaching programmes everywhere are designed to bring about. And since analysis of the perceived language product into what are thought to be its constituent parts yields an inventory of language constructs, then these – and the reasoning here is quite understandable – are what need to be 'taught' if that product is to be realized. This description of the entire procedure, however, is meant to stand somewhat as a reflection not only of how we look at language but, even more important, of how we see the world around us, for it is the way in which we perceive such 'reality' that ultimately determines in a large sense what kind of phenomenon we imagine 'language' itself to be. And of course it is this perception *of* language that must in turn lead to the assumptions *about* language upon which we base everything that we finally do *with* language – including teach it. Here it would be worth recalling momentarily our previous metaphorical distinctions.

In much current language teaching where grammatical consciousness-raising plays a role, the metaphor of language as a *machine* is an apt image for what is brought to consciousness. For just as with a machine – where it is the behaviour of the parts that collectively determines the behaviour of the whole – it is ostensibly the behaviour of the language constructs that collectively determines the workings of the formal language system as a whole, or so we are often led to believe. If in addition to the machine metaphor, however, one also brings into focus the image of language as an *organism*, then the part-whole relationship is turned upside down: it is now the behaviour of the whole that determines the behaviour of the parts.[1] This is the relationship that will prove the more important to us as we continue to explore the implications of grammaticization for consciousness-raising.

Our periodic excursions into metaphysics are part of an attempt to sort out some of the multi-faceted language complexity along the way to meaningful decision-making with regard to grammatical consciousness-raising. From this sorting-out procedure have steadily emerged the broad outlines of particular kinds of association, which we now want to make more explicit. Thus, in one interpretation of the nature of language we have the *machine* concept yielding a language *product* whose prime manifestation is a language *construct*. In our other (and not necessarily contradictory) interpretation we have the *organism* concept embodying language *processes* among which is all-important *grammaticization*. From the grammatical-*product* model it is not difficult to derive pedagogical implications. Indeed, these are evident for all to see in the mass of available 'grammatically oriented' commercially produced language materials. What, then, are the implications for grammatical consciousness-raising of the grammatical-*process* model?

2 Attention to the grammatical process

Since grammaticization is a process, it has no 'edges'. The learner cannot therefore 'grasp' it or 'get a handle' on it. Nor can he, to use some familiar terminology, manipulate it, transform it, restate it, delete it, etc. These are activities associated with the kind of C-R that arises more naturally out of approaches associated with a product model. Although we may make use of such activities in the process of grammaticizing in particular circumstances, they are not something that one 'does' *with* grammaticization. The pedagogical procedures to be associated with C-R for the grammatical-process model are ones that must arise naturally from the nature of grammaticization itself. But since no two languages reveal anything like either the same range or the same depth of grammaticization, it therefore follows that what C-R procedures are right for the learning of any one language will not be quite right for any other. Notice that it is not a question of 'right' choices to be made within some inventory of pedagogical-grammar 'techniques'. With each target language standing as the unique embodiment of its own index of grammaticization, there can be no such all-purpose inventory. Indeed, the very notion of an 'inventory of techniques' is one that is more to be associated with the raising-to-consciousness of language constructs. Much better suited to our purposes here would be the understanding that just as grammaticization is a visible manifestation of the organic side of language, so must the attendant C-R procedures be likewise organically conceived. Again, the nature of grammatical consciousness-raising within a grammatical-process model can derive only from the nature of the processes themselves.

What, then, does such C-R activity actually look like? Although this question is addressed with considerable detail in Part Five, it will be useful here at least to sketch some broad outlines of how one might go about the task at hand. How, for example, are the unique grammaticization characteristics of any target language raised to consciousness such that the learner's path to maximal utilization is that much more illuminated?

If we take English to be the L2, we have a target language whose syntactic possibilities are an example *par excellence* of grammaticization. One of the important determinants of this, unlike so many other languages, is the fact that 'every English sentence must have a subject', to use the popular parlance. The requirement is so strong in fact that even if no propositional content is available to 'fill' subject position, then we fill it with the so-called 'dummy' elements *it* and *there* (**It**'s raining; **There**'s water on the floor). What the learner has to learn, however, is not just this rather rigid stipulation concerning subjects, but also the fact that his various choices of what is to be the subject will trigger very different grammatical consequences for the rest of the sentence. As a very simple example of this, consider the sentence possibilities with the verb *take up* and the nouns *sofa* and *room*. Although the semantic relations among the three are such that there can essentially be only one meaning conveyed that makes sense, the possible syntactic relations are a different story. If we select *sofa*, for example, as subject of *take up* we will have (before making any further grammatical adjustments) *Sofa take up room*. On the other hand, selection of *room* as subject will trigger the passive: *Room is taken up by sofa*. The actual choice, of course, is governed not by the syntax but by discourse factors, e.g. the principled arrangement of 'new' and 'old' information (see Chapter 6). Notice, then, that the necessary grammatical 'cleaning up' of our two skeletal sentences will not be the same for each, and that the differences will also follow from what we chose to be the subject. Thus, although we can have skeletal *Sofa take up room*, we cannot have skeletal *Room take up sofa*. 'Promotion' of *room* to subject position now forces the passive, and maintenance of the proper semantic relations among *take up, sofa*, and *room* requires that agent *sofa* be expressed grammatically as *by sofa*. The further choice of proper determiner (*the, a, this*, etc.) will come about from the interaction of the grammar (e.g. count/mass noun, singular/plural) with the discourse (e.g. old/new information). Again, the point to be emphasized in all this is that the discourse-motivated choice of noun-phrase material to function as grammatical subject of the sentence carries in its wake the necessity to grammaticize those other portions of the sentence whose semantic relations would otherwise be altered.

The very processes we have just described may also constitute the basis for raising the grammatical consciousness of the learner. That is, it will be a fairly simple matter to present to him (or have him devise for himself) semantically conceived 'propositional clusters' consisting of verb + associated noun-phrases, very much on the order of what we have done above. With the learner's discourse-determined selection of appropriate grammatical subject, a given cluster then 'metamorphoses' (i.e. grammaticizes) into an SVO sentence, the consciousness-raising occurring as the learner is guided through the grammaticization that is thereby triggered in other parts of that sentence. If the propositional clusters appear in the absence of a discourse context, then the selection of a noun-phrase (where there is more than one in the cluster) for 'promotion' to subject may be arbitrary. The value of having the context, however, is that, at the same time the learner is working through the grammatical consequences of his lexical choices, he is also becoming cognizant of the *extra*-grammatical factors that motivate these choices. In other words, from the very start he learns not just *how* to grammaticize (e.g. form the passive) but also *why* one momentarily chooses this grammatical means (the passive) over some other (the active).[2]

The propositional-cluster principle for consciousness-raising represents a powerful means for enabling the learner to come to grips with the five concomitants of English grammaticization discussed in Chapter 4. Let us elaborate a little on this with regard to the phenomena in question.

Topic and subject

The act of conferring 'subjecthood' upon a designated noun-phrase, together with the grammaticization that this entails (e.g. morphological marking of subject-verb agreement), serves to engender 'understanding' of the grammatical properties that distinguish **subject** from **topic** and facilitates the learner's *reanalysis* of topic as subject in the early part of his development.

Word order

The activity of moving elements, under the constraint that movement must be into 'grammatically definable' sentence positions, reinforces the notion of word order as a reflection of grammatical as opposed to semantic relations.

Syntactic-semantic distance

The procedure of 'extracting' noun-phrases for subjecthood from deep within the propositional cluster, thereby attenuating form-meaning relationships in the resulting sentence, strengthens understanding of this pervasive characteristic of English.

Noun-to-verb ratio

Propositional clusters can be devised with more complex verbs (i.e. that have more associated noun-phrases) and clusters can be embedded within clusters, thereby drawing the learner's attention to the heavy use of verbal nouns for the compression of more propositional content into smaller grammatical space.

Coordination and subordination

The activity of rendering into well-formed sentences propositional clusters containing embedded material to be realized as relative clauses serves to steer the learner profitably through a 'paratactic' phase to 'syntactic' subordination.

Exploitation of grammaticization for consciousness-raising can lead in several directions and we have just been exploring some of that ground here. We will return in Part Five to a more in-depth and detailed look at these possibilities. Before moving on in the next chapter to other aspects of the relationship of second-language grammar to the learning/teaching experience, however, a few final thoughts are in order.

3 Epilogue

The proposals for consciousness-raising activity that we have begun to advance here, as well as all that is still to come, are meant to be consistent with *what* we believe the nature of language system to be, and *how* we think interlanguage development relates to that system. Although we are still a long way from truly understanding the language-acquisition process, it is perhaps not unreasonable to speculate that the ultimately most desirable means for raising consciousness will come as close as possible to replicating in some general sense the nature of acquisition itself. Our essential ignorance of the acquisition process notwithstanding, there is at least some certainty about ways in which acquisition does *not* proceed. We know of no evidence to support the notion, for example, that grammatical constructs are 'learned' as one would learn (i.e. commit to memory) a collection of facts in some academic discipline like history, law, or mathematics. Grammatical 'learning' of this kind *can* take place, of course, in special circumstances – e.g. knowledge obtained by a professional linguist who is trained to analyse languages – but where such knowledge seems to result in enhanced ability to use the language in question, the critical factors very likely are ones other than the instantaneous recall of a grammatical construct for 'plugging in' to the propositional content about to be transmitted within a discourse setting. As one researcher, R. Hurtig, has written, 'the sentence (clause) is the on-line perceptual unit while the discourse (idea set/logical event space) is the unit of cognitive (semantic) memory. Put in other terms, the discourse is the cognitive organiz-ational unit while the sentence (syntactic structure) is the production planning unit' (Hurtig 1977, pp. 103–4). Grammar thus perceived has also been described as a 'strategy' for the processing of discourse (Givón 1979). It is observations such as these that strengthen the concept of language that we have attempted to instil throughout these pages – that is, language conceived as an *organism*.

In Part Three we will again explore the possibilities of C-R by looking at grammatical form in relation to discourse function and semantics.

Activities

1. It was noted that the 'organism' metaphor of language points to a reversal of the traditional part-whole relationship – where the behaviour of the whole now determines the behaviour of the parts. Can you come up with other phenomena outside language in which this same part-whole relationship would seem to hold?

2. Consider the following 'propositional cluster':

blame – accident – weather – police

How many different ways can this cluster now be realized as a full sentence? Devise different discourse contexts that would render each choice an appropriate one.

3. Pick a convenient topic and assign one group of students to write a paragraph about it with no time pressure, and another group (of the same proficiency) to talk about it for a few minutes each on tape. Then roughly compare the two sets of products in terms of subordination and coordination and the noun-to-verb ratio. Are there any notable differences?

Notes

1. This is in fact the part-whole relationship that obtains in quantum mechanics. I owe this observation to F. Capra (1982, p. 86). Not unrelated to this is the following claim in Hatch (1978, p. 404): 'In second language learning . . . it is assumed that one first learns how to manipulate structures, that one gradually builds up a repertoire of structures and then, somehow, learns how to put the structures to use in discourse. We would like to consider the possibility that just the reverse happens. One learns how to do conversation, one learns how to interact verbally, and out of this interaction syntactic structures are developed.'
2. H. G. Widdowson's view of grammar as 'a device for mediating between words and contexts' (Widdowson 1986, p. 12) is not inconsistent with our treatment here.

Questions to Part Two

1. How relevant to your own language-related activities are the metaphors of language as machine and as organism? Are both metaphors useful as conceptualizations of language?

2. How would the native languages of your students (or your own native language) be described with reference to the classification features outlined in Chapter 4?

3. In Chapter 4.4, a comparison was made between two written texts (examples (4) and (5)) in terms of noun-to-verb ratio. What factors other than language proficiency do you think may also affect this ratio (i.e. factors having to do with task performance) and in what way?

4. What other examples of 'major lexical category confusion' (Chapter 4.4.4) have you encountered with language learners? Can they be analysed as examples of grammaticization in progress?

5. In what ways may 'product' and 'process' be considered part of the same general phenomenon?

Part Three
The reaches of grammar

Isolated material particles are abstractions, their properties being definable and observable only through their interaction with other systems.

Niels Bohr

In this book we have already touched on more than one way of looking at the phenomenon that we call 'language'. And we have seen that whatever conception of language we are disposed to carry around with us has a direct bearing on anything we say or do where something about language is involved – especially the teaching of it. If we are therefore 'saying' or 'doing' something that represents a pedagogical drawing of attention to characteristics of the formal system – i.e. the grammar – of someone else's native language, then that saying or doing cannot help but reflect our fundamental, probably unconscious, 'beliefs' about not only how language 'works' but also how it comes into being – as part of the mental capacity of a maturing infant as well as of a language-learning adult. As apt for language as for the physical world are the words of the scientist Fritjof Capra: 'Observed patterns of matter are reflections of patterns of mind.'

One such 'pattern of mind' that we have already discussed in previous chapters is the pattern overlaying a conception of human language that readily lends itself to the 'machine' metaphor. Language thus conceived consists of a network of separate 'components' (e.g. phonology, grammar, lexicon, semantics, discourse, etc.) that 'plug into' one another to the extent that the sum total of successful connections constitutes the cumulative 'mastery' of the language being learned. (Not unrelated to these components are the sub-parts of language production – pronunciation, vocabulary, grammar, conversation, etc. – that often define the content of the foreign-language curriculum.) The components themselves are closed systems, each with its repertoire of rules, features, characteristics, attributes, etc., and the systems range themselves in hierarchical fashion, i.e. phonology at the bottom, discourse at the top. This picture of language will be especially recognizable to anyone familiar with considerable linguistic research of a decade or so ago.

To the language model we have just recalled it is not difficult to conjure up one or two pedagogical analogues for grammatical consciousness-raising (C-R). Consistent with these observations about language organization would be an approach to language teaching in which first those portions of the target-language syntax that were identified as 'teachable' would be imparted to the learner in the form of explicit rules, arranged sequentially according to presumed 'order of difficulty', together with batteries of drills or exercises designed to reinforce the learner's newly acquired structural knowledge through classroom practice. Once the teaching of grammatical content had eventually run its course (and if enough hours still remained in the semester), the learner's attention would be drawn to models of written discourse classified as 'narration', 'argumentation', 'comparison and contrast', etc., in order that he might demonstrate ability to 'utilize' his assumed late grammatical knowledge through the grafting of grammatical constructs on to a discoursal framework. This approach to grammatical C-R in pedagogy was not so long ago quite in vogue, and it is important to realize that the whole enterprise subsumes a concept of language organization that is at once hierarchical and componential.

Similarly, another and more recent pedagogical analogue to language organization viewed as a collection of interconnected components is the approach to language syllabus design deriving from isolation of language units identified as 'notions' and 'functions'. The prime motivation for development of the 'notional-functional' syllabus was (a) the observation that grammar-based approaches did not seem to lead the learner to a functional use of the language, coupled with (b) a belief that the *end* of language learning (conceived as ability to give grammatical expression to categories of meaning) should also constitute the *means* for teaching it. The starting point for syllabus design was thus defined in terms of *behavioural objectives* articulated in the form of an elaborate taxonomy, e.g. semantico-grammatical categories (time, location, etc.); categories of modal meaning (certainty, commitment, etc.); and categories of communicative function (argument, judgement, rational inquiry, etc.). This taxonomic edifice reveals further subcategorization all the way to extensive, basic endvocabulary – the ultimate lexical instantiations, at the bottom of the hierarchy, of the kind of 'communicative need' specified at the top. It then remained only for meaning thus derived to receive its grammatical realization in order for all the language 'ingredients' necessary for communication to be available to the learner (see Wilkins 1976).[1]

Notional-functionalism is therefore an example *par excellence* of the 'componential' view of language.

Language described as a network of discrete components is a language description that serves as one possible answer to the question 'What is language made up of?' There is another and more far-reaching kind of question we might want to ask, however, and that is 'Why is language the way it is?' – or, to tailor the question to our more immediate concerns, 'Why is *grammar* the way it is?' That is, what is the relationship of grammar to the rest of language? What larger functions within human language does grammar serve? Why, among all the various properties of grammar across the entire range of known languages, do different subsets of such properties cluster in particular languages? Finally, what are the consequences, for learning and teaching, of the particular clustering of grammatical properties that obtains in English? It is an attempt to address these questions from a discoursal and semantic viewpoint that will concern us throughout Chapters 6, 7, and 8.

6 Grammar and discourse

It is commonly said that 'one picture is worth a thousand words'. What we probably mean by this is that real-world physical phenomena that can be taken in by the eye are rendered more accurately as a pictorial image than as a verbal description. Faithful 'depiction' of the place in which you find yourself right now, as you read this, for example, will be far easier to transmit to someone else as a photograph or drawing than as a stretch of prose. Images, unlike language, do not have starting and ending points. With our eye we take in a lot of things both randomly and simultaneously, whereas with language we can listen to only one thing at a time and generally read from left to right and from top to bottom. An image therefore exists only in space; it manifests no intrinsic 'ordering' of content for purposes of attention. Language, however, exists in time; limitations upon our capacity to 'attend' to language are such that language content has to be 'strung out' in *non*-random order. Images are thus *spatial*; language is *temporal*.

If language served no purpose other than merely the verbalization of what we can see, then obviously pictures would always be preferred. But language *does* serve other purposes – everything from the creation of a poem to the exercise of control over our social environment.[2] Language makes possible the most routine and inconsequential of human interaction, e.g. a simple greeting – as well as the most arresting and momentous, e.g. the *Declaration of Independence*. The range of possible expression with language, to repeat a popular cliché, is infinite; yet language accomplishes this with finite grammatical means. What actually is it then that is 'accomplished' in language through these grammatical means?

1 The given-new principle

Language, as we have said, is *temporal*. It is strung out in linear fashion, and these 'stretches' – whether they be phrases, sentences, paragraphs, whole texts, or whatever – have beginnings and endings.

The obvious consequence of this is that whatever language material appears in these stretches has to be in some kind of sequential *order*. Perhaps the kind of order most familiar to us would be that signalled by the sorts of language stricture that we can recall from elementary school: 'Don't end a sentence with a preposition.' 'Put the subject before the verb.' 'You shouldn't split an infinitive.' 'I before e, except after c' . . . and so on. And for more recent examples, throughout our discussions of grammaticization in Chapter 4 we talked of **basic word order** and of possible deviation from that order. Indeed, much of what we build into the expression of language rules of every variety involves an ordering of some kind.

The ordering of language material applies not only to grammatical elements but also to 'chunks' of information, or **propositional content**, that grammatical structure conveys. Strictly speaking, it is often possible to arrange propositional content in more than one order while at the same time maintaining grammaticality. Yet it is only one of these possible orders that is usually felt somehow to be 'right'; the alternative arrangements have something awkward or infelicitous about them. As an illustration of this, we will again look at a piece of writing produced by a learner of English. The passage (A) is part of a description of the house where the learner spent her childhood:

(A) ¹My father's house had four bedrooms and two sitting rooms.
²A large garden was in front of the house. ³My father had planted a lot of flowers in the garden. ⁴These flowers were roses and tulips, etc. . . .

Now compare (A) with passage (B), the learner's second effort, where the only thing that has changed is the order of information within two of the four sentences:

(B) ¹My father's house had four bedrooms and two sitting rooms.
²In front of the house was a large garden. ³In the garden my father had planted a lot of flowers. ⁴These flowers were roses and tulips, etc. . . .

Comparison of the two passages reveals of course that (B) is clearly more felicitous than (A). Since the only difference between the two is the order in which information has been placed within two of the four individual sentences, we are entitled to ask what it is about that order that can bring about such a contrast in felicity. The answer has to do with our ability as language users to process the language in the two passages in question. One of the things that makes language processing possible at all is the arrangement of information in linear order such that what we are hearing or seeing in the text for the first time is linked to something else with which we are already familiar. These two kinds of information are usually referred to as **new** versus old, or **given**.[3] Smoothly flowing discourse is characterized among other things by the extent to which new and given form a 'chain'. The simplest chain is created across sentence boundaries when what is introduced in one sentence as new starts the next sentence as given, thereby establishing its relevance to what has preceded. (Given may also be linked to a previous given.) If we let given be represented by 'g' and new by 'n', we can represent the above two passages schematically and thus more easily compare them in terms of this chaining effect:

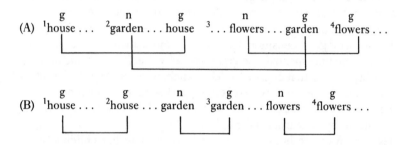

Notice the unevenness of the chain in (A) with its overlapping lines of reference. Thus, what makes (A) more difficult to process than (B) is that in sentences 2 and 3 the new information (n) occurs *before* the given (g). When we read the passage, *garden* in sentence 2 and *flowers* in sentence 3 therefore have to be held in suspension, so to speak, until their links with the previous content – through *house* in sentences 1–2 and through *garden* in sentences 2–3 – can be established. With the more natural ordering of given and new in (B), no such 'suspension' is required and the passage is more easily processed for comprehension. Passage (B) can of course be further improved by means of what in pedagogy is called 'sentence-combining', and we will have more to say about that in Chapter 12.

Before we consider the grammatical processes that figure in the ordering of propositional content illustrated in (A) and (B), let us look at one more brief sample of how the given-new principle works in written discourse. Our text in this instance is taken from standard English and the language therefore reveals more formal sophistication. This time the middle sentence is displayed as a choice among three possible alternatives:[4]

(C) [1]Our next task was to look for those elusive particles.

| [2a]Without a microscope, such particles are difficult to detect. | [2b]Such particles are difficult to detect without a microscope. | [2c]It is difficult to detect such particles without a microscope. |

[3]The particular kind of instrument needed can be found in an ordinary laboratory.

It can readily be seen that of the three options for sentence 2, it is 2b that forms the best link between sentences 1 and 3. Again, it is the arrangement of given and new information in sentence 2b that determines our choice, and a schema like that which we used for passages (A) and (B) will perhaps help to make this clear:

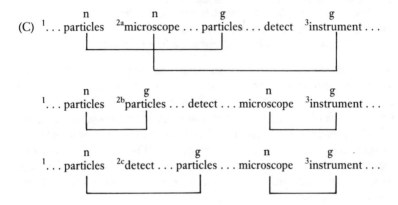

Sentence 2a is a poor link because the positions of given (g) and new (n) are the reverse of what they need to be. Sentence 2c has given and new properly ordered and is certainly an improvement over sentence 2a. Example 2b goes one better, however, by locating given at the beginning of its sentence for an even smoother link.

Notice that what the succeeding sentence picks up as given need not necessarily be an actual copy of what was introduced in the preceding sentence as new. The link between *microscope* and *instrument*, for example, is one of **hyponymy** (*microscope* being a subclass of *instrument*), and other kinds of relationship can establish such links as well (e.g. part-whole, synonymy, anaphora, etc.; these concepts are discussed at greater length in terms of **cohesion** in Chapter 7). The extent to which such relationships can be made transparent is largely determined by grammatical processes, and these are what we now want to catch a glimpse of. (Our fuller treatment will wait until Chapters 9 and 10.)

Consider once again the improvements that we opted for in passage (B) and the selection that we preferred in passage (C2). The most felicitous choice of sentences within each passage reveals an order of propositional content that is most compatible with the given-new principle. In what way does the order differ from that in the less appropriate (but still grammatical) sentences that we passed over, and what grammatical processes bring about these differences? The contrast between passages (A) and (B) is traceable to the arrangement of content in sentences 2 and 3, which are repeated here for convenience:

(A) ²A large garden was in front of the house.
     ³My father had planted a lot of flowers in the garden.
(B) ²In front of the house was a large garden.
     ³In the garden my father had planted a lot of flowers.

In (A) the sentence parts are in what one might say is their most 'basic' or 'neutral' order – the order that would obtain were there no context to dictate otherwise. In (B), however, a **locative adverbial** (in the form of a prepositional phrase) has been moved to the front of the sentence in both sentence 2 and sentence 3 (*in front of the house* in sentence 2, *in the garden* in sentence 3). The locatives have been **fronted** for a smoother text because contained in the locatives are items of given information (*house* and *garden*) that form a tie with the previous sentence.

A closer look, however, at the movement process for these pairs of sentences uncovers an interesting grammatical fact – one that typifies the pervasiveness of the grammaticization phenomenon in English. Although a locative has been fronted in each of the two sentences 2 and 3, this fronting is not the only movement that has taken place in sentence 2. It will readily be seen that the verb *was* has also moved: it has been drawn to the other side of its subject, in effect changing an SV construction to VS (*was* + *a large garden*). Contrast this with what happened – rather, what did *not* happen – in sentence 3: fronting of the locative (*in the garden*) did *not* trigger in sentence 3 a permutation of subject and verb. That is, for sentence 3 in (B) we do not find *In the garden* **had** *my father planted a lot of flowers*. The obvious question to ponder at this juncture is why fronting of a locative should effect verb-movement[5] in sentence 2 but not in sentence 3. The answer has to do with the relationship of the locative phrase to the main verb of its sentence. Notice that the semantic relationship in sentence 2 between *in the garden* and *was* is 'tighter' than the relationship in sentence 3 between *in front of the house* and *had planted*, which do not even occur adjacent to one another. In fact, the connection in sentence 3 is so loose that the sentence could stand alone *without* the locative and still be grammatical (*My father had planted a lot of flowers*). Yet nothing of this sort is possible of course with sentence 2; in other words, we cannot have a sentence like **A large garden was*. We may therefore say that fronting of locatives, as in sentences 2 and 3 of passage (B), will trigger movement of the verbal element as well where locative and verb form a tight semantic unit. Later, we will see that this principle is not limited to the fronting of locatives alone.

The examples of fronting that we have been discussing – (B2) versus (B3) – represent two kinds of possible movement in English which, taken together, begin to tell us something about a much broader concern; the interrelationship of grammar, semantics, and discourse. Very briefly, then, in terms of the language phenomena that we have just examined, we may roughly characterize this interrelationship as follows:

1. discourse requirements partially determine the general order of major information blocks within the sentence;
2. semantic requirements partially determine the amount of grammaticization that attends the movement of sentence constituents in the satisfaction of those discourse demands; and
3. grammatical requirements are such that grammaticization is invoked in order that this whole propositional complex be processable as human language.

2 Grammatical processes

Let us momentarily return for a brief look at the grammatical processes at work in the discourse of passage (C), above. The task in (C) was to choose among three possible arrangements of propositional content for the version of sentence 2 that best accommodates to its discourse setting, represented by sentences 1 and 3, and we saw that the choice had to be sentence 2b (*Such particles are difficult to detect without a microscope*). The most useful procedure for examining the grammatical processes that result in sentence 2b is one where we first attempt to identify the most basic grammatical and semantic relationships. That is, what really is it of which *be difficult* is predicated? Since it doesn't make sense to say that *such particles* are *difficult*, we look further and settle on the interpretation where what is predicated of *difficult* is the full infinitive phrase, *to detect such particles*. But this is not yet quite enough, for the true meaning narrows to 'detection' *without a microscope*. Thus, we can now construct a sentence, in the absence of any discourse context, in which the grammatical and semantic relationships are in the closest possible alignment – where the grammatical elements are in their most 'basic' order: *To detect such particles without a microscope is difficult.*

We now have a 'basic' version of sentence 2, passage (C), that is different from the three alternatives laid out – sentences 2a, 2b, and 2c. Let us then call this basic version sentence 2d. It is worth repeating here that the differences between sentence 2d and the three alternative versions sentences 2a–c have to do with the number and kind of grammatical processes involved; the propositional content of all four sentences remains identical. What then has taken place grammatically that distinguishes our 'basic' version, sentence 2d, from its three alternatives?

Compare sentence 2d first with 2c (*It is difficult to detect such particles without a microscope*). What is different in 2c is that what is predicated of *is difficult* – namely, *to detect such particles without a microscope* – has been shifted to the right side of the verb phrase, the spot that it has vacated – namely, subject position – now being occupied by the 'dummy' element *it*. This kind of shift is common in English where the subject of the sentence is grammatically complex. The shifting itself is usually referred to as **extraposition** (see Chapter 9.4) and the construction resulting after extraposition is, generally speaking, easier to process for comprehension than its non-extraposed counterpart.

Compare sentence 2d next with 2b (*Such particles are difficult to detect without a microscope*). In a sense, 2b is a step farther removed from our basic 2d than 2c was, and the easiest way to appreciate the contrast between 2d and 2b is to identify that step. What distinguishes 2b from 2c then is that the object of *detect* in 2c – *such particles* – has been **extracted** (see Chapter 9.4) from within its infinitive phrase and 'lifted' or **raised** (see Chapter 9.2.3) into the subject position otherwise held by 'dummy' *it*. Notice, however, that although a succession of grammatical processes has rearranged the propositional content of 2d such that *particles*, the **given** element, now occurs early in the sentence, there has been a price to pay for doing so. That is, a semantic unit – *to detect such particles* – has been split apart.

Finally, compare sentence 2d with 2a (*Without a microscope, such particles are difficult to detect*). Just as it was easiest to understand the grammatical processes involved in the previous alternatives by, in a sense, 'deriving' them one from another, beginning with 2d, so we may extend this tactic to 2a. In other words, the best means of 'getting from' 2d to 2a is by way of 2c and 2b, on the route we have so far traversed. Since we have already arrived at 2b by this route, what 'gets us from' 2b to 2a – that is, what distinguishes 2a from 2b? It should be obvious that the distinction arises from the location of the prepositional phrase *without a microscope*: in 2a it has been fronted.

We will pause here momentarily and take stock of the grammatical processes of passage (C) to which we have been calling attention, and their relationship to semantics and to discourse. The grammatical processes necessary to effect movement of various constituents in the sentence versions of sentence 2 offer a useful sampling of the kinds of constituent movement that English grammar embraces. (We will come back to this in more depth in Part Four.) With syntax and semantics initially closely aligned in 2d, we then witnessed a step-by-step wrenching apart of the two – from **extraposition** in 2c, through **extraction** and **raising** in 2b, to **fronting** in 2a – such that the version we finish up with, 2a, has its semantic relations in utter disarray. What induces this semantic confusion, however, is the 'pressure' of discourse to establish and maintain referential links across sentence boundaries and consistent with the **given-new** principle, in order that whole texts be rendered amenable to rapid processing for comprehension. The more distant the syntactic-semantic relations, the more that grammaticization needs to be brought into play – grammaticization as the primary means for processing discourse.

The extent to which English tolerates such 'distance' between grammar and meaning sets English apart from many other languages of the world. Thus, although the average learner of L2 English comes to the learning task automatically equipped with some general knowledge of how best to arrange information blocks in accordance with the given-new principle, he encounters a complicated language-particular means for accomplishing this – namely, English grammaticization – that is very alien to him. Assimilation (or 'internalization') of these grammatical processes is perhaps the single most challenging grammatical task of his English-language learning experience. This task of assimilation readily lends itself to pedagogical consciousness-raising and we have already caught a first glimpse of some means for achieving it – the 'propositional cluster' – in Chapter 5. We will return for another look at this notion in Chapters 8 and 12.

3 Thematization

We have now discussed at some length the notion that the material of language expression, unlike pictorial images, has to occur in some kind of linear sequence in order for it to be comprehended. And by definition, of course, linear sequences have beginnings and endings. There is thus something of an 'unravelling' effect to language expression wherein at the beginning of the ordering operation one of several possible conceptual 'threads' is selected to start things off. Pulling on that particular thread then unravels in some kind of sequence the rest of the language material associated with the expression of that concept. It is to the starting point of this unravelling that we will now briefly turn our attention.

3.1 *Initial theme*

What starts things off in a sentence is determined by several possible considerations, and one of these is already familiar – the 'given-ness' of a piece of propositional content, or the general tendency of the language user to have the **given** precede the **new**. So far we have considered fairly simple, clear-cut examples of what can be regarded as given in a sentence (e.g. a single noun-phrase). Given, however, is often more extensive than this; that is, there may well be more than one part of a sentence that can qualify as given. Since it is physically impossible for more than one item to occupy the initial position of any sentence at the same time, it follows that it may sometimes be necessary to choose what should start the sentence off from among competing candidates in propositional content, all of which can qualify as given. We actually encountered an instance of such 'competition' in one of our previous examples of learner English – the third sentences of passages (A) and (B), where *given* is shown in *italic-type*:

(A3) *My father* had planted a lot of flowers in *the garden*.
(B3) In *the garden my father* had planted a lot of flowers.

The garden is given because it was introduced, or 'raised to consciousness', in the previous sentence of the original passage. *My father* is given because it was introduced in the first sentence of the original passage. We thus had *my father* and *the garden*, both given and in contention as candidate to start the sentence off. In other words, they are both potential **themes** for the development of the rest of the sentence's propositional content. The theme, it is often said, is the 'point of departure' for the sentence, or 'what the sentence is about'.[6] As for the contention between (A3) and (B3) as the appropriate

sentence for their original discourse, recall that we earlier opted for
(B3) and noted that it represented a 'smoother link' between the
sentences that preceded and followed. We can now see clearly that
this 'smoothness' comes about because *the garden* in (B3), rather than
my father in (A3), is more 'what the sentence is about'. *The garden*
is thus the appropriate theme with which to start 'unravelling' the rest
of the sentence content.

So far we have seen how the propositional content of sentences
often tends to arrange itself in terms of earlier **given** and later **new**
information and we have just noted that the point of departure for
the development of sentence content is what we may refer to as the
theme (even the 'empty' theme of non-meaning-bearing *it* and *there*).
It would seem then that at the beginning of every sentence should
be thematic material, and that is in fact most often the case. Indeed,
there are some languages in the world (e.g. Russian and Mandarin
Chinese) in which it *must* be the case. English is not one of these
languages, however, and what this means in terms of English grammar
is worth probing here a little.

3.2 *Initial rheme*

If every sentence in English were said to contain a (**given**) **theme**, then
we would be hard-pressed to explain the existence of sentences like
A man stood in our path, which are not only grammatical but also
perfectly common. Our dilemma arises from the fact that although *man*
in this example appears in thematic position, the indefinite article *a(n)*
cannot accompany given information. We are thus forced to conclude
that although thematic material *normally* appears at the beginning of
the sentence, it is also possible in English for **non-thematic** or **rhematic**
material to occupy that position as well. Again, it is important to
remind ourselves that this characteristic of English is not shared by
a lot of other languages. Not surprisingly, also, it is a characteristic
that learners of English absorb comparatively late (Huebner
1983).

If subject position in English can accommodate rhematic as well as
thematic material, then obviously these two functions cannot always
be identified by their position in the English sentence. The user of
the language must therefore resort to something else in order to keep
them separate – namely, definite and indefinite articles, part of the
determiner system. It is thus the indefinite article, *a*, and not sentence
position, that marks *man* as rhematic in *A man stood in our path*. By
the same token then, the definite article (*the*) is needed to identify

thematic material, since theme in English does not have exclusive
rights to subject position. This is a particularly good example of one
important facet of the English determiner system, and it is somewhat
sobering to discover that to understand how this bit of grammar works
requires that we look beyond grammar itself to an aspect of discourse:
thematization.[7]

3.3 *Movement and rhematicity*

English has other grammatical reflexes as well that are attributable
to the theme/rheme distinction, and we will look at one more of these.
Suppose we take our previous example – call it (1):

(1) A man stood in our path.

and expand it a little by attaching a relative clause to *man*:

(2) A man *who looked in need of help* stood in our path.

To most native speakers of English, (2) now sounds slightly awkward,
because what look like natural candidates for theme (*in our path*) and
rheme (*A man who* . . .) are at the wrong ends of their sentence. We
would therefore want to move things around, perhaps invoking the
kind of fronting (of *in our path*) that we saw in Section 2. This would
give us:

(3) *In our path* stood a man who looked in need of help.

There is another option for moving the elements of (2) around,
however, and it occurs fairly commonly, especially in conversation. In
this version we perform the unusual task of breaking up the rhematic
material by 'detaching' that part with 'high rhematicity' (the relative
clause *who looked in need of help*) from the part with 'low rhematicity'
(the head noun *a man*) and shifting the relative clause to the right:

(4) *A man* stood in our path *who looked in need of help*.

Notice at this point that we have yet another example of where a
grammatical operation has split apart two elements that belong
together – the head noun and the relative clause – all for the sake
of getting thematic and rhematic material into more appropriate
positions while still preserving the SV order of subject before verb
(*A man* + *stood* . . .).

How can we be sure that it is thematization requirements that have
brought about the movement within (4) and not some other principle?
To demonstrate that theme/rheme considerations are indeed at work
here, all we need do is construct another sentence like (2), only this

time with the propositional content of main clause and relative clause interchanged:

(5) A man who stood in our path looked in need of help.

If we now split apart the noun-phrase containing the relative clause as we did in (4), we will have:

(6) *A man* looked in need of help *who stood in our path.*

which to most people is unacceptable. What has happened of course is that we have taken a movement rule reserved only for material with high rhematicity – like *who looked in need of help* in (2) – and applied it instead to material with low rhematicity: *who stood in our path.*[8] Again, then, a grammatical operation in English – detachment of a relative clause from its head noun – becomes understandable only with reference to a principle outside of grammar itself: **thematization.**

3.4 *Theme, grammar, and learning*

As one might guess, theme/rheme considerations play a role in the *learning* of English as well. Decisions as to what is to be the theme – the point of departure for what follows – has important grammatical implications for how the propositional content in the rest of the sentence is to be expressed. These implications are grammatical ones because, as we have already seen, rearrangements of sentence content can often preserve crucial semantic relationships only through the use of grammatical devices. Thus the learner of English, especially in the early stages, faces a dilemma of sorts. On the one hand, his prior language experience (as a native speaker of his own mother tongue) has resulted in unconscious awareness that thematic material (where it is present) serves as the most efficient departure point for sentence development; on the other hand, his thus far meagre target-language experience has begun to awaken in him a realization that the purchase of thematic options in English carries a grammatical price tag – namely, grammaticization, whose intricacies he has hardly yet begun to grasp.

In a context where the most 'natural' thematic option is something other than the grammatical subject of the sentence, the learner's alternatives are essentially three (with many gradations and with differential mother-tongue influence):

1. he can resort to the simple expedient of selecting an appropriate sentence-initial theme with no further regard for the grammatical consequences elsewhere in the sentence;

2. he can select that theme and make an abortive attempt to perform some of the necessary concomitant grammaticization;
3. he can opt for a less appropriate (but otherwise 'normal') theme – the grammatical subject of the sentence – and thereby have to call upon no more than his rudimentary knowledge of 'basic' grammatical formations.

To illustrate what these options might mean in the (idealized) simplest and most concrete terms, consider the following situation. The topic on which the learner is writing is 'How one chooses a wife or a husband', the content of the sentence in question is *ages – must be similar*), and *must* is the thematic element. Exercising option (1) above may yield *Must be the ages similar*; option (2) may give the learner *It must be similar the ages*; and option (3) will be *The ages must be similar* (Rutherford and Altman 1984). Which one of the options (or combination thereof) is actually exercised will depend upon a number of factors, including how far the learner has already progressed, the grammatical organization of his mother tongue, and the nature of the discourse he is engaged in (e.g. crucial or routine, planned or unplanned, etc.).

4 Topicness

We have already noted that **theme/rheme** considerations enter into the learning of the English *determiner* system – particularly the use of definite and indefinite articles – and we have also called attention to the fact that the grammatical organization of the learner's native language can have a bearing on how that learning takes place. One aspect of such 'grammatical organization' that we touched on in Chapter 4.1 was that wherein the native language shows a preference for **topic-comment** constructions (as distinct from, but possibly in addition to, **subject-predicate**) (Li and Thompson 1976). **Topic** in such languages, and **theme** as we have been discussing it above, have much in common. In fact there is evidence (Huebner 1983) that when speakers of a **topic-prominent** language begin to learn English, they will tend to interpret the first noun-phrase in an English sentence as **topic**. Since by definition topic is always definite, and since it often occurs first in the sentence,[9] anything additional that marks it as topic would therefore be redundant. Hence there is no need for the definite article with English 'topic' (i.e. thematic noun-phrase) and accordingly we find that in the earliest production of such learners it routinely does not appear.

'Topicness' would also seem to provide a means for plausibly analysing interlanguage examples such as (7):

(7) I need to write a letter to my friend and send Ø today.[10]

where 'Ø' marks the position of the obligatory object (pronoun) in target English. Non-occurring major constituents such as the missing direct object in the second conjunct of (7) are a common feature of topic-prominent languages. In such languages noun-phrases that are co-referential with what is perceived as (discoursal) topic can often be deleted. On the other hand, in subject-prominent languages like English, where co-reference obtains with regard to (syntactic) **subject** or **object**, the co-referent would appear as a pronoun. Thus, if the interlanguage of (7) represents a topic-prominent system, then *letter* will be the 'topic' that controls deletion of *letter* as the object of *send*. (See Chapter 10.3.1 for a more detailed account of these principles.)

The foregoing discussion of given/new, theme/rheme, and topic/comment has touched upon the interrelationships of these concepts and the ways in which they may serve to shed light upon the nature of the learner's developing L2 competence. They may also serve to bring more clearly into focus the learner's need to sort out those features of the target language that are controlled by discourse from those that are controlled by syntax. For these controls will not be the same from one language to another.

Before we turn to the matter of consciousness-raising with regard to 'grammar and discourse' (Chapter 8), we will devote some attention in the following chapter to the relationship between grammar and semantics.

Activities

1. It has been pointed out by the researchers Clark and Haviland (1977) that a sequence of sentences like *Agnes saw somebody | It was Agnes who saw Maxine* is a violation of the given-new contract. In their words (pp. 14–15):

> in two-sentence sequences like this, the first sentence sets up a context, a set of propositions in memory. The second sentence is then interpreted relative to the first. It induces the listener to search for an antecedent to its given information in the propositions stored in memory from the first sentence. If the listener cannot find an appropriate antecedent without restructuring the second sentence, he will consider the speaker to have breached the given-new contract and judge the sequence to be awkward or inappropriate.

Look closely at the two columns of utterances below. Consider the pairing possibilities for any sentence in the first column with any in the second. Make a note of all pairs that represent observance of the given-new contract. Call this 'group one'. Note down also the pairs that make sense but violate the given-new contract. Call this 'group two'. Compare your results with someone else's to see whether your intuitions are the same. Do the two groups differ if writing is considered separate from speaking (intonation)?

a. John did something.
b. John sliced the salami with something.
c. Somebody did something.
d. John did something to the salami.
e. John sliced something with an axe.
f. Somebody sliced something.
g. John did something with an axe.
h. Somebody sliced the salami.

1. John sliced something with an axe.
2. John sliced the salami.
3. John sliced the salami with an axe.
4. What John did to the salami was slice it.
5. What John did was slice the salami with an axe.
6. What John did was slice the salami.
7. It was the salami that John sliced.
8. It was with an axe that John sliced the salami.
9. What John sliced the salami with was an axe.
10. It was John who sliced the salami.

2. Some early interlanguage is characterized by a tendency to have sentence constituents in their basic or 'unmarked' positions, e.g. with little or no application of movement rules. In the following writing samples of early L2 English (L1 Arabic), for instance, we see that a choice of constituent order other than the one chosen would have made for better observance of the given-new principle:

a. A wedding ceremony always takes place in the evening. . . . *Also, hundreds of goats, sheeps, and camels are killed in this night to be cooked for the guests.*
b. One day I found a girl whom I fell in love with her . . . *I began to smile since that day.*

Scan some samples of learner writing and see if you can identify: (1) infractions of the given-new principle where constituents have been retained in 'basic' positions; and (2) satisfaction of the given-new principle through the placement of constituents in other than 'basic' positions but with little or no grammaticization.

3. Find some L2 English writing samples produced by learners whose mother tongues contrast as to degree of word-order freedom (e.g. Spanish and French, Russian and Japanese, etc.). Note whether within the English sentences there appear to be differences in distribution of thematic and rhematic material that correlate with the differences in L1 word-order freedom. If you find such differences, can you plausibly attribute them to L1 transfer?

Notes

1. For the componential approach carried to its extreme, see Munby (1978).
2. See Frawley and Lantolf (1984) for evidence for this from L2 acquisition research.
3. The role of 'given' and 'new' in English discourse is far more involved than might be apparent from the limited treatment of the subject that we have to settle for here. For some further discussion of this and other discourse principles to be touched on in this chapter, see Clark and Haviland (1977) and Chafe (1972).
4. The idea for this layout comes from Gleason (1965).
5. To be linguistically precise, it is the 'AUX' node whose movement is triggered by fronting. The rule is thus termed 'AUX-attract'.
6. For a more detailed discussion of theme, see Halliday (1967, 1968). For a shorter, less technical treatment of theme, see Chapter 14 of Quirk *et al.* (1972).
7. For a detailed analysis of 'thematization strategy', see Candlin and Lotfipour-Saedi (1983).
8. This is the kind of analysis that is proposed in Ziv (1975). See Leech 1983 for an explanation in slightly different terms.
9. See Givón (1984), however, for arguments that the unmarked universal order is not topic-comment but rather comment-topic.
10. This kind of example is cited in Schmidt (1980).

7 Grammar and semantics

In Chapter 4 we had our first look at characteristics of English having to do with what we labelled 'syntactic-semantic distance', or the various degrees to which semantic relations and their surface-syntactic realizations may diverge. And in Chapter 6 we touched on this again in discussing the semantic 'price' that must be paid with the invocation of grammatical movement rules to satisfy discoursal requirements – that price being disruption to one extent or another of the semantic relations. What we are really saying then is that the effect of such movement rules is to bring about a surface 'misalignment' of what in underlying structure was a close 'fit' between syntax and semantics.[1] Since syntactic-semantic distance correlates to a considerable extent with the ease or difficulty with which language may be processed for production and comprehension, then it should not be surprising to learn that degree of distance has a bearing on learnability (see Kellerman 1979).

There are other aspects of semantic relationship in English that learners find challenging (where 'challenging' here and throughout is used with general reference to features of target-language formal organization). With some of these aspects the challenge stems from the straightforward need simply to learn a new syntactic network for the realization of semantic concepts – as would be the case for the learning of *any* new language. Other aspects, however, seem very special to English and here the learner's challenge turns out to be commensurately 'special' as well. In Chapter 9.6 we will look at this in the light of the learner's need to parse the language for comprehension.

1 Verb-argument revisited

One challenge confronting the learner has to do with the semantic relationship obtaining between a sentence's main verb and associated noun-phrases (NPs) – *verb-argument relations* in linguistic terms – and with the possibilities in English for such NPs or *arguments* to serve as subject of the sentence. Thus, consider the following examples:

(8) a. The child *broke* the window with a hammer.
    b. The hammer *broke* the window.
    c. The window *broke*.

In this set of perfectly good English sentences there are several things worth noting:

1. all three examples have the same main verb, *break*;
2. *break* has a different subject in each of the three;
3. *window* occurs in all three and the semantic relation between *window* and *break* – 'objective' – is always the same.

Notice then that what has changed throughout the three examples is not the **semantic** relations between *break* and the various NPs but rather the **grammatical** relations. That is, we find *window* occurring, for example, as direct object in (8a–b) but as subject in (8c). We see *hammer* as object of a preposition in (8a) but subject in (8b). Yet what, one may ask, is the 'challenge' in all this? Sentences (8a–c) are so common in English that a native speaker hardly bothers to think about them.

We call attention to these examples because two of the three, (8b) and (8c), have highly unusual characteristics. Even quite advanced learners of English in fact often deny that they can even be grammatical. We will take the three in turn to see why this is so.

Among the various semantic arguments contracting relations with their verbs, there is one that universally lends itself most readily to service as grammatical subject. That is the 'agent', and the semantic relation we term 'agentive'. In (8a), then, *child*, contracting an agentive relation with the verb *break*, occurs naturally as subject of that sentence. We can put this another way: of the three arguments that are potential candidates for 'subjecthood' in sentences like (8a–c) – i.e. agentive *child*, objective *window*, and instrumental *hammer* – it is selection of *child* as subject (as in (8a)) that somehow feels 'basic'. The association of agent with subject is a strong tendency that ranges across languages in general,[2] and there is actually a rather straightforward explanation for this. Since agents are usually animate and objects *in*animate, it is more likely that the agent (e.g. child) will be 'doing something' to the object (e.g. window) than vice versa.

With (8b) and (8c) it is a different story, however. In many other languages it is not possible to have an argument that bears the instrumental relationship serving as subject of its sentence. Nor can objectives serve this way unless the verb is specially marked, i.e. as passive, as can also happen of course in English (*The window was broken*). Not surprisingly then, learners of English typically find sentences such as (8b) and (8c) very strange. Their reaction to seeing or hearing such examples is often something like 'But a hammer has to be thrown *by* somebody', or 'But windows don't break by themselves!' Thus, the tendency of the learner is to want to 'correct' the examples to perhaps *The hammer broke the window by the child* and *The window* **was** *broken*. (Notice that there is an additional problem for the learner: that with instrumental subject, the agent cannot be expressed at all.) The special ways in which English realizes syntactically these *verb-argument* relations therefore poses a challenge to the learner (see Chapter 9.3.1).

2 Collocation

Another challenge facing the learner of English is one having to do with the ways in which semantic relations are preserved over syntactic formations that differ in category, in size, and in rank. It is a question, grammatically speaking, of 'what goes together with what' – that is, **collocation**[3] – and the challenge is greater for learners whose mother tongue makes less use of grammatical morphology than does English.

For our point of departure in discussing grammar, semantics, and collocation, we will take an example of learner production that we encountered in Chapter 4 – one of the examples that illustrated the learner's early heavy production of verbal elements:

(9) The problem is the *destroy* of nature.

We said earlier that the problem revealed by examples like (8) is possibly one of what is sometimes referred to as 'major lexical category confusion' and it was suggested also that such examples can be regarded as a 'way stage' in the development of learner-language grammaticization. We can also look at (9) from the perspective of collocation. That is, *the* doesn't 'collocate' with *destroy*. We don't want to suggest, however, that this particular learner somehow thinks that *the* can occur with verbs, for that would not be very plausible given that nothing else in his production confirms this. Rather, it would be more reasonable to suppose that the English morphology that distinguishes (or derives) verbal nouns from verbs has not yet been learned. Yet it should be added that the use of *destroy* in (9) is, from the learner's standpoint, not really a bad guess; after all, many verbal nouns in English are not distinguished morphologically at all (e.g. *need, push, stop, love, charge*, etc.).

Yet the challenge facing the learner of the grammatical requirements attending semantic collocation is even wider than that exemplified in (9). Consider the following semantically equivalent pair of
sentences in standard English:

(10) a. The two brothers *very closely resemble each other physically*.
    b. The two brothers *bear a very close physical resemblance (to each
       other)*.

The two sentences contrast grammatically in their verb-phrases, and
what brings about this contrast is the choice of main verb in each:
resemble in (10a) and *bear (a resemblance)* in (10b), where we find the
effected object construction (Chapter 4.4.3). This is only the start
of things, however, for these verb choices in turn trigger a chain of
grammatical consequences for the rest of the lexical items in the two
examples. The pivotal elements are of course *resemble* in (10a) and
resemblance in (10b), for all the residual semantic collocations in the
two examples must now manifest morphological marking that produces
different grammatical compatibility within the two. Thus, *closely*
(resemble) in (10a) must appear as *close (resemblance)* in (10b), though
the adverb *very* (as a modifier of both adjectives and adverbs) remains
unchanged. However, *physically*, the modifier of the entire verb-
phrase in (10a), must occur in its adjective form *(physical)* and appear
within the analogous noun-phrase that it modifies in (10b). In these
two sentences, then, we have an excellent example of English grammaticization working to preserve semantic collocation.

Although our chosen examples involve fairly complex syntax, it is
not difficult to conjure up natural pairs of a simpler kind (***Consider
this matter* carefully** / *Give this matter* **careful consideration**). It is
also possible to have pivotal elements other than finite verbs (*It is*
clearly evident *that . . .* / **There is** **clear evidence** *that . . .*) or other
than verbal nouns (*I* **heavily emphasized** *that . . .* / *I made it* **heavily
emphatic** *that . . .*). In any event, the need for preservation of
semantic collocation within differential grammatical frameworks poses
a considerable challenge to learners of English at all proficiency
levels. In Chapter 8 we will take up the matter of collocation with
regard to grammatical consciousness-raising.

3 Lexical properties

3.1 *Synonymy and syntax*

All language learners, it would seem, make at least some use at some
time of a dictionary, whether desk-size or pocket-size, bilingual or

monolingual, up-to-date or obsolete. A not uncommon and entirely understandable procedure for the use of the dictionary would be the following: the learner wishes to compose a passage – let us say as part of a written description of a laboratory experiment – with roughly the meaning of 'When you heat the mixture, it _____ white.' His learner-language lexicon does not contain a suitable change-of-state verb to complete the sentence, however, and he therefore consults his bilingual dictionary. He looks up the verb he would have chosen in his native language and finds several English 'equivalents' – *alter, change, turn,* and *convert.* Since his dictionary is too small to provide either samples of usage or lexico-grammatical information, the learner has to guess which of these four (ostensibly synonymous) entries fits the context he has composed. His guess here – as often will be the case – happens to be wrong, and he winds up producing the sentence *When you heat the mixture, it* **changes** *white.* Since 'change' *is* a change-of-state verb, however, and since the sentence makes perfectly good sense, it is well to consider exactly what is wrong.

Given the context that was to accommodate an appropriate change-of-state verb (*When you heat the mixture, it _____ white*), the proper choice among the four verbs provided (*alter, change, turn, convert*) could only have been *turn(ed)*. We might therefore conclude that only *turn* has exactly the 'meaning' that we want in this particular instance. Although there is certainly some truth in this, one can also note that only *turn* can occur with an adjective (colour) complement, producing what some grammarians call a 'resulting copula' (Quirk *et al.* 1972); in other words, only *turn* has the grammatical properties that we want as well. *Change* and *turn* (both used in their change-of-state sense) therefore contrast in ways that have as much to do with grammar as with semantics. We have *turn* **white** (adjective) but *change* **colour** (noun), *turn* **thick** (adjective) but *change* **consistency** (noun), *turn to* **liquid** (noun) but *change into* **a liquid** (noun-phrase). It is in fact common to encounter apparent synonyms in English that manifest quite distinct sets of grammatical properties.

3.2 *Zero-derivation*

Learning the vocabulary of a new language and learning how properly to employ that vocabulary in normal language use is no simple task, although avenues of simplification do exist (see below). Take, for example, the matter of vocabulary – and specifically verbs – containing the feature of **causation**. In English, **causative** verbs display a wide variety of morphological marking: adjective + *en* (*soften*), adjective

+*ify* (*humidify*), adjective + *ize* (*humanize*), phonological change
(*cause to fall* = *fell*), etc. One also naturally has recourse to the actual
verbs of **causation** itself – *cause, force, have, make, get, effect, bring about*,
etc. – and the different grammatical properties associated with each.
However, by far the most common device for producing causatives in
English is what is sometimes referred to as **zero-derivation**
(Hurford and Heasley 1983) – in which intransitive verbs are
employed as causatives with no morphological change. We thus have
The door **opened** as well as *X* **opened** *the door* (i.e. *X caused the door
to* **open**), *The wax* **melted** and *X* **melted** *the wax* (i.e. *X caused the
wax to* **melt**), *His head* **moved** and *X* **moved** *his head* (i.e. *X caused
his head to* **move**), etc.

It should not be surprising then to discover that early in their
development learners of English also make extensive use of zero-
derivation for the formation of causatives.[4] It is a procedure that
requires minimal grammatical knowledge, and indeed we find the
learner over-applying zero-derivation for the creation of highly
innovative though non-targetlike causative constructions:

> The shortage of fuels *occurred* the need for economical engine.
> This construction will *progress* my country.[5]
> If you don't have enough money [for the dowry], you will have to
>   borrow some or it will *lose* your *face*.
> Careless currency devaluation will *go back* us to old habits.

Here again then, we have examples of vocabulary (i.e. the verbs *occur,
progress, lose face, go back*) in which 'meaning' is not a problem for the
learner, but in which one of the concomitant grammatical properties
(namely, non-participation in the zero-derivation of causatives) has
not yet been assimilated.

3.3 *The lexicon and learnability*

Having duly noted the 'challenges' posed to the learner by the
intricacies of predicate-argument relations, semantic collocation, and
lexical properties, we need to recognize as well those aspects of the
lexicon whose learning will automatically be *simplified*. As early as
Chapter 4 we called attention to the kinds of relationship – syntactic,
semantic – obtaining between a verb and its corresponding verbal
noun, and in this chapter we have explored this area further. It will
be evident then that awareness by the learner of the syntactic and
semantic properties of given lexicon (e.g. for a verb, the number,
identity, and semantic make-up of its possible arguments) will automatically mean knowledge of corresponding lexicon in another major

category (e.g. verbal nouns). In other words, what the learner already knows about, for example, the verb *decide* will constitute knowledge as well about the noun *decision*, or vice versa. In the words of one current researcher, C. Adjémian:

> the acquisition of a lexical rule itself will then in fact *simplify* the task of acquiring a native command of the lexicon since it will express a generalization, thereby reducing the need for memorization and the deciphering from contextual clues each time a new item occurs. Under this theory the learner has the ability to *predict* what certain properties of new lexical items should be.
>
> Adjémian 1983, p. 254

4 Cohesion

In this chapter so far, our attention has been drawn to aspects of semantics the scope of whose grammatical reflexes is fairly restricted. Discussion, in turn, of **verb-argument** relations, **collocation** and **lexical properties** has progressively narrowed our area of inquiry from the full sentence to single lexical items and their immediate context. Other grammatico-semantic phenomena of interest to us are broader than this, however, and these are what we now want to look at.

4.1 *Kinds of cohesion*

Reflect for a moment upon the following very short English text – only two sentences, as a matter of fact – and consider what kinds of inference and association are necessary for its successful interpretation:

(11) One characteristic of wars in general is that often nobody wins. Somebody did, however, in the American Revolution, but even this conflagration is said to have taken its toll on both sides.

The comprehension of this passage entails, among other things, that the following relationships be perceived: of hyponymy, as between *war* and *American Revolution*; of anaphora, as between *American Revolution* and *conflagration* and between *conflagration* and *its*; of contrast, as signalled by *but*; of contradiction, as conveyed by *somebody did*; and of major category to surrogate, as between *win* and *do*. Moreover, *conflagration* must be seen to be in a subject relationship to *take*, what is 'said' in the passive must be understood as something like *This conflagration took its toll*, and *its toll* must be perceived as in an object relationship to *take*. Even more, of course, could be pointed out, such as the kind of syntactic-semantic distance that we discussed in Chapter 4.[6]

The kinds of relationship specified above are examples of what is often referred to as **cohesion**, or what it is that 'ties' sentences together such that we perceive them collectively as constituting a single text. We may identify the examples from (11) in terms of the broad categories of cohesion outlined in the theoretical work of M. A. K. Halliday:[7]

1. **Reference** (of *its* to *conflagration*). Commonly **anaphoric reference** (e.g. referential pronouns) but also personal pronouns and demonstratives (including **deictics**).
2. **Substitution** (of *did* for *won*). A replacive grammatical relation between linguistic elements. Substitution can apply as well to nouns and clauses.
3. **Ellipsis** (of *win* in *did (win)*). The omission of 'understood' elements that are formally retrievable from the text. Ellipsis can also occur with nouns and clauses.
4. **Conjunctive ties** (as with *but*). Connecting clausal elements by means of 'additives' (*and*), 'adversatives' (*yet*), 'disjunctives' (*or*), 'temporals' (*then*), etc.
5. **Lexical ties** (as of *war* to *American Revolution*; as of *American Revolution* to *conflagration*). Commonly, simple **reiteration**, but also **synonymy** and **hyponymy**.

4.2 *Cohesion and learner production*

How then does the average foreign-language learner fare in coming to grips with this network of comprehensive grammatico-semantic relations that we call 'cohesion'? What can we observe in the learner's early attempts at writing a foreign language that bear on the question of cohesion?[8] Some observations of this kind we have already made – for example, when we discussed interlanguage characteristics relating to grammaticization in Chapter 4. We noted there the over-reliance upon **conjunctive ties** at the expense of 'tighter' subordination. To this we can now add that the conjunctive tie overwhelmingly preferred in this 'over-production' is *and*, that problems abound for the learner in the appropriate use of *and*, *but*, and *so*, and that conjunctive ties also appear in the learner's text where they are not called for (Beebe 1979).[9]

From the learner's standpoint, of course, the early heavy dependence upon conjunctive ties in written discourse makes a lot of sense, since conjunction requires much less of the kind of grammaticization that he hasn't yet learned, as we have already seen. We may also note in connection with the ubiquity of *and* in learner language that of all the conjunctive ties *and* has the greatest **polysemy** or widest range of meaning. Although the commonest sense of *and* is that of simple 'additive' conjunction, *and* can also carry the meaning of *so, then,* and *furthermore*. We thus have a range of meaning for *and* something like the following (Staal 1968):

(12) The clerk was rude,   *and* ['additive'] insensitive.
                      and (*so*) was treated rudely in return.
                      and (*then*) apologetic.
                      and (*furthermore*) even used vulgar language.

From *and* one can thus coax a substantial amount of semantic 'mileage', even in native-speaker English. It should therefore not be altogether surprising that *and* bears an unnaturally heavy semantic load in the learner's early written production.

Another relatively simple means of achieving cohesion in interlanguage is the mere reiteration of a lexical item. Reiteration is a ready-made tactic for binding textual matter where synonymy and grammatically governed anaphora, ellipsis, and substitution are still beyond the learner's present competence, and we find that he makes extensive use of it:

(13) a. About four years ago we had a revolution in *my country* which not only over shaddowed *my country* but everywhere.[10] [Farsi]
    b. This *temple* is famous because it is the biggest *temple* in the world. It is not difficult to *go there* because you can *go there* any time. [Indonesian]
    c. It is obvious why *I came to the United States. I came to the United States* to continue my higher education. [Mandarin Chinese]

Where the learner (unconsciously) perceives cohesion as governed not by grammar but by discourse, however, we may find him more readily resorting to the tactic of ellipsis. As we saw, for example, in Chapters 2, 4, and 6, there is evidence (Schachter and Rutherford 1979)[11] that learners whose mother tongue is topic-prominent (e.g. Mandarin Chinese, Japanese, Korean) will, in the course of learning English, often produce language such as (14a), understood as (14b) but usually erroneously analysed as (14c) or an abortive attempt to render the English passive:

(14) a. All people can choose their mate in their own way. *These ways* almost can classify two types.
    b. ... *These ways* almost [one/we] can classify [*them*] (into) two types.
    c. NOT ... These ways almost *can be classified* ...

In (14a) then, *these ways* is to be analysed as topic, and ellipsis of *them* thus comes about through co-reference to (discourse-defined) topic and not to (syntax-defined) subject. (In Chapter 10.3.1 we will encounter ellipsis *vis-à-vis* topic and object.) Also consistent with the structure of topic-prominent languages is the ellipsis in (14a) of an 'understood' subject element such as 'one' or 'we', as reanalysed in (14b).

In any discussion of the role of cohesion in learner-language development it is important to recognize that learner progress is not to be measured in terms of the *quantity* of cohesion devices manifested. Such progress is to be seen rather in the *extent* to which the learner's cohesion devices represent an appropriate fit to their context and are adequately distributed throughout the text.[12]

5 Postscript

One of the prevailing themes of this book is the need to maintain a 'systems' view of language phenomena and its relation to consciousness-raising. Another such theme is that systems do not exist in and of themselves but rather are 'definable and observable only through their interaction with other systems', to quote the physicist Niels Bohr. The kind of 'interaction' to which our attention has been drawn in this and the previous chapter involves three such 'systems' – syntax, discourse, and semantics – and we have indeed seen that one cannot in all practicality probe any of the three to the exclusion of the other two. Although it is the *syntactic* system that we choose as our main reference point for this volume, the three systems are thus all interrelated. The nature of these interrelationships is therefore what we are really talking about when we speak of the 'challenges' to the learner, as we did at the beginning of this chapter. The four aspects of grammatico-semantic relationship touched on here – **verb-argument, collocation, lexical properties,** and **cohesion** – thus constitute a challenge precisely because they arise not from a system *per se* but from the interaction of one system with another.

Activities

1. The following passage (an expansion of example 13b, Section 4.2) is taken from a piece of writing produced by an Indonesian speaker learning English. Consider the possibilities for achieving more cohesion in this passage (if necessary, through altered placement of theme and rheme). What kinds of thing could be done? Of these possibilities, which ones would you guess (all things being equal) the learner is likely to acquire sooner? Later? Why do you say this?

Many people come to my country. If a visitor comes to my country, I will take him to Borobudur. Borobudur is a big temple in island of Java, Indonesia. This temple is famous because it is the biggest temple in the world and it is very old. It is not difficult to go there because you can go there any time and you can go by plane, or by car.

2. It is interesting to note that the American political groups supporting the right of individuals to own firearms have exploited for propaganda purposes the kind of 'unnaturalness' that we said many learners identify in English syntax. Thus, to counter the slogan of the gun-control advocates ('Guns kill people'), the pro-gun lobby has devised the slogan 'Guns don't kill people; people kill people'. How would you describe this 'unnaturalness' in formal terms?

3. The fact that English has verbs, including 'change-of-state' verbs, that can occur as both **transitive** and **intransitive** (e.g. *open, close, freeze, melt, burn*, etc.) is not all that strange when one realizes that the semantic relations expressed therein make a lot of sense. We refer here to the identical relationship between the object of, for example, the transitive *melt* (*The sun melted the ice*) and the subject of the intransitive *melt* (*The ice melted*). In fact, in a small number of languages – called **ergative-absolutive** – these identical semantic relations receive the same morphological coding. In the *melt* example, in other words, *ice* would be marked morphologically as **ergative** in both the 'transitive' and 'intransitive' constructions. Nevertheless, many learners still find sentences like *The door opened* strange, whereas they are likely to consider *The ice melted* quite natural. Can you think of any possible explanations for this?

4. As we have said, although some learners find strange a sentence like *The door opened*, there are other pale reflections in English of 'ergativity' that never seem to pose a problem. Take, for instance, the question of adjectives formed from verbs through affixation of *-able/-ible* (*teachable, edible*, etc.). Such formations are typically built upon transitive verbs and the semantic relations are of the kind: *teach* X : X *is teachable, eat* Y : Y *is edible*. In other words, the relation reflected is that of verb-object. Yet there are also a small number of intransitive verbs that can take this suffix (e.g. *perish, agree*, etc.). Now, however, in the resulting construction the relation reflected can only be **subject** verb: X *perishes* : X *is perishable*. The pattern of English suffixation with *-able/-ible* is thus an instantiation (albeit a minor one) of the close relation between 'object of a transitive verb' and 'subject of an intransitive' (i.e. **ergativity**) that we can observe elsewhere. Given these facts, since we may now assume that some learners of low proficiency

will be reluctant to accept as grammatical sentences of the form 'X *broke*' ('Things don't break by themselves'), do you predict that they would also have trouble with 'X *is breakable*'? In other words, are they likely to interpret the semantic relation between 'X' and *break(able)* as **agentive**? Why not?

5. The linguist James McCawley has noted that the nature of the lexicon is not such as to allow the possibility of lexically-internal syntactic structure. That is, there could never exist, for example, a verb *blick* meaning 'kiss a girl who likes', such that the sentence *I blicked spaghetti* could mean 'I kissed a girl who likes spaghetti'. From this, one should not conclude, however, that the lexicon isn't necessarily complex in other ways. For example, it is common in an American business office nowadays to hear (of an executive to his/her secretary): *Send this memo to Schultz and* **copy Cohen**, where *copy* can mean only something like 'make a copy of ____ and send it to'. Can you think of any other lexical examples like this? Would a learner of English be likely to find this more complex sense of a verb like *copy* strange?

Notes

1. This descriptive terminology is adapted from Hawkins (1985).
2. Overriding even the subject/agent correlation is the subject/theme correlation; see Tomlin (1985), p. 61:
   'Syntactic subject in English has a dual function. Its primary function is to encode **thematic information**. Its secondary function is to encode the semantic role **agent**. What this means is that when several NPs compete for the subject relation, the one representing the most thematic information will win. If no NP can be established as the most thematic, then the subject will take the agent.'
3. 'Collocation' is being used here in a sense somewhat broader than that reflected in the work, for example, of J. R. Firth (1957) and his modern disciples.
4. See van Hest *et al.* (1984) for empirical research on this topic.
5. The first two examples are taken from Scarcella (1984). See Selinker, Swain, and Dumas (1975) for reports of a similar phenomenon in the acquisition of L2 French by English speakers.
6. This material has been adapted from Rutherford (1982). The original idea for this kind of analysis comes from Munby (1978).
7. See Halliday and Hasan (1976) for a book-length development of this concept.
8. Some of the observations to follow are taken from Scarcella (1984).
9. See also Neuman (1977).

10. The unusual frequency of the phrase *my country* (in lieu of the name of the country itself) in interlanguage perhaps stems from its appearance in frequently assigned topics for writing – e.g. 'A famous tourist attraction in my country', 'The greatest problem facing my country today', etc.
11. See Hatch (1983, Chapter 7) for a useful discussion of syntax and discourse in L2 acquisition from a psycholinguistic perspective.
12. See Scarcella (1984) for evidence of this.

8 Discourse, semantics, and grammatical consciousness-raising

Previous discussions of grammatical consciousness-raising throughout these chapters have emphasized the need for being aware of certain overriding principles – principles of learning as well as of language. One of these would be the recognition that successful learning does not occur in a vacuum, that what is to be learned – the as yet unknown – must be linked in some meaningful way to what has previously been learned – the already known. Another such principle would be the importance of maintaining wherever possible a close relationship between consciousness-raising procedures and the nature of the language-learning process as we presently know it. Still another would be the requirement that whatever is selected for raising to consciousness be at the very least not inconsistent with the essence of language organization itself.[1] We will presently see that observance of these principles meshes quite well with the practice of deriving consciousness-raising activity from the interrelationships among syntax, semantics, and discourse.

It will be useful here at the outset to look again at what we have already noted (Chapter 6) of these interrelationships. Recall (1) that the ways in which we, as humans, interact with each other through language conspire to bring about within **discourse** the arrangement of whole chunks of propositional content in preferred sequences; (2) that crucial **semantic** relationships destined for destruction in the placement of these 'chunks' are rescued through grammaticization; and (3) that **grammar** thus ensures that the entire discourse/semantics complex becomes processable for comprehension. What, then, do these 'reaches' of grammar into semantics and discourse imply for consciousness-raising? Or how does consciousness-raising connect to this network in a principled way?

1 Consciousness-raising and linear order

Consider again what it is that the learner already brings to the language-learning experience that can provide the connection with what is yet to be learned. The learner's linguistic contributions range themselves on a scale marked at one end by his unconscious 'knowledge' of universal language processes (e.g. the effort to preserve semantic relations, the need for establishing and maintaining relevance, the requirement that language be processable in real time, etc.) and at the other end by the current state of his 'knowledge' (conscious or unconscious), such as it may be, of the language he happens to be learning. All of these contributions have to do significantly with the linear ordering of elements – what the sequence should be, how the sequence gets that way, and why (where there is a choice) the sequence should be one way and not another.

One approach to bringing to consciousness the important aspects of the linear ordering of sentence constituents would utilize the 'propositional cluster' principle discussed in Chapter 5. We noted then that the pedagogical potential of this principle included the engendering of learner sensitivity to the use of English basic word order for the expression of grammatical rather than semantic relations. There were hints as well that the principle could facilitate in a natural way the raising-to-consciousness of aspects of ordering that embrace stretches of language larger than the sentence. We now want to develop these notions in more detail.

The fundamental idea behind the propositional-cluster approach is the need for consciousness-raising activity in which the exercise of grammatical options can be carried out by the learner in a manner that is consistent with principles of target-language organization. In English, in particular, the choice of material to fill the major-constituent positions of subject and object of a verb produces a grammatical 'ripple' effect throughout the sentence precisely because the major sentence-constituent positions are definable in grammatical terms. It is the *motivation* for those choices of material, however, that takes us beyond sentence boundaries and touches on some of the discourse and semantic phenomena encountered in Chapters 6 and 7.

As an illustration of this more global interpretation of the propositional-cluster principle, let us take a tiny bit of text from a sample of technical writing – something similar in style to passage (C), Chapter 6.1:

(15) Below is a photograph of the sun taken with a special telescope. The dark patches on it are called sunspots.

We observe right away that the two sentences of (15) 'hang together', so to speak; that is, they constitute a text. What binds them together, or what establishes their **cohesion**, are the links that extend across the sentence boundaries: pronominal *it*, the **definite article** accompanying *dark patches* and occurrence of *dark patches* in **thematic** (i.e. sentence-initial) position. Additionally, *call* is in the **passive** because *dark patches*, interpretable semantically only in an **objective** relation to *call*, appears as subject of the sentence. The propositional-cluster principle displays this text (15) in such a way that the second sentence comes into being only as the learner brings to bear (perhaps even unconsciously) the kind of knowledge of cohesion just cited. Displayed for the learner, then, we would thus have something like (16):

(16) Below is a photograph of the sun taken with a special telescope.

    call – dark patches on sun – sunspots

The learner's task, of course, is (1) to decide which of two available noun-phrases (*sunspots* and *dark patches on sun*) is to become subject of *call* and place it in that position; (2) mark *call* as **passive** since the subject now bears the objective relation to *call*; (3) distinguish **given/new** and **theme/rheme** by means of the appropriate choice of determiners (**the** *dark patches* . . ., Ø *sunspots*); (4) replace repeated *sun* with **referential** *it*; and (5) adjust for subject-verb agreement (*patches* . . . *are*). The decision as to what shall be the linear order of major constituents for the skeletal sentences of (16) is thus given over to the learner. His verdict must be a principled one, and once having reached it he must see to it that the intra-sentential grammatical events triggered by that decision are fully played out.

There are other types of consciousness-raising activity that serve to sensitize the learner to the importance of discourse as the prime influence upon the linear ordering of information chunks. A number of these activities are quite simple in conception and can be devised very quickly from almost any existing text. (See Chapter 12 for fully worked out examples.) One example of this consists of the display of the sentences of a paragraph in list form and in a scrambled order, the task of the learner being to re-create the original paragraph with the sentences in their appropriate order.[2] Another kind of activity would utilize something like the layout of text exemplified in passage (C), Chapter 6, wherein the learner would simply 'trace a path' through sets of alternative versions of the sentences, the link-up of each selected version with its predecessor being determined by principles of discourse and semantics. Still another sort of activity would present the learner with a three-sentence text, the middle sentence of which, though well-formed, runs afoul of the given-new principle, i.e. its information blocks are inappropriately positioned. The task of the learner is therefore to rewrite that middle sentence in such a way as better to accommodate it to its (discourse) context, with whatever grammatical changes this would entail.

One can hardly stress enough here that for consciousness-raising activity involving aspects of language form that are shaped by extra-grammatical forces – in fact, a great deal of the language – those forces (e.g. discourse and semantics) need to comprise the context in which the learner performs that activity (see Chapter 11).

2 Consciousness-raising and constituent relations

The history of consciousness-raising in language pedagogy is, as we have already seen, as long as the history of the field itself. Moreover, it is obvious that C-R does not necessarily mean the same thing for different researchers and practitioners. Whereas for some it may represent mere exposure to language embodying a particular structural phenomenon, for others it could represent the formal articulation of some rule of pedagogical grammar. What most C-R (including 'grammar-based') approaches have in common, however, is a preoccupation with *what* it is that should be called attention to. This typically involves the isolation of grammatical constructs and decisions concerning their protocol for display purposes.

The emphasis throughout these pages has been upon a form of C-R in which what is drawn attention to, for whatever purpose and to whatever extent, does not exist in and of itself. It is C-R in the service of a concept of language in which the notion of **relationship** is held to be paramount. We have already opened discussion of the possibilities for C-R at points where the grammatical system intersects those of discourse and semantics – grammatical relations on a grand scale, so to speak. It is also then worth noting our prospects for guiding the learner through C-R where *smaller*-scale relations are concerned. It turns out that the principle of **cohesion** provides an ideal framework for some meaningful C-R of precisely this kind.

Let us look again at the passage that appeared in Chapter 7 as example (11), repeated opposite as (17), but this time with the clausal elements in list form and the referential links identified via connecting lines, the broken line representing **hyponymy**.

Obviously, texts of virtually any length would be amenable to this sort of treatment and no doubt also the connecting-line conventions might be improved upon. It is then but a short step, of course, to the invention of C-R activity in which the learner himself is asked to

(17) One characteristic of *wars* in general is that often nobody *wins*.

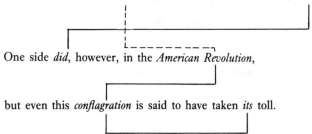

One side *did*, however, in the *American Revolution*,

but even this *conflagration* is said to have taken *its* toll.

connect the referential material in question – either verbally or by means of some convention like that in (17). Or he might be given the text with all anaphoric elements replaced by their lexical referents and asked to make the appropriate cohesive **substitution, ellipsis**, etc. himself. C-R can also be narrowed to cohesion involving only one grammatical subcategory, e.g. indefinite non-specific noun-phrases, and we will encounter an example of this in Chapter 12.

C-R activities arise quite naturally as well where constituent relations bear upon grammaticization and the lexicon. In Chapter 7, for instance, we looked at learner attempts to grapple with the kinds of grammatical shift that accompany the conversion of lexicon from one major category (e.g. verb) to another (e.g. noun). That is, to take a very simple example, sentence-internal grammatical context will often require that a verb-phrase consisting of verb + adverb, like *summarize briefly*, appear instead as a noun-phrase (*brief summary*), thus entailing the conversion not only of verb to noun but also of adverb to adjective. One can think of it as lexical **collocation** moving intact through grammatical prisms, so to speak, where the semantic relations are 'reflected' but the grammatical relations 'refracted'. The 'before' and 'after' states of this grammatical shift, conversion, or 'refraction' are not unlike stages in the L2 learner's course of syntactic development.

It is useful, then, to devise contexts in which the learner has to make this kind of conversion for himself, and this is actually very easy to do. It will be sufficient, for example, to provide (1) a sentence with a portion of the verb-phrase highlighted in some way (e.g. *General Motors **contributed sizably** to the political campaign*); (2) the main verb of the corresponding **effected object** construction (*make*) (see Chapter 4.4); and (3) the beginning of the sentence to contain the rewriting (*General Motors . . .*). The intended rendition by the learner will then of course be *General Motors made a sizable contribution to the political campaign*.

The learner has to know how not only to subject lexical collocation to grammatical 'refraction' but also, as we have seen, to select contextually appropriate lexicon among options that are seemingly semantically (and grammatically) equivalent. One effective C-R procedure that can at least sensitize the learner to the delicacy of proper lexical choice and concomitant semantic and syntactic relations relies heavily upon the learning principle wherein the new material is fitted to the old. One can, quite simply, display in paradigm form the lexicon having the shared properties in question (perhaps the feature [possession], for illustration purposes), the item(s) to be learned juxtaposed to the already familiar. The paradigm might thus conceivably consist of *keep, possess, own, belong to,* and *have,* and different sentential contexts will be devised wherein by turns only one (or at the most perhaps two) of the items is a possible choice. For example:

(18)

He	~~keeps~~ ~~possesses~~ ~~owns~~ ~~belongs to~~ has	a book that	~~keeps~~ ~~possesses~~ ~~owns~~ belongs to ~~has~~	me.

Contexts can of course even be devised in which the options represent other lexical categories, e.g. derived nouns, adjectives, etc. It might also be possible, with perhaps a little more effort, to compose whole texts containing enough lexical items with shared semantic properties that the text would be convertible to a 'cloze' exercise to be completed with items from precisely that lexical set. The C-R possibilities in the realm of lexical relations are in fact extensive, and we will see more examples of this in Chapter 12.

Among the other facets of constituent relations that can plausibly lend themselves to C-R, we will for now focus on that having to do with the grammatical realization of **verb-argument** relations. Recall that use of 'propositional-cluster' activity requires that discourse principles motivate the learner's choice of position for placement, within any sentence, of a noun-phrase contracting a semantic relation with its associated verb (Section 1). The resulting linear order of constituents is thus partially determined by extra-sentential forces, and the semantic relationship (viz. *objective*), only one or the other of these be for the most part unambiguously marked by means of prepositions (Chapter 5.2; but see also Chapter 9.5). It is the C-R potential for this grammatical 'marking' of semantic (case) relations that we will touch on here.

In essence, we want the learner to be aware that fundamental **verb-argument** relations are preserved throughout grammatical 'refraction'.

In other words, and by way of illustration, the learner needs to 'know' (even subconsciously) that semantic relations among lexical material are the same for, say, the sentence *Germany invaded Poland* and the noun-phrase *Germany's invasion of Poland*. One fairly straightforward way of engendering such awareness is through the practice of converting whole sentences into noun-phrases, most profitably as part of a general procedure of embedding sentential material within other propositions. Thus, with a main verb like *solve* contracting with its three associated arguments the semantic relations of **agentive** (X), **objective** (Y), and **instrumental** (Z), we might have either X *solved* Y *with* Z or X*'s solution of* Y *with* Z. But of course also Y or Z can, alternatively, occur to the left of *solve/solution* (Y *was solved by* X *with* Z; Z*'s solution of* Y (**by* X), etc.), or in the complex noun-phrase version there may even be *no* lexical material to the left of the head noun (*the solution of* Y *by* X *with* Z). In such circumstances the learner's activity could conceivably be, given the full sentence with all lexical items supplied, to insert the identical lexicon into matching skeletal complex noun-phrases in which only the verbal noun and the semantic case-marking prepositions are provided, as in (19):

(19) a. _____'s solution of _____ with _____
    b. _____'s solution by _____
    c. _____'s solution of _____ (**by* _____)

This is also a useful means for bringing to consciousness the grammatically neutralizing effect of the possessive *'s* in _____ *'s solution*, where *'s* marks any of the three relations: **agentive** (*the man's solution*), **objective** (*the problem's solution*), and **instrumental** (*the computer's solution*).

We should hasten to add that decisions as to which of the alternatives such as represented by (19a–c) one would choose in actual language use can be incorporated as well into appropriate pedagogical activity. That is, given that although, for example, *the discovery of the drug* and *the drug's discovery* are two syntactic realizations of the same semantic relationship (viz. **objective**), only one or the other of these otherwise ostensibly equivalent grammatical renditions will be likely in a context where either *discovery* or *drug* serves as head of a relative clause: *the discovery of **the drug which can cure** ...* (**the drug's discovery **which can cure** ...*), *the drug's **discovery that occurred only two days ago*** (*?the **discovery** of the drug **that occurred only two days ago***). Moreover, the version of noun$_1$ *'s* noun$_2$ will not be possible where noun$_1$ has substantial premodification: *the discovery of **the potent and relatively inexpensive drug** (*the potent and* *relatively inexpensive drug's discovery*). Learner activity consisting in selection among appropriate/possible and inappropriate/impossible alternatives of this kind should not be difficult to conjure up (see Chapter 12).

3 Postlude

In these discussions of C-R, as in any such discussion, one is occasionally apt temporarily to disregard one or another of the fundamental assumptions of grammatical C-R developed earlier and their relation to language learning. It is therefore useful periodically to remind ourselves just what it is that we are doing, or trying to do, and what we are not doing, or not trying to do, in our recourse to grammatical C-R in pedagogy. Consider once more then that C-R is the means to an end, not the end itself. That is, whatever it is that is raised to consciousness is not to be looked upon as an artifact or object of study to be committed to memory by the learner and thence recalled by him whenever sentences have to be produced. Rather, what is raised to consciousness is not the grammatical product but aspects of the grammatical process, and C-R activity must strive for consistency with this principle. It is a concept of the role of C-R that first of all has relatively little to do with the answer to the question 'How does one form a particular construction?' and a great deal to do with the answer to the questions 'What is it that one does with this bit of grammar?', 'What has to be done grammatically in order to have this block of information in position X?', 'What grammatical/morphological changes are required for the preservation of lexical collocation in environment Y?','Why does one say or write it this way rather than that way?', etc. It is also a conception of the role of C-R that is consistent with the 'top-down' (rather than a 'bottom-up') principle of grammatical function – that is, that grammar is the on-line processing component of discourse and not the set of syntactic 'building blocks' with which discourse is, as it were, 'constructed'. Finally, it is a conception of the role of C-R that aligns with the notion that to teach a language is not to teach a body of knowledge but to teach how to learn, or to teach learners how to become better managers of their own learning (Allwright 1984a). Just as we have grammar, broadly speaking, in the service of language *use*, so also we have grammar, through C-R, in the service of language *learning*. This symbiosis should not be lost sight of.

Activities

1. The following mini-texts, (A) and (B), each consist of three sentences. Note that the first sentence of (A) is syntactically the 'mirror image' of the last sentence of (B), and likewise the last sentence of (A) and the first sentence of (B). The two middle sentences are also mirror images of each other. Can you explain what is occurring **thematically** to produce these effects? Can examples of this kind be shaped into C-R activity?

(A) [1]Air coming up from the lungs causes the vocal cords to vibrate. [2]The vocal cords stretch across the larynx. [3]The larynx is the upper part of the respiratory tract.

(B) [1]The upper part of the respiratory tract is called the larynx. [2]Stretching across the larynx are the vocal cords. [3]The vocal cords are caused to vibrate by air coming up from the lungs.

2. A very useful classroom routine for focus on theme-rheme/cohesion, etc., and one that is extremely easy to conduct, requires nothing more than a sample of good, formal writing pitched to the learners' proficiency level. Expose the learners to the opening paragraph plus the first sentence of the second paragraph and ask them to guess the general outlines of information to come next (e.g. a clarification, an example, an elaboration, etc.). Then reveal that withheld text, for comparison purposes, and do the same with the opening of the next paragraph, and so on.

With very little more effort, exercises can also be devised of the following sort, where the learner has to choose the contextually appropriate next sentence from among (a), (b), and (c) (Rutherford 1977, p. 280);

This substance has some interesting properties.
a. Therefore, ...
b. Notice first that ...
c. Even more can be said ...

Find a target-language text of your own choice and devise a similar exercise of several items.

3. Select any sequence of a few sentences that constitute a text, arrange the sentences in list fashion with a space between each, and draw lines (as in example (17), p. 101) to connect all those pairs of items manifesting a referential relationship. How might this kind of activity be made more suitable as a C-R procedure for learners of low proficiency?

Notes

1. See also Candlin (1983).
2. For a methodologically innovative way of utilizing the scrambled-sentence device to maximum learner benefit, see R. E. Gibson, 'The Strip Story: a catalyst for communication', *TESOL Quarterly*, vol. 9, no. 2 (June 1975), pp. 15–51.

Questions to Part Three

1. The 'given-new principle' has been observed to apply to a wide range of languages. What natural aspects of human communication might be contributing to this wide application?

2. Rough correspondences are to be noted among various sets of terms referring to the organization of discourse: topic/comment, theme/rheme, given/new, etc. Why do you think there are so many of these? Why don't we just settle on one?

3. In Chapter 7.3.1 we noted occurrences of interlanguage like *When you heat the mixture it **changes** white*. To what extent might heavy reliance upon a small bilingual dictionary be contributing to the appearance of such examples?

4. It was pointed out in Chapter 7 that knowledge by the learner of the grammatical characteristics of a verb like *decide (on something)* will also extend to the noun *decision (on something)*. Does this principle apply as well to other parts of speech? For example, what about verbs and adjectives?

5. Are problems of cohesion to be seen only in the interlanguage of relatively advanced learners or do we see them with beginners as well?

6. In many commercially produced textbooks for teaching languages the learner is asked to change or 'transform' active sentences into passive sentences, or vice versa. What is wrong with a procedure of this kind? What false notions about language might the learner pick up through this kind of activity?

7. In Chapter 8 much is made of grammatical consciousness-raising for certain aspects of discourse and semantics. Would the C-R instruments displayed necessarily be appropriate for all learners in all circumstances? Do you see any *problems* with these kinds of C-R activity?

Part Four
The shape of English grammar

The world thus appears as a complicated tissue of events, in which
connections of different kinds alternate or overlap or combine and
thereby determine the texture of the whole.

Werner Heisenberg

Some people think best in formulas, and other people think best in
shapes.

Benoît Mandelbrot

Each of the three preceding parts of this book has approached the
topic of English grammar and consciousness-raising from a distinct
perspective. In Part One we considered English grammar in relation
to general characteristics of language organization and language
processing. In Part Two we looked at the implications for identification of the language learner's task in terms specifically of grammaticization phenomena. And in Part Three we discussed
relationships between the grammatical system and the systems of
discourse and of semantics. We now want to return to the topics of
English syntax *per se* and of the more precise nature of the task that
confronts the learner of English in his movement towards some kind
of linguistic competence in the target language. In Chapter 9 we look
at grammatical competence in English from a language-*typological*
perspective. In Chapter 10 we do so from a language-*universal*
perspective.

9 English and language typology

At various points in the preceding chapters of this book we have found it useful to make passing reference to certain over-arching conceptual frameworks within which to relate the formal systems of two or more languages. The kinds of 'framework' we are talking about here are essentially the means at our disposal for grouping large numbers of languages on the basis of shared gross characteristics. When those shared characteristics amount to sets of principles that delineate no language 'groups' at all – or rather, when they delineate only one group: the group that consists of *all* languages – then we may properly speak of **language universals** (see Chapter 10). When those shared characteristics delineate more than one group, then we are identifying those groups according to formal *type*; that is, **language typology**.[1] It will be useful to review here the kinds of typology that have already surfaced in previous discussion.

1 Four typologies

It is instructive at the outset to realize that we have to talk about 'typology' in the plural. Human language is so vast and so labyrinthine, and the sheer quantity of individual languages so great, that collectively they accommodate to no single classificatory system that linguists have yet been able to conceive. We must therefore have recourse to more than one such system if we are to gain the most comprehensive insight into the principled ways in which human languages may vary. There are in fact perhaps four typological systems or frameworks that have been proposed at one time or another in modern linguistic research,[2] although among them can be found a good deal of overlap.

The typology most frequently invoked in the linguistic research literature is that built upon the possible basic word orders of the sentence constituents S(ubject), O(bject), and V(erb) – sometimes referred to as **canonical word order** (see Greenberg 1966 and this volume Chapter 1.2). English, along with most other European languages, manifests the order SVO, and S (unlike, for example, Spanish and Italian) is obligatorily present (see Chapter 10).

For a number of known languages, however, the syntax-definable category 'subject' is less significant than the discourse-definable category 'topic' – i.e. sentences in such languages are plausibly to be analysed as topic-comment rather than subject-predicate (or occasionally both, or even (but rarely) neither). These contrasts have given impetus to the positing of the typological distinction **subject-prominence** (S-p) versus **topic-prominence** (T-p) (Li and Thompson 1976), with English identified of course as S-p (see Chapter 4.1).

The basic order of canonical constituents is always subject to the pressure of natural extra-sentential forces, however, that can effect permutations of these constituents in various languages and to varying degrees. On the one extreme would be total freedom in the ordering of canonical constituents to satisfy pragmatic demands; on the other would be word order rigidly maintained in the service of grammatical relations. These tendencies have led to the establishment of the typological distinction **pragmatic word order** (PWO) versus **grammatical word order** (GWO) (Thompson 1978), with English identified as solidly GWO (see Chapter 4.2).

Closely related to PWO/GWO is another language distinction drawn with respect to the degree of 'transparency' of semantic relations and their syntactic realization. Languages can be characterized by their propensities for preserving 'directness' in syntactic-semantic relations or for tolerating 'indirectness'. Capturing these tendencies then is the typology of **syntactic-semantic distance** (Hawkins 1985) with English located well towards the 'distal' end on the 'proximal/distal' scale of syntactic-semantic relations (see Chapter 4.3).

General analyses of English syntax can thus appeal for descriptive power to one or another of at least four (somewhat overlapping) typological frameworks: **canonical word order, topic-/subject-prominence, pragmatic/grammatical word order**, and **syntactic-semantic distance**. In the remainder of this chapter we will explore some of the further implications of typologically-defined English grammar and their relation to language learning.

2 Structure preservation

We have just noted once again that English is an excellent example of what has often been called a **grammatical word-order** (GWO) language, in which word order serves primarily the function of preserving grammatical structure. The structure whose preservation we refer to is of course that of SV(O), and it would be well to take a closer look at how some of this is accomplished.

2.1 *Interrogatives*

Perhaps the best example of such preservation is one of the most common and frequently discussed aspects of English grammar: question formation. Although the details may vary here and there, most ESL grammar-teaching materials cite the general requirement for 'inversion' of subject and **auxiliary** (including *be*) or (if only an inflected main verb is available for inversion) the created 'tense-carrier' *do*. Such statements certainly are pedagogically plausible generalizations of English question phenomena for those wishing to be given the 'rules'. There is another way, however, to view what is often looked upon by learners as a bizarre and perversely complicated formation for simply asking questions in English, and that is in terms of the strong tendency of English grammar to preserve its canonical word order. Thus, consider for a moment the relationship between a declarative sentence like *John smokes* and its corresponding yes-no question, *Does John smoke?* If we abstract away the question-making paraphernalia of 'tense-carrier', '*do*-support', 'inversion', etc., we can readily see that the meaning-bearing **lexical** elements *John* and *smoke* are in the order SV for both declarative *and* interrogative. In other words, SV canonical word order (where V is interpreted as **lexical verb**) has been preserved. Thus, although it is accurate to say that question formation in English involves the inversion of subject and auxiliary including (if necessary) the invocation of '*do*-support', the net structural effect of this otherwise cumbersome operation for forming questions is to maintain the subject before the (lexical) verb.

2.2 *Clefting*

Structure preservation in English can also be seen in the so-called 'focus' constructions:[3] **cleft** (*if* **it's** MONEY **that you want**, ...) and **pseudo-cleft** (*if* **what you want is** MONEY, ...) where the 'focused' element (*money*) is in upper case. Whereas many other languages (e.g. Russian, Spanish) can achieve 'focus' merely by rearranging canonical constituents such that the focused element appears in (salient) sentence-final position (*si* **quiere Usted dinero**, ... = *if – want – you – money*),[4] written English resorts to highly grammaticized constructions like **cleft** and **pseudo-cleft**. It is important to realize, however, that this grammaticized clefting creates structures that serve to maintain canonical SV(O). That is, cleft sentences collapse the propositional content into a **head + relative clause**-like structure (e.g. *money that you want*) and create a new subject (viz. 'dummy' *it*) and verb (viz. 'copula' *be*). Pseudo-cleft sentences create a new main verb ('copula' *be*), place the focused element to the right, and collapse the non-focused part of propositional content into a **headless relative clause** which then serves as the new subject: *if what you want is Money* . . .). Again, one of the effects of all this is the maintenance of SVO structure.

2.3 Raising

Often called attention to in linguistic research is the fact that the English language sets itself apart from most other languages by its extensive battery of 'movement' rules. It is a collection of rules that allow the positioning of information blocks to satisfy discourse requirements while at the same time ensuring that canonical word order is preserved. In Chapter 5.2 we encountered an example of one subset of such movement rules – the subset labelled **raising** rules. The term 'raising' has to be understood with reference to the phrase-structure configuration posited for English syntax whose branching structures create hierarchical relations between elements 'higher' and 'lower' within the configuration. For an example of this, compare the sentences (1a) and (1b):

(1) a. They believed that *the war* was over.
    b. They believed *the war* to be over.

The structural difference between the two sentences is seen most clearly if we consider that (1b) has been derived from the structure underlying (1a).[5] In this sense then, *the war*, which is the subject in the (lower) **subordinate clause** *that the war was over* in (1a), has been raised to become the object in the (higher) **main clause** *They believed* . . . in (1b). *War* has thus been **raised** from **subject** of a lower clause to **object** of a higher clause and, accordingly, the operation is referred to as **subject-to-object** (S–O) **raising**.

Languages generally require **raising** rules to the extent that word-order freedom is constrained, and thus some languages do not have such rules at all (e.g. Russian, Hungarian). In other languages (e.g. Hebrew, Egyptian and Lebanese Arabic, Turkish) the only kind of raising possible is what we have just seen – namely, **subject-to-object** (Eckman 1977). English can go further than this, however. Again with **raising** in mind, compare (2a) and (2b), (3a) and (3b):

(2) a. It seems that *the war* is over.
   b. *The war* seems to be over.
(3) a. It's easy to forget *the war*.
   b. *The war* is easy to forget.

With regard to (2a–b), we can observe that *the war*, as subject of the (lower) **subordinate clause**, *the war is over* in (2a), has been raised to become subject of the (higher) **main clause** (. . . *seems* . . .) in (2b). Since *war* has been **raised** from lower-clause **subject** to higher-clause **subject**, we may properly refer to the operation as **subject-to-subject** (S-S) **raising**. With (3a–b), the **raising** of *war* is from **object** of (lower) infinitival *forget* in (3a) to **subject** of higher-clause . . . *is easy* . . . in (3b), and this operation then will be **object-to-subject** (O-S) **raising**.[6]

Several further remarks are in order here. First of all, although all three kinds of **raising** (S-O, S-S, O-S) are possible in English, the number of languages for which this is also true is very small; among the well-known languages, for example, one could cite French and to some extent German. Second, the occurrence of raising data across languages can be displayed as an **accessibility hierarchy** of the following sort: S-O > S-S > O-S. That is, any language evincing one of these three kinds of raising will also evince anything higher in the hierarchy (i.e. to the left), though not necessarily anything lower (i.e. to the right) (Eckman 1977). Third, subjects and objects derived through raising do *not* contract semantic relations with their main verbs – note . . . *believe the war* in (1b), *the war seems* . . . in (2b), *the war is easy* . . . in (3b). Indeed, the proliferation of raising in English has been linked by some researchers (see Hawkins 1985) to the comparable propensity of the language to tolerate the occurrence of non-agentive subjects in general (see Section 3; see also Chapter 7.1). Finally, it can readily be seen that all these derived structures (1b), (2b), (3b) maintain SV(O) word order. Thus the three raising rules discussed here are examples *par excellence* of how canonical *constituents* may be rearranged while canonical *structure* is still preserved.

We first touched on these syntactic characteristics in our discussion of syntactic-semantic distance (Chapter 4), and we noted then that learners of English face greater challenges for those aspects of the language wherein semantic relations and syntactic relations manifest little coincidence. **Raising** phenomena then bring these learning challenges into particularly sharp focus. There is evidence, for example (Kellerman 1979), that learners will reject structures such as (1b)/(2b)/(3b) as ungrammatical, *even when such structures are grammatical in the learner's native language*. In other words, the learner will usually prefer that language structure in which syntax and semantics display the greatest **isomorphism**. To the extent that isomorphism must give way to structure preservation, as is so evident in English,[7] then the challenge posed to the learner is that much greater.

3 Diverse subjects[8]

In previous chapters we have often drawn a distinction between characteristics that seem to be generalizable to all or most languages and those that appear to be language-specific. We have also noted that on occasion the general tendency and the specific instance can work at cross purposes. There is a particularly striking example of this to be seen in English canonical word order *vis-à-vis* the general pattern of arrangement of information in discourse. Recall that whereas the language-general tendency is to order **theme** before **rheme**, the rigidity of English SVO structure will pull the other way in those instances where **theme** does not happen to coincide with **subject**. One of the ways in which English resolves this tension involves movement rules of the kind that we have looked at in the previous section. That is, English grammaticization licenses the movement (e.g. **raising**) of constituents out of and into basic syntactic positions to satisfy theme-rheme requirements while at the same time preserving SVO structure. Resolution of discourse-syntax tension in English is accomplished in other ways as well – some of these having to do with the diversity of possible semantic relations between subject and verb.

3.1 *Non-agentive subjects*

In Chapter 7, we called attention to the fact that the verb-argument relation **agentive** is universally the semantic relation that most naturally maps on to syntactic subject and verb. We also noted that the semantic relation **instrumental**, for example, can achieve this mapping in English and that such instrumental-subject SVO constructions are often perceived by learners as strange.

It happens that subject-verb in English can take the mapping of other non-agentive verb-argument relations as well. Consider the following:

(4) a. *July and August* are hot in Los Angeles.
    b. It is hot in Los Angeles *during July and August.*

(5) a. *Los Angeles* is hot during July and August.
    b. It is hot *in Los Angeles* during July and August.

(6) a. *This camper* sleeps four people.
    b. Four people (can) sleep *in this camper.*

(7) a. *Ice cream* keeps for a long time.
    b. You (can) keep *ice cream* for a long time.

In all the (a) examples, the subject bears a semantic relation to its verb that is highly unusual; that is, verb-argument relations of these kinds cannot be borne by subject-verb in many other languages, where something like the (more 'natural') (b) forms would be the only alternative. The subject of (4a), for example, is a **temporal**; that of (5a) is a **locative**, as is that of (6a). Note that the subject of (7a) is **objective** without conversion of *keep* to the passive, not unlike examples such as *The door opened* and *The window broke* that we encountered in Chapter 7.

Non-agentive subjects such as the above are generally late acquisitions for the learner, and an example of learner progress in this area will serve as illustration. The propositional content represented by *teach electronics – they – I – in that school* would appear in the early production of most learners as a sentence with **agentive** subject:

(8) *They* taught me electronics in that school.

If discourse context suggests *school* as the more appropriate theme, then the learner might subsequently be expected to front the **locative prepositional phrase** while still retaining agentive *they* as subject:

(9) *In that school* they taught me electronics.

Only in the later stages of acquisition (and with the same thematic requirement) are we likely to see the **locative** supplant the **agentive** as subject of the sentence:

(10) *That school* taught me electronics.

Learner production of non-agentive subjects like those in (6a) and (7a) is even rarer, though the examples in standard English of these and others are copious: *My guitar broke a string, This shirt buttons in back, The book sold like hotcakes, A dollar won't buy you much*, etc. Again, however, the advantage of **non-agentive** subjects to the language user is that he is thereby afforded one more option for satisfying discoursal theme-rheme requirements within the severe canonical word order restrictions of English.

3.2 *Passive*

The commonest construction allowing (indeed, requiring) a non-agentive subject is of course the **passive**. The most frequently occurring, or 'basic', passive is that triggered by selection of **objective** as the semantic relation to be mapped onto subject-verb (e.g. *A letter was written*). English is notable, however, for its tolerance of participation in the passive by other semantic relations. These include **dative** (*The mayor was written a letter*), **benefactive** (*The waiter was left a tip*), various prepositional-phrase **locatives** (*This bed's been slept in*), and assorted other relations represented in **phrasal verb** constructions (*The plan was asked for/believed in/looked at/talked about*, etc.). The task of the learner then, over time, is to be able freely to select thematic candidates for subjecthood while at the same time (a) distinguishing **agentive** subjects from **non-agentives**, and (b) knowing whether or not, for non-agentives that happen not to be **objective**, passive is triggered at all. This in addition to learning the **passive** grammatical apparatus itself.

The learner's rhematic options increase with expansion of his verb lexicon to include reciprocal pairs like *buy/sell, lend/borrow, give/get, teach/learn*, and others like *rob/steal*. The pair affords a wider choice because although the two members are semantically similar, they have different verb-argument assignments. It is the pairing then, as if to create a single verb (as indeed is the case in some other languages), that widens the options for theme-rheme assignment – again, within the canonical word-order restrictions of SVO English. *Rob* and *steal*, for example, each have three associated **arguments (agentive, objective, ablative)**, but it is only for *rob/steal* as a *pair* that all of the three may serve as (thematic) subject of the sentence. Thus:

(11) a. X robbed me of $100.
    a'. X stole $100 from me.
    b. I was robbed of $100.
    b'. *I was stolen $100 from.
    c. $100 was stolen from me.
    c'. *$100 was robbed me of.

In general then, the more **arguments** available, the wider the choice for candidates as subject (i.e. theme) of the sentence. The learning experience in English therefore involves not just the acquisition of verbs with more than one (or two) associated arguments but also sensitivity to the tolerance of English for these diverse arguments to be mapped onto subject-verb.

4 Extraction

We have thus far looked at English movement rules from the standpoint of **structure preservation** (Section 2) and **verb-argument mapping upon subject-verb** (Section 3). We also want to consider rules with regard to the syntactic locales from which elements are extracted and to those in which they are deposited. One such **extraction** rule involves the formation of **relative clauses**.

4.1 *Relativization*

The area of interlanguage syntax that has to date been investigated perhaps the most thoroughly of all is **relativization**. The function of relativization across languages[9] is a uniform one – namely, noun-phrase modification. The gross structure of relativization across languages (for those languages whose relativization resembles, even remotely, that of English), many details aside and using the relative clause *the child who(m) we talked to* as example, can be stated as

a) the embedding of sentential matter to a noun-phrase (i.e. the head noun) with which one noun-phrase in the (lower) embedded sentence is **co-referential**:

(12) *the child* [We talked to *the child*]

b) suppression of the lower shared noun-phrase, or substitution of a relative marker (depending upon the language):

(13) the child [We talked to *wh*-]

c) extraction of the relative marker and movement (in most languages) to sentence-initial position:

(14) the child [*wh*- we talked to Ø]

d) deposit, for some languages, in the position of the extracted noun phrase/relative marker of a pronominal trace:[10]

(15) the child [wh- we talked to (*him*)]

Moreover, **extraction** may include larger constituents (e.g. a prepositional phrase) of which the noun-phrase/relative marker is a part:

(16) the child [*to wh*- we talked Ø]

The shared noun-phrase underlying the **relative clause** can bear the following syntactic relations to the rest of its clause:[11]

(17) a. S(ubject):   the person *who called us*
      b. D(irect) O(bject):   the person *who(m) we called*

c. Non-D(irect) O(bject):   the person **who(m)** *we called* **to**
                            the person **to whom** *we called*
d. POSS(essive):   the person **whose son** *we called*

It has been noted many times in the linguistic research literature that the relativized syntactic positions displayed in (17a–d) constitute a cross-linguistic **accessibility hierarchy**, representable as (18):

(18) S > DO > Non-DO > POSS

We interpret (18) to mean that if a language can relativize on a given position, then it necessarily relativizes on any position higher (i.e. to the left) in the hierarchy, though not necessarily lower (i.e. to the right). Furthermore, the accessibility hierarchy also applies to the occurrence of **pronominal traces** in these relativized positions across languages. Thus, if a language leaves pronominal traces in a given relativized position, then it necessarily leaves pronominal traces in any relativized position lower in the hierarchy (i.e. to the right), though not necessarily higher. English, of course, relativizes on all four positions and leaves no pronominal traces. (But see Activities for this chapter, p. 126, item 5.)

Not surprisingly then, the language learner's acquisition of relative clauses also proceeds in general accord with the accessibility hierarchy. That is, learner production of relative clauses in terms of accuracy and frequency – as well as learner perceptions of relative-clause grammaticality – develops from the top down or, with reference to (18), from left to right. Furthermore, learner propensity for leaving pronominal traces in relativized positions has a distribution that is yet again consistent with the hierarchy – the occurrence of traces for a given position implies traces as well for any position lower in the hierarchy, though not necessarily higher – and elimination of these traces in the course of learner progress also proceeds from top to bottom.[12]

The learner's persistent tendency to leave hierarchically distributed pronominal traces in relative clauses is, of course, not to be regarded as linguistic perversity on his part, as we first noted in Chapter 4.3. It is through recourse to this trace procedure that the learner is able to bring semantic relations and syntactic form into closer alignment and thereby extend his command of the language. Pronominal traces in relative clauses thus render usable to the learner relativized positions lower in the 'accessibility' hierarchy that would otherwise be for the time being *in*accessible to him. For many learners of English then, the pronominal trace is a *necessary* path to full acquisition of relative clauses.

Learner tendency to leave pronominal traces will be even more pronounced in relative clauses of greater complexity – that is, where the element to be extracted (i.e. relativized) is located lower than the first level of embedding, as in (19), with a hypothesized learner-rendition as in (20):

(19) a. **the child** [We think [that *the child* has measles]]
    b. **the child** *who*(*m*) we think ~~that~~ Ø has measles
(20)   *the child who* we think that *he* has measles

In general, evidence of extraction in learner language will co-vary with both the derivational depth of the extracted element (i.e. the more embedding, the less extraction) and the recourse to pronominal traces (i.e. the more embedding, the more traces). One measure of progress, therefore, would be the learner's increasing ability to handle aspects of English extraction phenomena without the processing 'crutch' provided by redundant trace-elements.

The relative clause phenomena that we have been discussing here have one thing in common, and that is that in all the examples in question the relative clause and its head noun are adjacent. In our earlier discussion (Chapter 6.3) of grammar and discourse, however, we saw that **adjacency** of the relative clause is not an absolute requirement in English and we will now briefly consider a few other aspects of the adjacency question, postponing the rest until Chapter 10.

4.2 *Discontinuity and dislocation*

More than once in these pages we have encountered instances in English where syntax and discourse exert a 'pull' upon each other, and seen the kinds of 'compromise' often reached. A good illustration of this would be the relative clause characteristics from Chapter 6, cited above and recaptured here as example (21):

(21) *A man* stood in our path *who looked in need of help.*

We noted before that the **rhematic** strength of the relative clause was sufficient to detach it from its head noun (*a man*) and shift it to the right. It is important to note also, however, that whereas languages classifiable as more PWO than GWO (e.g. Spanish, German) might let rhematic concerns bring about a shift to the right of the *entire* noun-phrase (i.e. head noun + relative clause), English must hold back the head noun in order that it fulfil the strong grammatical requirement of keeping subject position occupied. Thus, the syntax-discourse struggle over the positioning of a noun-phrase consisting of head noun + relative clause – syntax pulling to keep it in (sentence-initial) subject position, discourse pulling to shift it to (sentence-final) rhematic position – is resolved through a 'compromise' in which the noun-phrase is split, one part given to syntax, the other to discourse. One obvious but important effect of this split is thus the emergence of **discontinuity**, or the break-up of a noun-phrase containing a relative clause.

The kind of 'shift' we are talking about is usually referred to as **extraposition**, with the element in question being **extraposed**. As it turns out, the occurrence of extraposition in English is much wider than merely the above relative-clause type, for it is easy to find common examples of its extension to noun-phrase modification in general:[13]

(22) a. *A rumour* circulated *that he was a spy.*
  b. *The problem* arose *of what to do about it.*
  c. *The time* had come *to address the issue.*
  d. *A committee* has been formed *consisting of X, Y, and Z.*
  e. *What business* is it *of yours?*
  f. *All of us* were upset *but you.*
  g. Did *you* do that *yourself?*

In all these cases (save for the question examples of (e) and (g)), what prevents the (subject) head noun from extraposing along with its complement is the rigid requirement of English that subject position not be left empty. Again, however, fulfilment of the requirement produces sentences containing **discontinuous** elements.

What happens then in cases where the **extraposable** material is not attached to any head noun? English abounds in syntactic phenomena of this kind, most typically where the sentence subject contains a clausal element, as in (23):

(23) a. *That you say something to them* is important.
  b. *For you to say something to them* is important.
  c. *What you say to them* is important.

In such cases, there are two forces that work together to rearrange the order of subject and verb-phrase – namely, the relative difficulty of processing subjects that are themselves clauses and the tendency to position rhematic material sentence-finally.[14] Extraposition *implements* these forces and, accordingly, the subjects in (23) are moved to sentence-final position. But since these (clausal) subjects include no head noun, there is nothing to leave behind in subject position in the course of extraposition. The problem is solved, of course, through the *creation* of a 'head noun' to perform this function – namely, non-referential ('dummy') *it* – and thus from the structure underlying (23) we derive (24):

(24) a. *It* is important that you say something to them.
    b. *It* is important for you to say something to them.
    c. *It* is important what you say to them.

Although the overriding pressure of English to maintain SVO structure in the course of these **extraction** operations is most evident in the case of **subject** (S) extraposition, there are abundant common examples to be found with **object** (O) extraposition as well. Analogous to (24), then, clausal objects can extrapose as in (25):

(25) a. We consider *it* important *that you say something.*
    b. We make *it* a rule *never to say anything.*
    c. We'll leave *it* undecided *whether we should say anything.*

For **extraposition** of clausal elements from both subject and object position, non-referential *it* thus provides the otherwise missing head noun *cum* syntactic place-holder.[15]

The examples of discontinuity we have been discussing all involve movement of something to the right, usually to the end of the sentence. Movement to the beginning of the sentence is also common in English, and such leftward shift of (thematic) noun-phrases is referred to as **left dislocation** if a pronominal trace is planted in the vacated position, **topicalization** if it is not:

(26) *Max*, I can't stand *him*.   (Left dislocation)

(27) *Max*, I can't stand.   (Topicalization)

Although in writing, topicalization is far more common than left dislocation, it is useful to note that in both examples we have two of the relatively few instances when English SVO order is rearranged (viz. to OSV). Observe, nevertheless, that all-important SV is still present. Therefore, the reader or listener will instantly abandon any processing of (initial) *Max* as subject upon encountering the full SV clause-structure that immediately follows.[16] Thus, **topicalization** – as well as the other extraction phenomena treated here: **dislocation**, **extraposition**, and **relativization** – does not alter basic grammatical relations within English clause-structure.

4.3 *Extraction, raising, and the learner*

We spoke earlier (section 2.3) of the 'challenge' to the learner posed by the results of syntactic **raising**, wherein adjacent grammatically related elements bore no corresponding semantic relation. Learners typically judge such constructions as ungrammatical and, in terms of production, usually fall back upon alternative means of grammatical expression in which the relation between syntax and semantics is more direct. (For example, the learner is likely to prefer *It is easy to convince John* to *John is easy to convince*.)[17] The learner's approach to English **extraction** phenomena, however, is somewhat different. The difference has to do with the fact that although extraction, like raising, produces structures in which there is some **distance** between semantic representation and syntactic realization, it is *un*like raising in that (a) the destination of extracted constituents is not a definable grammatical position (e.g. subject, object); and (b) the question of an extracted element not contracting a semantic relation with an adjacent element to which it is grammatically linked does not therefore arise. In the case of extraction then, the learner's tactic is to devise means, when needed, for following the extraction 'trajectory', for retaining a sense of syntactic/semantic connections by relating the 'landing site' to the 'extraction site'. Hence, his recourse to pronominal traces in the extraction sites of relativized noun-phrases. Hence, his earlier preference for left dislocation over topicalization.[18] Hence, his relatively fewer problems with noun-phrase extraposition, where the extraction site is automatically marked with non-referential *it*. **Raising** affords the learner no such avenues of adjustment.

5 Obliteration of grammatical cues

The operations in English represented by **raising, extraction, non-agentive subject**, etc., all amount to varieties of constituent rearrangement that serve to widen the gap between syntax and semantics. Also contributing to that widening is a phenomenon of another kind, one in which the grammatical cues to semantic interpretation are not merely obscured but are actually obliterated. Consider the following example:

(28) He'll see that the door is locked.

Note that (28) is ambiguous; it can mean either (a) *He'll notice . . .* or (b) *He'll ensure . . . .* Note further that meaning (b) has a variant form – namely, (29):

(29) He'll see *to it* that the door is locked.

What we have with *see* in (28), then, is not lexical ambiguity, as for example with the multiple meanings of *charge* or *drive* or *count*, but rather syntactic ambiguity, resulting from certain grammatical operations. To illustrate, we might sketch the underlying forms for meanings (a) and (b) of (28) as follows:

(30) a. He'll see [that the door is locked]
     b. He'll see to [that the door is locked]

The realization of (30a) as (28) is fairly straightforward, and the realization of (30b) as (29) involves the already familiar extraposition plus introduction of *it* as syntactic place-holder (since a clause cannot be object of a preposition). How, then, does (30b) also get realized as (28), to render the above ambiguity? The answer is that English has another way of avoiding the unacceptable clause-as-object of a preposition, and that is to delete the preposition:

(31) He'll see ~~to~~ [that the door is locked]

Hence (30b) can be realized as (29) via extraposition or as (28) via preposition deletion. It is thus the preposition deletion of (31) that reduces underlying *see to* to surface *see* and brings about the ambiguity of (28).

It will scarcely come as a surprise to note that if the full form of a particular verb is *see to*, then to have it appear in actual use as *see* will make slightly more demands upon one's faculties of semantic interpretation. Yet English regularly suppresses such grammatical clues to semantic relations, as in these additional examples:

(32) a. I'm *surprised* ~~at~~ that the door is unlocked.
        (cf. What I'm *surprised at* is that the door is unlocked.)
     b. He *insists* ~~on~~ that you lock the door.
        (cf. What he *insists on* is that you lock the door.)
     c. They *convinced* me ~~of~~ that the door was locked.
        (cf. What they *convinced* me *of* was that the door was locked.)

Semantic relations are also less explicit in English compounding (e.g. *book shelf*) than in the analogous 'prepositional postmodification' (*shelf for books*), where the presence of the preposition obviates any possible ambiguity. Not surprisingly, therefore, the learner's early reach for explicitness and semantic 'transparency' leads to a preference for prepositional postmodification over compounds.[19]

English prepositions then perform an important function in the expression of semantic relations, and the tendency for syntactic concerns often to squeeze them out does nothing – shall we say – to enhance their learnability.[20]

There are other grammatical cues that can regularly be dispensed with in English, and we have examples of them in the course of **relativization** and **complementation**:

(33) a. the door (*that*) I unlocked
   b. the door (*that*) I put a lock on
(34) I think (*that*) I forgot to lock the door.

Object relative clauses can typically delete the relative marker *that*, as in (33); complements can typically delete the complementizer *that*, as in (34) (though not after all verbs and not at all in noun complementation). Again, the effect of such deletion, of course, is to render syntactic and semantic relations less explicit and we therefore find that in his early production the learner will usually exercise the option of retaining these grammatical cues.

6 Typological characteristics and language parsing

Many of the phenomena discussed in this chapter support the notion that English displays an uncommon propensity for obscuring the relationships between form and meaning, and we have often spoken of the 'challenges' to the learner that are inherent in such a language characteristic. For any given instance of challenge, however, the language phenomenon in question will pose different task constraints for the learner, to the extent that he is trying to produce language or trying to comprehend it. For example, although English sentences in which 'raising' rules have applied (e.g. *Vocabulary is easy to forget*) will often baffle the learner in the early stages, he will always have recourse to a non-raised, more 'transparent' paraphrase (i.e. *It's easy to forget vocabulary*) for production purposes. This will obviously not be the case when the learner has to *comprehend* language containing the structural phenomenon in question, for his **parsing** abilities will necessarily be tested without recourse to paraphrased alternatives. Thus, we may well consider for a moment the more general implications of some of the previously discussed typological characteristics for language parsing, or the ability to impose a structural analysis upon incoming language data.

There is widespread recognition that the pattern of language acquisition for the L2 learner is one wherein, among other things, hypotheses about the organization of the target language are formed, tested out, and then often abandoned in favour of more reasonable ones. The interesting question is what it is that leads the learner to abandon one hypothesis in favour of another. It is difficult to believe that the reformulation was induced by the sudden availability of certain crucial data, for we have no reason to think that such data were not present in what the learner was exposed to all along. Rather, it has been suggested (Zobl 1986) that the crucial data were there but simply *not noticed* until the learner had developed the ability to parse the particular kinds of language embodying grammatical principles represented by precisely those data. As the learner improves his performance in the target language, what we are therefore likely seeing with the attainment of higher levels of language complexity is the attainment of higher levels of processing (e.g. parsing) capability. A case in point might well be represented by the speaker of (topic-prominent) Mandarin Chinese learning (subject-prominent) English, where the L1-induced 'misparse' of English subject-predicate as topic-comment is later rectified as the learner's developing target-language knowledge embraces those properties associated with subject as distinct from topic, e.g. subject-verb agreement, agentness, participation in movement operations, etc. One can thus readily understand why learner-misparse of basic word order (e.g. English SVO) does *not* normally occur, because from the start the unfailing presence of SVO – with its major constituent breaks – makes minimal demands upon the learner's parser (Zobl 1986).

7 Postscript

In this chapter we have been talking about English in terms of gross features that cut across a range of syntactic phenomena and that serve to paint a very rough grammatical picture of English – features amounting to the sets of (interrelated) characteristics that go to make up the 'vocabulary' of language typology. We have thus noted that English exhibits a fairly rigid SV(O) order with S obligatorily present, that it utilizes word order in the service of grammatical rather than semantic relations, that it tolerates an array of non-agentive arguments as subject of the verb, and that all of this conspires to spawn a surface grammatical structure that is at some remove from its corresponding semantic representation. Moreover, we have frequently defined 'tasks' and 'challenges' of the learner of English in terms of entry into this maze where grammatical clues to meaning are often wanting, where the syntax seems to ride roughshod over the semantics. What can be done then to aid the learner as he threads his way through this grammatical labyrinth?

The most sensible approach to this problem – and one that is consistent with what is known of the nature of learning, the nature of language organization, and the nature of language acquisition – would be to devise the sorts of activity in which the learner can experience for himself the impact upon surface grammar of crucial formal features of the language that we have here identified in typological terms. One set of such activities, utilizing the 'propositional cluster' principle, has already been described (Chapter 5) and will be further extended and elaborated in Part Five. We will then also examine other aspects of consciousness-raising wherein the learner may be helped to a more rapid understanding of how meaningful use of English is achieved within a system where form and meaning are often far apart. In the interim, however, we will return in the next chapter to an examination of English grammar from the perspective of language universals.

Activities

1. English, as we have seen, routinely creates (a) transitive verbs out of intransitives (e.g. **zero-derivation** of causatives, as in *He's walking the dog*) and also (b) intransitives out of transitives (e.g. with change-of-state verbs, as in *The door opened*). It is easy to find examples in interlanguage of innovative constructions of the (a) category but not at all of the (b) category. Can you suggest any reasons why this might be the case?

2. It is not difficult to contrive contexts for little exchanges containing reciprocal pairs like *teach/learn*, *buy/sell*, *give/get*, *borrow/lend*, etc. For example:

> Bob: My mother *taught* me all I know.
> Sue: Hey Cathy, Bob says he *learned* all he knows from his mother.

Try your hand at this with one or two of the other pairs. How might this sort of thing be exploited for learner activity?

3. In the written English especially of Japanese-speaking learners one often finds sentences like *As for* _____, (sentence); *Speaking of* _____, (sentence). In the written English especially of Spanish-speaking learners one often finds sentences like *In this place happened the* _____; *Was very interesting the* _____. What typological characteristics of the mother tongues might be contributing to interlanguage characteristics of these kinds?

4. The following 'limerick' is usually attributed to Abraham Lincoln:

> In beauty I'm not a great star;
> Others are handsomer far.
> But my face I don't mind it,
> Because I'm behind it;
> It's the folks out in front that I jar.

The limerick contains, among other things, one example each of **adverb fronting**, **clefting**, and **left dislocation**. Can you identify them?

5. Now that we've discussed the tendency of some learners to leave pronominal traces in positions of extracted noun-phrases, consider the following kind of sentence commonly found in native-speaker English: *New York is a city you have to spend a lot of time in Ø to appreciate Ø*. The two 'Ø' mark positions of extracted noun-phrases that are co-referential with *city* (and the second Ø is an instance, in linguistic terms, of a 'parasitic gap'). However, native speakers of English will, as often as not, leave a pronominal trace in one of these two positions. Which of the two is it (i.e. what sentence would be produced?) and why is it that one rather than the other?

6. Language-teaching texts often contain exercises in which the learner is asked to combine two sentences into one containing a relative clause, e.g. *I know the girl* + *The girl likes opera* → *I know the girl who likes opera*. Occasionally in such texts we also find items like *I know the girl* + *Mary is taller than the girl* → *I know the girl who Mary is taller than*. Apart from the general problems posed by context-less language manipulation, what is intrinsically wrong with getting the learner to produce a sentence like this last example? (This is a question that has to do with the very function of relative clauses.)

7. Wh-questions in English can manifest deep extraction. Compare (a) and (b):

(a) *What* did you think he would do Ø?
(b) *What* do you think he would have wanted to suggest that we do Ø?

Do you think that deep-extraction phenomena of this kind have any implications for C-R? Why (not)?

Notes

1. Comrie (1981, p. 31) explains the universal/typological symbiosis in the following terms:
    > . . . both [universals and typology] are concerned with variation across languages, the only difference being that language universals research is concerned with limits on this variation, whereas typological research is concerned more directly with possible variation. However, neither conceptually nor methodologically is it possible to isolate the one study from the other.
2. For discussion of the more traditional 'morphological typology' – i.e. classification of languages in terms of *fusional* versus *agglutinative*, *isolating* versus *polysynthetic* – see Comrie (1981, Chapter 2).
3. Many of the comments here concerning GWO are adaptations of those to be found in Thompson (1978).

4. Spanish also has clefting, of course (*si **es dinero que** (Usted)* **quiere** ...), but greater word-order freedom affords options in Spanish that can be rendered in written English *only* by clefting.

5. In Chomskyan UG, (1a) and (1b) would be argued to have different (though similar) underlying structures. Hawkins (1985), drawing upon contrastive data in English versus German, opts for a 'raising' analysis, and it is the Hawkins position that we have adopted here.

6. The pairs in (1), (2), and (3) necessarily obscure an important derivational principle for the raised elements – namely, that the raised element must bear the same relationship to the main verb of the higher clause as did the (lower) clause from which it was raised. This principle is called the 'Relational Succession Law' (see Perlmutter and Postal (1974)). Thus, the more immediate underlying structures for the (b) examples of the pairs (1–3) would (informally) be something like the following:

(1c) They believed [The war was over]
(2c) [The war is over] seems
(3c) [One forgets the war] is easy

Object-to-subject raising (example (3b)) is often referred to as 'tough movement', and what is raised can also be object of a preposition: *Computers are hard to write letters with.*

7. Thompson (1978; p. 31) offers an interesting comment concerning transformational-generative grammar, structure preservation, and the English language:

... English lends itself particularly well to being described in terms of such [structure-preserving] transformations precisely because pre-verbal position is so crucial as a signal of grammatical subject. In fact, one could go so far as to say that it is no accident that the formal system that we know as standard transformational grammar was the result of trying to account for the grammatical structure of English. That is, it is quite natural that an apparatus with rigidly ordered SVO 'deep structures' and a host of operations whereby these deep structures are transformed into other SVO structures should have been developed, given that the language on which it was based was English.

8. Some of the data in this section are drawn from Hawkins (1985).

9. The phenomenon designated 'relativization' takes on a wide variety of forms cross-linguistically. To quote Newmeyer (1983, p. 102):

... among other ways, relatives may be formed by complete nonreduction of the clause (as in Bambara), by gapping the co-referent noun phrase (as in Japanese), by changing word order (as in English), by nominalization (as in Turkish), by use of a resumptive pronoun (as in Hebrew), by use of a relative pronoun (as in Spanish), or by coding the verb (as in Philippine languages).

10. These are often called 'resumptive pronouns'.

11. These four categories are a reduction (Comrie 1981) of the usual six. *Non-DO* is a conflation of *Indirect Object* and *Object of Preposition*, and the sixth – *Object of Comparative* – is rare.

12. See Gass (1984). The genitive (POSS) does not always conform to this hierarchy, however. See Zobl (1983) for an explanation of this in terms of the 'projection principle'. Moreover, Gass (1979) has shown that the pattern of pronoun retention is different at the upper end of the hierarchy – though not at the lower end – and that this difference is attributable to native-language influence.

13. These examples are modifications of those to be found in Quirk *et al.* (1972, pp. 966–7). Quirk *et al.* label the phenomenon 'postponement' and provide additional examples of it with comparatives: *More people own houses than used to, He was so angered by the reprimand that he quit.* Leech (1983) discusses examples like these in terms of pragmatics and with reference to a 'principle of clarity' and a 'maxim of transparency'.

14. Quirk *et al.* (1972) refer to these forces as 'end weight' and 'end focus'.

15. Extraposition has sometimes been likened to a kind of movement rule, found more commonly in unplanned language use, called *right dislocation*, where the dislocated material has more the feeling of an 'afterthought':
     (a) He's a scoundrel, **that man**.
     (b) He's a scoundrel, **he is**.
     Quirk *et al.* (1972, p. 971) refer to these as 'noun-phrase tags'.

16. In written English one often encounters instances of topicalization whose syntax is quite complex and consequently where more processing time is demanded of the reader. Quirk *et al.* (1972, p. 947) provide a good example: *Everything – or nearly everything – that the Labour movement exists to stop the Tories from doing Labour will be asked to support the Cabinet in doing.* Examples (26) and (27) are products of what in linguistics are known as 'root transformations' (Emonds 1976).

17. See Kellerman (1979).

18. See Fuller and Gundel (1985).

19. It might also be noted that prepositional postmodification (i.e. head-adjunct) is also in alignment with the head-adjunct order of VO.

20. Mackenzie (1981) identifies what he terms 'adpositional usage' and 'verb valency' (cf. predicate-argument) as two of the foremost problems confronting the learner.

10 English and language universals

We began this book with a consideration of two kinds of unconscious 'knowledge' with which the learner comes to his language-learning experience already equipped. These we termed 'knowledge how', i.e. *how* to bend the target language to purposeful activity in the course of learning it – and 'knowledge that', i.e. *that* language itself obeys sets of universal constraints upon the shape that any individual language may assume. It is this latter 'knowledge', its manifestation through English, and its relation to language learning that we want now to examine more closely.

1 The acquisitional feat

The most useful way to begin a discussion of language universals takes us along a route that is by now rather familiar to many language professionals; one moves into the discussion through consideration of the seeming enormity of the language learner's task. The essence of this undertaking is that much target-language structure must somehow be learned in the absence of data that would otherwise have been thought to be crucial. This is as true for the learning of a second language as it is for the learning of one's mother tongue. For not even in the most comprehensive and carefully contrived formal L2 curriculum would there be even sufficient opportunity merely to *expose* the learner to the vast array of target-language processes and constructs and their possible intercombinations and interrelationships. Language learning then is in no way the result of the learner's having come in contact, even over a period of time, with tokens of all the formal attributes of the language system in question.

The central question is thus the following: how is it that the language learner is able to infer the existence of attribute X of the language he is learning if no evidence for X is known ever to have been present in the data available to that learner, and no principles of 'analogizing' or 'comparing' can possibly render the necessary accounting?[1] An example of this kind of knowledge was presented in

Chapter 1 – namely, the principle that formal rules of language must be **structure-dependent**. By this principle alone one could rule out as a possible question in English, for example, **Is Mary is the one who still saying 'no'?* (Cf. *Is Mary the one who is still saying 'no'?*) Learners do not violate the structure-dependency principle, though there is *a priori* no reason why operations that do violate should not constitute one of the initial target-language hypotheses to be tested out by them.

There are other constraints upon language form that do not appear to be 'learned', and some of these, as they pertain to the second-language learner, will be identified in Section 3, below.

2 A theory of universal grammar

If the learner cannot conceivably have 'learned' a general principle or a constraint through exposure to the data of the language being learned, then whence has such 'knowledge' come? The prevailing view among generative linguists (not without some amount of contro-versy) is that the learner has to have been born with it – that his predisposition to limit in principled fashion the number and kind of hypotheses to be entertained in the course of learning a language is a genetic endowment of the human species. Since no natural languages are known to violate these precepts, we may properly speak of them as **language universals,** or as constituting collectively a **universal grammar** (UG). Since it is a grammar that has never been 'learned', we may properly equate universal grammar with every learner's tacit knowledge of the limits upon the principled ways in which language may take shape.

Although this is not the appropriate place for a detailed look at UG as currently conceived (see Chomsky 1984),[2] it will nevertheless be useful at least to sketch some of its broader outlines. The theory of UG, in contrast to earlier versions of transformational-generative grammar, is in actuality a 'highly structured and restrictive system of principles with certain open parameters to be fixed by experience' (Chomsky 1981, p. 38). This relatively small set of principles and their parameters, unlike the earlier batteries of highly language-specific transformations, interact in such a way that only slight adjustments in their application suffice to render large differences among the many and diverse languages that are presently known. The sorts of prin-ciple invoked are ones, for example, that constrain the movement of elements within the sentence, that specify the interpretation of the relationship between a referent (e.g. pronoun) and what it can and cannot refer to, that limit deletion to 'recoverable' items, and a few more. With a very small set of base phrase-structure rules and only one multi-purpose movement transformation, UG thus massively overgenerates but is subsequently 'reigned in' by means of universal constraints and conditions upon the output of its derivations.

Inasmuch as UG has been posited as the genetically inherited predisposition of the child to learn his mother tongue, there has since arisen the very natural question of whether UG constraints are still in force for the learning of languages beyond the first. Or, to put it another way, is there evidence that violations of those principles and constraints can occur in L2 interlanguages? We have already considered one such principle – namely, **structure-dependency** – and noted more than once throughout these pages that no violations in interlanguage have been attested. Let us then turn our attention to several of the other constraints.

3 Universal constraints and interlanguage

Investigation of interlanguage in terms of Chomskyan UG is of very recent origin, partly because of fast-changing developments in UG research itself. Consequently, not very many definitive results have yet emerged from second-language empirical studies by the relatively few scholars working within the UG paradigm. Of the UG precepts that *have* been looked at in terms of interlanguage, two will be taken up in this section: the **conjunction-reduction principle** and the **subjacency condition**. The further question of interlanguage and a **parameterized UG** is the focus of Section 4.

3.1 *The conjunction-reduction principle*[3]

Languages may typically delete one of two identical major constituents in conjoined sentences. Thus, in an SVO language like English the conjunction of *Max writes stories and Max plays baseball* would be *Max writes stories and Ø plays baseball*. This can be represented formulaically as SVO + _VO, where S (*Max*) in the second conjunct has been deleted. We will call this (35a):

(35) a. SVO + _VO (Max writes stories and Ø plays baseball)

The conjunction of *Max writes stories and Mary writes poetry* would give *Max writes stories and Mary Ø poetry*, represented as SVO + S_ O, where V (*writes*) in the second conjunct has been deleted. Call this (35b):

(35) b. SVO + S_O (Max writes stories and Mary Ø poetry)

Since deletion of this kind 'reduces' one of the two conjoined sentences, the operation may be labelled **conjunction-reduction**.[4]

So far we have seen examples of reduction obtained through deletion in the second conjunct of S and of V. What of the other at least theoretically possible deletions in SVO English? Let us display them here as (35c–f):

(35) c. **__VO + SVO   (**Ø Writes stories and Max plays baseball)
   d. **S__O + SVO   (**Max Ø stories and Mary writes poetry)
   e.   SV__ + SVO   (Mary writes Ø and Max reads poetry)
   f. *SVO + SV__   (*Mary writes poetry and Max reads Ø)

Notice first of all that (c), (d), and (f) are not possible in English. Thus, if we describe (a) and (b) (where deletion occurs in the second conjunct) as 'forward deletion', then it is clearly the corresponding 'backward deletion' of (c) and (d) that is ruled out. Note also that acceptability with the forward- and backward-deletion examples in (e) and (f) is reversed (the possible linguistic explanations for which will not concern us here).[5] What is really of importance, however, is that whereas all the starred examples represent impossibilities for English, only the examples with double stars (**) are impossible in *all* languages. In other words, the conjunction-reduction pattern of (35f), although not possible in English, would be acceptable in many other languages.

The **conjunction-reduction principle** reflected in (35) is a **language universal**. As such, then, we would expect to find no evidence for examples like (35c) and (35d) in interlanguage, and that is precisely the case. Learners of English do not produce such constructions, nor do they identify them as acceptable when asked to render a grammaticality judgement. Example (35f), however, is a different story. This is an instance of not a language-universal violation but a language-particular one and it occurs in interlanguage frequently, especially in the production of those whose mother tongues are typologically topic-prominent (e.g. Mandarin, Japanese).[6] Interlanguage thus provides additional evidence for the universality of a conjunction-reduction principle as reflected in (35).

3.2 *The subjacency condition*

In our earlier look at **discontinuity** and **dislocation** (Chapter 9.4.2) we noted examples like *A **man** stood in our path **who looked in need of help**, All of us were upset **but you**, What **business** is it **of yours**,* etc., where part of the noun-phrase subject of the sentence has been detached from its head noun and shifted to the right, or **extraposed**. The 'before' and 'after' situations can be shown as in examples (36a) and (36b), respectively:

(36) a. *All of us but you* were upset.
     b. *All of us* were upset *but you.*

If we construe extraposition here to mean 'shift to the end of the sentence', however, we will run into trouble, as in (37c):

(37) a. [[That *all of us but you* were upset] is obvious]
     b. [[That *all of us* were upset] *but you* is obvious]
     c. *[[That *all of us* were upset] is obvious] *but you*

From these examples one has to conclude that extraposition cannot move an element across more than one sentence boundary, as has happened in (37c). As it turns out, (37c) would be disallowed in *any* language and is illustrative of a set of universal constraints upon movement that is termed the **subjacency condition** Chomsky 1984). In Section 4.3 we will see that the kinds of boundary that limit movement in general are not necessarily the same from one language to the next.

Does the subjacency condition have any relevance to second-language learning? Let us attempt to address this question by noting first that the direction of movement of the phrase *but you* in (36) and (37) is to the right. 'Rightward movement' is characteristic of languages, like English, whose structure is 'right-branching', e.g. O(bject) is to the right of V(erb), relative clauses are to the right of their head nouns, noun-phrases are to the right of their prepositional heads, etc. Learners of English whose mother tongue is 'left-branching' – i.e. having OV word order, relative clause to the left of the head noun, noun-phrases to the left of their postpositional heads, etc. – would therefore find the rightward movement of English a totally new language experience, since any movement analogous to (37) in their left-branching native languages is to the left. Such learners, then, with nothing in their language experience to guide them, should not be expected to be able to identify ungrammaticality among examples like those of (37). And yet they can. It has been shown, for example, that learners of English whose native language is (left-branching) Japanese will limit rightward movement in accord with the subjacency condition as exemplified in (37).[7] Since the learner's 'knowledge' of this constraint exists in the absence of any data encountered in either his L1 or his L2, the knowledge must therefore form part of his innate capacity for language acquisition. In other words, the **subjacency condition** is part of **universal**

grammar. We have here then another good example of evidence for a language universal – viz. the subjacency condition – being drawn from L2 interlanguage. We will return to this in Section 4.3.

4 Parameterized UG and the L2 learner

In our discussion of UG theory (Section 2) we saw that certain of its principles and conditions consist of **parameters**, or sets of options, that remain open until fixed by 'experience', i.e. the childhood experience of learning one's native language. One such parameter would perhaps be the order of the basic constituents S(ubject), O(bject), and V(erb) – where, for example, the setting of that parameter for the child learning Hebrew would be VSO, for French SVO, for Iranian (Farsi) SOV, etc. A **parameterized UG** thus conceived[8] offers some interesting considerations for the learning of a second language.

Assume first that the learner's L1 setting for some parameter P will, in the absence of any data, constitute his initial hypothesis for the setting of P in L2 as well. Where the actual settings for P differ for the pair L1/L2, assume further that one aspect of the learning of L2 will involve the resetting of P to the L2 mode. The question to ask then would be whether L2 interlanguage manifests characteristics that are plausibly to be attributed to the as yet unsuccessful attempts by the learner to reset parameter P to the specification of the L2 target. In other words, do L2 learner intuitions offer evidence to support the theory of a parameterized UG? The results of a number of current studies point to such evidence and we will briefly look at a few of these here. In Section 5 we will take up the matter of a parameterized UG and consciousness-raising.

4.1 *Branching direction*

In Section 3.2 we touched on the tendency for individual languages to exhibit some amount of internal consistency in **branching direction** – a manifestation of the basic order of **head + adjunct** for any phrasal category. Since there are always only two possible orders (**head-adjunct** or **adjunct-head**), the situation will always be one in which a given adjunct branches either to the right of the head (**right-branching**) or to the left (**left-branching**). As we noted, languages in which the 'adjunct' O(bject) precedes the 'head' V(erb) – i.e. OV languages – are thus left-branching, and in most such languages the adjunct-head sequence for other phrasal categories will tend to follow suit (e.g. relative clauses to the left of the head noun, noun-objects to the left of their **postpositional** heads, etc.). For VO languages, on the other hand, the pattern is reversed – i.e. relative clause to the right of the head noun, noun-objects to the right of their **prepositional** heads, etc. (There are other languages, however, which show something of a mixture of the two patterns. German and Dutch, for example, have SVO in main clauses but SOV in subordinate clauses. Mandarin has, in addition to VO and OV order, prepositions and postpositions, pre-head relative clause but post-head noun complement, etc. English also shows some inconsistency, which we will touch on presently.)

The positioning of subordinate clauses tends also to adhere to the pattern of branching direction. That is, in left-branching languages the natural position of subordinate clauses is to the left of the main clause:

(38) *When Jim arrived*, I left.

And in right-branching languages the natural position is to the right:

(39) I left *when Jim arrived*.

There is evidence that branching direction is a parameter that will need to be reset in the course of the learning experience where L1 and L2 contrast in this respect (S. Flynn 1984). Learners of English whose native language, like English, is typologically VO (e.g. Spanish) apparently have little difficulty in either comprehending or producing structures like (39). On the other hand, learners whose native language is OV (e.g. Japanese, Mandarin), when asked to repeat sentences like (39), tend in the early stages of learning to render them as coordinations (i.e. *I left; Jim arrived*). And of course one might guess that the relative learning difficulties for sentences like (38), where branching direction is the reverse, is likewise the reverse for learners within these same language groups. Thus, some aspects of second-language learning seem to be facilitated to the extent that the branching directions of native language and target language are the same.

Individual languages, however, seldom display *complete* internal consistency in their branching direction. English, for example, although manifesting the right-branching characteristics cited above, nevertheless places adjectives, possessives, and deictics (*this, that,* etc.) to the *left* of their heads. It is therefore worth investigating what L2 learners do upon encountering, in a target language like English, both patterns – 'basic' **head-adjunct** and 'deviant' **adjunct-head**. There is evidence (Zobl 1982), for example, that French-speaking learners of English at an early stage produce something like (head-adjunct) **friend for her* instead of (adjunct-head) *her friend*. Since *friend for her* corresponds to nothing at all in the surface structure of French, it is plausible to speculate that such a construction is the result of the learner's attempt to 'regularize' the general English head-adjunct pattern – that is, to 'bend' the aberrant adjunct-head order of English possessives into alignment with the general right-branching structure of the rest of the language. More such examples need to be identified, however.

4.2 *Null-subject*

There are a number of languages in the world (e.g. the Romance languages, minus French) in which declarative sentences like (40) – exemplified here in English for convenience – are very common:

(40) a. Maxine will arrive
    b. Will arrive Maxine
    c. Will arrive[3rd pers sing]

Such languages have SVO word order but incorporate a rule allowing the permutation of subject and verb-phrase, as in (40b), or the total suppression of 'understood' subject, as in (40c). Both options are considered in UG to be part of the same parameter, termed **null-subject**.[9] Spanish, for example, activates the **null-subject parameter**, while English does not.

Again then, in what way does the prior disposition of null-subject in one's L1 affect the learning of L2? To narrow the question a little more, what would we be likely to see in the interlanguage of the Spanish speaker learning English and of the English speaker learning Spanish? Although one might expect a straightforward carry-over or **transfer** into interlanguage of the L1 setting for null-subject, this turns out to be not quite the case. It is true that sentences like (40b) and (40c) do indeed appear in the L2 English of the Spanish speaker. Yet it is also true that the Spanish analogues of those sentences like-wise appear in the L2 Spanish of the English speaker, where we might have expected the English pattern to prevail – i.e. only sentences like (40a).[10] The probable explanation for this is actually a quite natural one. The English-speaking learner of Spanish has merely to notice the *presence* in his L2 of sentences like (40b and c) for evidence that null-subject is activated in Spanish. On the other hand, the Spanish-speaking learner of English has somehow to notice the *absence* in his L2 of sentences like (40b and c) for evidence that null-subject is *not* activated in English. Since it is perceptually more difficult to notice the absence of something than its presence, we find the 'transfer' into L2 of L1 null-subject disposition only in the second instance – the learning of English by Spanish speakers. In Section 5 we will recall these observations in the context of grammatical consciousness-raising.

4.3 *Movement and boundaries*

In Section 3.2 we observed that extraposed elements in any language cannot cross more than one sentence boundary – an example of the subjacency condition – as illustrated by (37c), repeated here as (41):

(41) *[[That *all of us* were upset] is obvious] *but you*

As it turns out, what counts in some languages as a 'boundary' to constrain movement can be that of a **noun-phrase** as well as a sentence, and 'movement' itself embraces not just extraposition but also the fronting of *wh-* elements for questioning. Thus, analogous to (37) will be (42):

(42) a. [He bought [_____ books]]
     b. *How many books* [did he buy]?
     c. **How many* [did he buy [_____ (of) books]]?

Note, then, that (42c), like (41), is not possible in English. In both examples a moved element (*wh-* in (42)) has crossed more than one boundary. The difference, however, is that *wh-* fronting in (42c) has crossed not two sentence boundaries (which is disallowed universally) but rather the boundaries of a sentence ([*did he buy* ...]) and a noun-phrase ([_____ *books*]). Again, what serves as a 'boundary' for the constraint upon movement in English will be not only sentences but also noun-phrases.[11]

We said earlier that what counts as a boundary for application of the **subjacency condition** will vary from language to language. In UG terminology, in other words, subjacency is **parameterized**, the particular parameter for any given language represented by what counts in that language as boundary for limits upon movement. French, for example, sets the subjacency parameter differently in that it does allow sentences like (42c), i.e. *Combien a-t-il acheté de livres?*[12]

The general question already raised by us in other contexts is therefore one that we want to reapply here. What happens in learner language where L1 and L2 have different settings for the subjacency parameter? For example, does the necessity for the French speaker to reset his L1 parameter (i.e. the kinds of boundary that constrain movement) in accord with that of L2 English constitute a problem?

What little work has been done in this area so far suggests that French-speaking learners tend at first to accept as grammatical the kinds of disallowed English sentence typified by (42c). This would seem to indicate, as in the previous sections, that parameter re-setting can pose a problem for the development of grammatical competence in a second language.

4.4 *Adjacency*

The last aspect of parameterization that we will take up here has to do with the proximity of elements bearing a close semantic relationship. In terms of **verb–argument relations** (Chapter 9.3) there is a general tendency in language to place noun-phrase arguments as close to the verb as possible – one aspect of the **adjacency condition**.[13] There is some variation in the applicability of this condition, however, in that (a) not all verb-argument pairs have the same degree of intolerance for intervening material, with **verb–object** generally being the 'tightest' in this respect, and (b) not all languages maintain the same relative tolerance scale for **adjacency**. English, for example, allows only an indirect object to come between verb and object (*I bought Mary a hat*, but **I bought yesterday a hat*) – related to the reservation of word order in English for signalling grammatical relations – while Hebrew, French, etc., are more tolerant of this. Facts like these suggest that adjacency is **parameterized**, where in English this parameter would be set for the 'strict' application of adjacency (i.e. virtual intolerance of intervention).

To return once more to our thematic question then, does L2 interlanguage offer any possible evidence that parameter resetting is involved in the learning of English tight adjacency? Since one of the very frequently occurring 'errors' in L2 English is precisely the break-up of verb-object with intervening lexical material, it is tempting to surmise that the parameter-resetting analysis is indeed the plausible one.[14] The kinds of learner example in question would be as in, for example, the written-language data of (43):

(43) a. The university here is very rich and can *pay* for education *more money*. [Arabic]
   b. Spain *had*, under military forces, *many countries*. [Spanish]
   c. The problem is the difference of the ideas to control their power and to *help* to live *their people*. [Korean]

Again, however, these are representative of interlanguage data that have only just begun to be looked at in UG terms.[15]

The concept of a **parameterized UG** thus serves narrowly to define

differences in mother-tongue and target-language conceptual structure – as we have just seen with regard to conjunction reduction,
null-subject, subjacency, and adjacency – and in so doing would seem
to offer a useful explanatory framework for consideration of the
effects of these phenomena upon interlanguage. We will now
briefly consider the possible relationship of these matters to grammatical consciousness-raising.

5 UG and consciousness-raising

In Chapter 1 of this book we asked what could constitute evidence
that the language-universal constraints posited for native-language
acquisition were still in place for the learning of a second language
as well. The evidence we cited was in a sense 'negative' evidence
– which is to say that in all the research on interlanguage to date
no violations of universal constraints have yet been documented. We
are now in a position to refine somewhat the answer to that original
question. That is, we have taken note of evidence in L2 interlanguage to support not just the general notion of UG but the more
precise concept of a **parameterized UG**. What, then, of UG and
consciousness-raising?

Although it would be premature at this stage of research in UG
to make firm pronouncements about the value of UG theory for grammatical C-R, there are several important points that deserve to be
recognized here. The employment of C-R in the pedagogical plan for
any language-learning experience requires that choices be made –
namely, the choices of what phenomena within the L2 grammatical
panoply to make light of. It follows that if discriminations of this kind
are to be made at all, then there needs to be, insofar as possible, a
principled basis for doing so. Where L1/L2 differences are
concerned, and for those areas of syntax amenable to the widest
generalizations, that principled basis might conceivably be a parameterized UG. This could certainly be the case for pedagogical situations in which the learner's native language and the target language
have different settings for some given UG parameter. More import-
antly, however, we would have the basis for rendering decisions as
to *whether any C-R is needed at all.* For instance, none might be
needed (a) where L1/L2 parameter settings coincide, or (b) where
such settings for a given parameter differ but L2 data needed to
trigger the re-setting are readily available to the learner. The (b)
situation would presumably apply, for example, to the need for
English speakers to reset the null-subject parameter in learning

Spanish or Italian (Rutherford and Sharwood Smith 1985), which they appear to do very early and without any difficulty.

What about those situations, however, where we believe that the data necessary to trigger a re-setting of some L1 parameter are *not* readily available to the learner? The familiar example here would be the speaker of (null-subject) Spanish learning (non-null-subject) English, as we discussed in Section 4.2. What is the nature of the actual *evidence* that the learner requires in order for his interlanguage grammar to phase out the generation of sentences such as *Was very interesting that book* in favour of *That book was very interesting*? It has been claimed by some researchers that the null-subject parameter is really a *cluster* of interrelated language properties that operate together – a cluster that includes, in addition to null-subject itself, the status of modals like *can, will, may*, etc. and of 'dummy' elements (i.e. *it* and *there*).[16] Interlanguage data (for Spanish speakers learning English) seem to indicate that movement from Spanish L1 null-subject to L2 English obligatory subject is 'triggered', so to speak, by the learning of the rudiments of English modality and of the need for 'dummy' syntactic place-holders like *it* and *there*. If this is so, then the obvious role for C-R in such learning situations would be to ensure that the modality and dummy-element data were appropriately available.

Needless to say, much yet remains to be worked out even beyond the notions of UG and parameterization sketched out here, to mention nothing of precisely how they may bear upon L2 learning or how they may contribute to principled decision-making for purposes of C-R. Nevertheless, although the incorporation of UG concepts into research in second-language acquisition and pedagogy has been minimal to date, the potential would seem to be promising.[17]

Activities

1. English speakers learning (SVO) French often pass through a stage of development where they produce sentences like **Je vois le*, before finally learning the correct *Je le vois* ('I see him'). French learners of (SVO) English, however, do *not* pass through an analogous stage of development where they produce sentences like **I him see* on the way to the correct *I see him*. (These data are taken from Zobl 1980.) If the starred French example is to be attributed to **transfer** from English, then why does transfer not work the other way as well to produce the (non-occurring) starred English example? Look

for an explanation in terms of canonical word order and branching direction.

2. Consider the following relative clause information for Japanese and English.[18]

Relative clauses are right-branching in English, an SVO language:

John owns the cat that killed the rat that ate the cheese that was rotten.

The bracketing of this would look something like

John own cat [Cat kill rat [Rat eat cheese [Cheese rotten]]]

Relative clauses are left-branching in Japanese, an SOV language, and a direct translation of this into Japanese would produce (disallowed) self-embedding:

John [Cat [Rat [Cheese rotten] eat cheese] kill rat] own cat

The bracketed representation of a *possible* Japanese version of the original sentence would be:

[[[John own cat] Cat kill rat] Rat eat cheese] Cheese rotten

The direct translation of this into (right-branching, SVO) English would produce self-embedding:

*The cheese that the rat that the cat that John owns killed ate was rotten.

The bracketing of this would look something like:

Cheese [Rat [Cat [John own cat] kill rat] eat cheese] rotten

Write out, in a fashion like that above, English and Japanese representations of the sentence:

This is the man that owns the company that bought the horse that ran the race that was televised.

Notes

1. See Hornstein and Lightfoot (1981, Chapter One).
2. For a more readable account of Chomskyan UG, see van Riemsdijk and Williams (1986). For a brief overview of L2 acquisition research within the UG framework, see Rutherford (1986).
3. Material in this section is based largely on the findings of Schmidt (1980).
4. In the linguistic literature the principle involved is narrowly construed to conjunction-reduction through deletion of V(erb), termed *gapping*.
5. See Harries-Delisle (1978).

6. A plausible accounting of (35f) in the interlanguage of such speakers is that O (*poetry*) in the first conjunct, identified as topic (i.e. what the sentence is about), permits ellipsis of co-referential O in the second conjunct, as is typical in topic-prominent languages. This is not unlike the kind of interlanguage ellipsis discussed in Chapter 7.4.2.

7. See Ritchie (1978).

8. It has been noted by more than one linguistics researcher that what constitutes a 'parameter' in UG is at the present time far from clear, with the parameterized status of word order itself somewhat controversial.

9. The null-subject parameter is referred to as 'pro-drop' in most of the linguistic literature. The necessarily technical explanation of the formal aspects of pro-drop would not be appropriate here. See van Riemsdijk and Williams (1986).

10. For evidence of this, see White (1985a), Rutherford and Altman (1984).

11. In actuality, what counts as a 'boundary' (i.e. 'bounding node') in English for the subjacency condition is not only S and NP but S-bar as well. For an explanation and deeper discussion of these matters, see Chomsky (1984). For a briefer treatment of subjacency parameters as they pertain to second-language acquisition, see White (1985c).

12. The explanation offered for the grammaticality of the French version of (42c) is that S is not a bounding node in French, although there is less than unanimity on this among linguistic researchers. See White (1985c) for a review of the arguments, as well as the background research for the remarks in general on parameterized subjacency and L2 acquisition in this section.

13. In UG theory, NP arguments are assigned case by the verb (or the preposition).

14. See White (1985b) for discussion of these matters. See also Selinker (1985) for a report on this question within a non-UG framework and with data from Hebrew.

15. The examples of (43) are somewhat problematical in regard to where the tightest adjacency obtains. It can be argued that a sense of constituency stronger than VO is revealed through *pay for education* in (43a), *have under military forces* in (43b), and perhaps strongest of all, the verb-complement construction (*help to live*) of (43c). True cases of lexical intrusion upon VO would thus more likely be on the order of *I bought yesterday a hat*, reported in, for example, Selinker (1985).

16. See Hilles (1986), whose analysis of null-subject (pro-drop) is based on Hyams (1983).

17. It has been suggested by White (1985b, p. 39) that the theory of UG may be able to help distinguish between L2 phenomena falling within domains roughly corresponding to what Krashen characterizes as 'acquisition' and 'learning'. That is, what can always be 'acquired' may well be what is outside the domain of UG – 'pragmatic competence and properties of discourse'. Belasco (1985) also cites the value in L2 acquisition and pedagogy of UG constraints.

18. The Japanese relative clause information comes from Kuno (1973).

Questions to Part Four

1. Although English canonical word order is SVO, certain limited movement rules of syntax do permit another order – viz. VS: *In front of the house* **was a large garden** (Chapter 6.1); *Into the valley* **rode the six hundred**, etc. What arrangement of S, V, and O is reflected in these lines from Robert Browning?

> Irks care the crop-full bird? Frets doubt the
>   maw-crammed beast?

Apart from vocabulary, do you think learners of English would have difficulty with the syntax of poetry like this? Why (not)?

2. Would you predict that a speaker of English will have difficulty *unlearning* the possibility of sentences like *Rome is hot in summer* in the course of studying another language that doesn't allow them (e.g. **Roma è caldo nel verano*)? Why (not)?

3. Evidence for an **accessibility hierarchy** was cited in connection with the relative-clause discussion in Chapter 9.4. How might classroom instruction affect learner observance of such a hierarchy? Do the predictions of the hierarchy square with your own intuitions about learner production or do they run counter to them?

4. In note 20, Chapter 9 it was noted that according to one researcher two of the biggest problems confronting the learner of English is the usage of prepositions and the proper deployment of verbs and their arguments. Do you agree with this, or do you feel that other aspects of English syntax are even more of a problem for L2 learners? Finally, is there any possible relationship between the above noted difficulties and the UG principle of case assignment (note 13, this chapter) by verbs and prepositions?

5. What does it really mean to say that English is a 'right-branching' language? Is this an absolute? That is, are there other languages that are *more* right-branching than English? What aspects of English word order are characteristic of *left*-branching languages?

6. It often happens that researchers come up with 'new' findings about how language works that language teachers have known about for some time. Is there anything in the discussion of **parameterization** that possibly exemplifies this observation? Is there anything else in this *book* that illustrates it?

Part Five
Grammar and the pedagogical programme

All things can be mastered by mindfulness.

Buddha

Our experience with second-language grammar throughout this book has by now in all probability left something of an imprint – that of a particular way of looking at grammar, of how the research findings tell us grammar may be learned, and of how these observations point to ways in which grammar may be raised to consciousness. The 'imprint' in question can also be viewed as a set of assumptions or beliefs underlying the whole enterprise of learning and teaching second-language grammar. We have thus far carried these principles forward to each new realm in which grammar exerts an influence and we are now about to do so once more – this time with respect to the pedagogical programme itself.

In considering the question of the place of grammar in language pedagogy it is very important that these beliefs and assumptions be permitted to inform our decision-making in this area, wherever appropriate. It might again be useful then to take note of some of these premises here before venturing to discuss the issues surrounding their manifestation in terms of curriculum and syllabus. Let us therefore begin with a list:

1. Language may be viewed as a network of interdependent systems (e.g. discourse, syntax, semantics, phonology, pragmatics, etc.) rather than as a multi-layered structure.
2. Grammar may be viewed as the on-line discourse-processing aspect of language rather than the set of constructs with which discourse is 'put together'.
3. Grammatical consciousness-raising may be viewed as the means to an end (e.g. the learner's acquisition of target-language grammaticization) rather than the end itself.
4. Acquisition of language form may better be facilitated by the learner's working through grammatical processes than by his working at assembling grammatical constructs.

5. Learning at least partially entails the continual forming, testing, and often revising of hypotheses by the learner.
6. Learning may best be accomplished by proceeding from the familiar (something the learner has already learned) to the unfamiliar (related phenomena that the learner has not yet learned).
7. Language learning may better be achieved through a programme that incorporates the raising-to-consciousness of aspects of language form (consistent with the foregoing) than through a programme in which grammatical C-R of any kind is purposely excluded.

How then does one go about bringing all this into play for the shaping of the actual pedagogical programme? We attempt to address this question with regard to the language curriculum in Chapter 11 and with regard to the language syllabus in Chapter 12.

11 Grammar and the language curriculum

It has been suggested that the design of any language-teaching curriculum be conceived as constituting the answers to three inter-related questions: 'What is to be learned?' 'How is learning to be undertaken and achieved?' 'To what extent is the former appropriate and the latter effective?' (Breen and Candlin 1980, p. 89). The 'appropriateness' of the answer to the first question is something that we need to establish at the start, for bound up in the matter of 'what is to be learned' is the question of 'What is (or are) the function(s) of language?' It is a question whose answer is not necessarily an obvious one.

1 Curriculum and 'communication'

Over the last decade or so, and in partial reaction to the deficiencies of audio-lingualism and traditionally-viewed teaching programmes, there have been increasing efforts to bring curricular objectives into alignment with language-functional aims and learner-behaviour specifications. We thus find that the goals of language-teaching programmes are often articulated in terms of 'communicative competence',[1] and much discussed in the pedagogic research literature of late are the so-called 'communicative approaches' to language instruction.[2] The fundamental premise of most such approaches, whether stated or not, is that the primary (perhaps even the only) function of language is that of 'communication', although seldom is the term itself given a very precise definition. Certainly, the viability of any 'communicative curriculum' will need to be linked in important ways to the validity of this premise; yet the premise itself represents a belief about language function that in fact is by no means shared by many other language professionals. One well-known researcher, F. Newmeyer,[3] for example, has this to say:

> Obviously, communication is a function of language – perhaps, according to some plausible but still undevised scale, its most important function. But communication does not appear to be the *only* function of language.

> Language is used for thought, for problem solving, for play, for dreaming, for displays of group solidarity, for deception, for certain specialized literary modes such as represented speech . . ., and possibly to fulfill an instinctive need for symbolic behavior . . .; in fact, language plays an integral role in virtually every conceivable human activity. Now one might, of course, choose to call all these attributes and abilities 'communication'. But doing so, it seems to me, takes from the word 'communication' any meaning other than 'acting human'.
>
> Newmeyer 1983, p. 100

If, because of its possible limitations, 'communicative competence' is an unfortunate choice of terminology for what we expect the learner to attain through the medium of classroom instruction, then it may well be that 'acting human' *does* better denote that expectation. Perhaps even more accurate would be 'acting like an ordinary human being'; better still, 'doing so in someone else's culture. In other words, if 'communicative' is to remain the defining adjective in construction with 'language teaching/curriculum/syllabus/approach, etc.', then it cannot but assume the all-purpose yet ill-defining sense to which attention is called in the above quote.

It follows then that there is nothing of intrinsic language organization that can be identified, isolated, and abstracted away for curricular representation as the formal exponent of some set of 'communicative functions', however these are defined. Nor can we perform grammatical abstractions in this manner for exponential correlates to *anything* identifiable outside the formal system. Grammar is in no sense amenable to such procedures, and this is as true for product- as for process-oriented concepts of language form. These observations argue then against any centrality within the curriculum for systems of 'communication' where decisions concerning grammatical focus are attendant upon 'communicative' points of departure. Indeed, they argue as well against the centrality of the curriculum itself in the full pedagogical plan. To quote one researcher, N. Hawkes, 'On the one hand curriculum studies might appear to be [the] superordinate discipline. On the other, the universal human faculty of language is surely more central and fundamental than any construct yet educed in curriculum theory' (Hawkes 1983, p. 86).

2 The centrality of language

Letting language itself be at the centre of the pedagogical plan would seem at first glance to represent nothing new. Hasn't this been the case, after all, for virtually the entire two and a half millennia of documented language teaching? With all that we have lately come to know about language 'functions' and learning objectives, wouldn't a return to promulgation of language supremacy *vis-à-vis* the curriculum represent a step backward? It will perhaps not be apparent to many how the answer to this kind of question can be a negative one.

Possible difficulties in accepting the value of a language-centred pedagogical plan would very likely stem from what we already know of so many such attempts in the past – attempts whose apparent failure to lead to desired goals has more recently, in the eyes of some language professionals, discredited the notion of *any* kind of curricular prominence for language organization. Although criticism of previous grammar-centred instructional plans is deserved, it is usually made for the wrong reasons, and it would be useful here to consider once more why this is so.

As already brought out at several points in previous chapters, there are two prime assumptions that are usually identifiable throughout the history of language-centred pedagogy. The first of these amounts to a belief about *language*, the second about *teaching* (and, by extension, *learning*):

1. the essence of language is an assemblage of hierarchically-arranged constructs;
2. the essence of language teaching/learning is the direct imparting of those constructs by teacher to learner.

Although we have already discussed at length the blatant theoretical flaws behind these widely assumed premises, it is worth calling attention here to the fact that the crystallization into curriculum structure of such a set of beliefs places in the way of the learner yet another very serious obstacle, and this time a psychological one – namely, the withdrawal of the target-language formal system from participation in the learner's 'ontogenetic experience', for want of a better term. It is the difference between guiding the learner in mentally working out the surface implications of L2 intrinsic formal organization on the one hand and handing him the inventory of surface constructs 'on a pedagogical platter', so to speak, on the other.

Not far removed, in some respects, from the kinds of thing we are suggesting here is the following statement from a recent journal article by M. Breen and C. N. Candlin on language-curriculum matters:

> In the past, it has seemed easier to somehow separate the learner from the knowledge to be learned – to 'objectify' the target language as something completely unfamiliar to the learner. This objectification of the language in relation to the learner has perhaps been encouraged by a narrow definition of what the object of learning actually is, and by an incomplete view of what the learner has to offer. We have tended to see

the target only in terms of 'linguistic competence' or textual knowledge, and we have limited such knowledge to the level of syntax without reference to structure above the sentence. Thus, ideational and interpersonal knowledge, which continually interact with textual knowledge and from which textual knowledge evolves, have tended to be overlooked or neutralised.

Breen and Candlin 1980, p. 93

'Objectification' is an apt term for the problem under study here. Where the thrust of our discussion departs from that of the above quote, however, is in precisely how and where objectification may be countermanded. Our position is that a remedy can and should be found within the grammatical system of the target language itself and not *a fortiori* by appeal to 'ideational and interpersonal knowledge' 'above the sentence', however valuable such an appeal might otherwise be. In other words, although in both instances it is a matter of seeking the solution to 'objectification' through widening the above 'narrow definition of what the object of learning actually is', the kind of 'widening' we would argue for here is that of one's concept of grammatical system itself.

This, then, is the appropriate place to begin a closer look at what it really means for us to let second-language grammar shape the outlines of the language-teaching curriculum.

3 The grammar-centred curriculum

We have already called attention more than once to the fact that there would seem to be at least one characteristic common to all instances of successful second-language learning. Logic dictates more than a mere correlation, however, i.e. that this characteristic would also have to be seen as the one indispensable prerequisite for such learning to occur at all. We refer here of course to the fact that the learner has to be exposed to the data from which hypotheses may be formed and meaningful generalizations drawn. This 'exposure' factor is a more crucial one than might be supposed and becomes even more so where the classroom is the only source of target-language data. The critical need for making these data available to the learner therefore places a special burden of responsibility upon the language curriculum and, by extension, the language syllabus.

The overriding responsibility in curriculum planning under these circumstances has three parts to it:
1. some kinds of decision must be made as to what aspects of the grammatical system are the major sources for data from which the learner may ascertain the most powerful formal generalizations;[4]

2. choice of language content, notwithstanding whatever *non-linguistic* criteria it needs to meet, must be such as to ensure the sufficiently timely appearance of the grammatical aspects identified in (1);
3. in bringing all this to the attention of the learner (i.e. consciousness-raising), great care and sensitivity must be exercised that the pedagogical instruments for C-R maximize the probabilities for learner receptivity (i.e. for 'input' to become 'intake', to cite a familiar phrase).

This tripartite responsibility then, although necessarily stated in grammatical terms, is seen here to have overtones for three different disciplines – linguistics, education, and psychology, respectively. Let us pursue this a bit further.

3.1 *Data identification*

It is incontestable that one cannot learn a language without direct contact with that language. No one could ever learn English, for example, given a vocabulary list and sets of rules for syntax, morphology, phonology, etc., no matter how accurate or how comprehensive. What then does direct contact provide for the learner? The seeming obviousness of the answer to this question – namely, samples of all the constructions to be found in the language – turns out not to be the case, given what we know about language and how it is learned. The complexity of language is such that if learning it required systematic direct contact with each of its possible constructions, actual learning time would exceed the average person's life span! Since logically it cannot therefore be necessary for the learner to encounter the exhaustive set of target-language constructions, what then *is* necessary? If direct contact is required but contact with the full set of formal tokens is *not* required, then what becomes necessary for learning is exposure only to some subset of the target language's formal range. From this subset of grammatical properties the learner is thus able to 'project' to grammatical phenomena that may not themselves have been present in the data to which he was exposed. (That the learner is able to do this has been reported many times in the research literature on language acquisition.[5])

One of the primary responsibilities of the language-teaching curriculum would therefore seem to be to come as close as possible to an identification of those grammatical properties of target-language lexicon considered of crucial importance for learner 'projection' to well-formed grammatical constructions. Furthermore, this task of identification cannot fail to take note of those learner predispositions that are destined to influence the projections in question – in other words, the learner's knowledge of his own mother tongue. Proper identification of crucial data would thus entail consideration, for example, of whether or not the learner might have to re-set some parameter of Universal Grammar in the course of learning his new language (as we noted in Chapter 10.4) and, even more specifically, whether exposure to particular data can sensitize the learner to a cluster of target-language properties associated with that parameter – e.g. modality, 'dummy' *it*, and obligatory subject for learners with null-subject mother tongues (Chapter 10.5).[6]

3.2 *Data availability*

In designing a curriculum it is not enough, of course, that we do our best to recognize those aspects of target-language intrinsic organiz-ation most likely to lead the learner to the entertainment of useful L2 hypotheses and the formation of the most valid generalizations. It is also essential that the instructional conditions be such as to make the data available to the learner – that is, that he be assured of access to such data at appropriate times during the learning experience. No two learners are alike, however, either in the state of their target-language knowledge at any given time or in their readiness at any time for additional data upon which to reform a hypothesis or arrive at a new generalization. Provision of data can therefore not follow any 'lockstep' schedule but rather must reveal some amount of ongoing differentiation.[7] Since exposure of the learner to crucial data should not occur with either randomness or rigidity, the important task of curriculum design with regard to data availability thus turns out to be a rather sophisticated one.

3.3 *Data dissemination*

Yet the identification of crucial target-language data and the act of making them available to the learner in timely fashion (i.e. input) are still not enough for the design of a grammar-centred curriculum as we envisage it here. One must also be concerned with the choice of pedagogical instruments by which the data in question – already identified and appropriately available – may be absorbed by the learner (i.e. intake). These 'instruments' are really the means for raising learner consciousness, or what we referred to in Chapter 2.1.1 as 'modes of operation'. Here and there we have cited particular examples of such instruments (e.g. scrambled sentences, connecting lines for referential relations, propositional cluster, etc.), but we also want to take note of their broader characteristics.

The handiest frame of reference for conception of the instruments of C-R derives from what would have to be their two extremes: natural appearance of a grammatical phenomenon in 'authentic' text on the one hand and its contextless explicit formulation on the other. Somewhere in between these poles would occur C-R in which the grammatical phenomenon would simply be 'highlighted' or otherwise given prominence of some kind, the learner expected to do no more than merely 'notice'. Much of the C-R activity exemplified in previous chapters, however, asks that the learner not only 'notice' but also perform an operation of some kind. In other words, it is C-R activity that is task-oriented, where the learner is actively engaged in solving problems.

In addition to selection of the appropriate C-R instrument one must also make decisions as to the proper *intensity* of exposure, i.e. how much attention, and for how long? There is a limit, however, to what may be specified in advance of the actual learning experience and the questions we have just raised have as much to do with methodology as with curriculum, although the distinction between the two is not always a sharp one. We will therefore offer a few comments here on methodology as it relates to a grammar-centred curriculum.

4 Methodology

Though it may seem paradoxical, what is to be taught in the kind of grammar-centred approach we have been discussing is not grammar at all. If the learner is actually 'taught' anything, we would have to say that he is taught 'how to learn' or, better still, 'how to manage his own learning' (Allwright 1984a).[8] Target-language grammar enters the learner's experience not as an objectified body of alien knowledge to be mastered or as obstacles to be overcome but rather as a network of systems in which the learner is already enmeshed, the full grammatical implications of which he alone has to work out on the basis of what he comes in contact with in interaction with what he himself contributes as an already accomplished language acquirer. Methodologically speaking, grammar in this sense is not so much 'in command of learning' as it is 'in the service of learning'.

Several other methodological conclusions follow from the pedagogical role we have chosen for grammar. Since no attempt is being made to force classroom learning procedures into a 'lockstep' pattern, there should thus be no barrier to learners developing at a pace consistent with their own predilections for hypothesizing, projecting, generalizing, and reanalysing. One beneficial consequence of this is that if each learner is following his own individual learning schedule, learning has little chance of being competitive. To the extent that learners often learn from each other as much as from their teacher, learning will in fact be *cooperative*. Diversified learning schedules of this kind also mean, however, that classroom events will tend to seem 'chaotic'. But it is 'chaos' only insofar as one assumes the teacher rather than the learner to be the manager of the learning, and teacher-directed learning is of course incompatible with the whole concept of the learning and teaching of second-language grammar that we have been developing throughout these chapters. Thus, the inevitable unpredictability and open-endedness of our approach to grammar is to be not deplored but instead welcomed, for only in this way can the learner profitably bring to bear upon his learning experience all aspects of the language faculty with which, as a human being, he is endowed.

5 Summary

We will depart from the customary narrative here and attempt a different kind of wrap-up for important aspects of the grammar-driven pedagogical programme outlined above. Following, then, is the sketch of such a programme (which we again label 'organic'), whose attributes are (1) grouped according to 'objectives', 'curriculum', and 'methodology', and (2) contrasted with an idealized sketch of the more traditionally conceived ('mechanic') grammar-centred pedagogy.[9]

Two views of the grammar-centred pedagogical programme

	Mechanic	Organic
OBJECTIVES:	Knowledge of language structure	Knowledge of language system
	Grammatical well-formedness	Grammatical understanding
	Grammar as an end	Grammar as a means
CURRICULUM:	Teacher organized	Teacher/learner organized
	Structures	Operations
	Linear	Cyclic
	Exhaustive	Selective
	Uniqueness	Relationship
	Hierarchic	Holistic
	Accumulation	Metamorphosis

Agglutination	Fusion
Product-oriented	Process-oriented
Language/learner distance	Language/learner proximity
Increasing complexity	Progressive reanalysis
METHODOLOGY: Teach grammar	Teach learning
Transmission by teacher	Interpretation by learners and teacher
C-R is an end (necessary and sufficient)	C-R is a means (necessary but not sufficient)
Memory	Understanding
Specific rules	General principles
Predictable, closed	Unpredictable, open
Objectification	Incorporation
Competitive, divisive	Cooperative, supportive
Rule articulation	Operational experience
Group-focused	Individual-focused
Grammar as an obstacle	Grammar as a facilitator
Grammar in command	Grammar in service
Speeding up (time needed for production)	Slowing down (time needed for reflection)
Cadential (lockstep learning)	Chaotic (differential learning)

Activities

1. With reference to the need for identification of target-language data that would be important from a learnability perspective (Section 3.1), what kinds of data might be crucial for a learner of English whose mother tongue is Russian, an SVO language of great word-order freedom and with no (definite or indefinite) articles?

2. Refer once more to the sketch of two grammar-centred curricula at the end of the chapter, specifically the 'organic' view. How much of what is listed there would be compatible with a communicative curriculum, however you wish to conceive it, and what would need to be changed or eliminated?

3. What further questions would you want to ask before designing a grammar-centred ESL curriculum for a small group of young adults whose native language is Japanese and who will be enrolled in a two-month summer programme at an American community college?

Notes

1. The term 'communicative competence,' is assumed to have first appeared in Hymes (1970).
2. Perhaps indicative of the recent popularity of these approaches

(especially in Britain) is the number of titles in language pedagogy – of books as well as articles – that contain the actual words 'communication' or 'communicative'. In addition to the following books – *The Communicative Approach to Language Teaching* (Brumfit and Johnson, eds. 1979), *Teaching Language as Communication* (Widdowson 1978), *Perspectives in Communicative Language Teaching* (Johnson and Porter, eds. 1983), *Communicative Syllabus Design* (Munby 1978) – there are, in the Johnson and Porter bibliography, over thirty journal articles alone whose titles carry the 'communication' theme.

3. Smith (1975, p. 113) takes a similar view. See Frawley and Lantolf (1984) for still another interpretation.

4. Wilkins (1984, p. 85) explains the teacher's share of this responsibility: 'The teacher should be ready to create the opportunity for more intensive use of, or exposure to, those parts of the language system that he or she judges to be sources of important generalizations.'

5. See Zobl (1983), for example, for an account of some of these. See also Kean (1984) for necessary further theoretical adjustments.

6. Sharwood Smith (1983, p. 402) writes that 'it is important to distinguish input to the *comprehension* system, where the listener/reader employs a whole network of linguistic and nonlinguistic knowledge sources, and input to the language acquisition, i.e. "grammar constructing" device, which will *not* be coextensive with the first type of input'.

7. Bialystok (1981) argues for differentiation on somewhat similar grounds. Individual language-learning experience varies to the extent of interaction among differential settings on two learning parameters: automatic/controlled and non-analysed/analysed. Preoccupation with only one of these dimensions would thus account for the shortcomings of a number of current 'non-traditional language programmes'.

    Harley and Swain (1984, p. 310) came to a similar conclusion with regard to learners of French in Canadian immersion programmes: 'In order to promote greater accuracy in the production of French by immersion students, we hypothesize that there is a twofold need:

    1. for the provision of more focused L2 input which provides the learners with ample opportunity to observe the formal and semantic contrasts involved in the relevant target subsystem (this does not necessarily involve explicit grammar teaching); and

    2. for the increased opportunity for students to be involved in activities requiring the productive use of such forms in meaningful situations.'

8. As a further comment on this principle in Allwright (1984b, p. 205), we read that '... there is a distinction worth making between practice opportunities as concerned with target-language phenomena, and as concerned with learning itself.'

9. This sketch is an extensive adaptation of one appearing as a handout to a lecture presented at USC in 1980 by Michael Breen (University of Lancaster).

12 Grammar and the language syllabus

If the language **curriculum** is concerned, in the broadest possible terms, with what is learned, how it is learned, and to what extent all of this meets certain standards of effectiveness and appropriateness, then the language **syllabus** is concerned with 'a particular specification of the content upon which teaching and learning would act' (Breen 1983, p. 58), to quote from one recent statement on this topic. It is to this question of 'content specification' that we will now turn our attention.

1 The question of syllabus content

Specification of the grammatical content of the syllabus is the result of any one of several methodological predispositions as to what is the driving force in language pedagogy. These forces, in turn, are usually perceived with reference to:
1. the *grammatical inventory* of language learning;
2. the *communicative goals* of language learning;
3. the putative *strategies* of language learning.

The notion of content in the long familiar 'grammatical syllabus' is a fairly straightforward one. What goes into such a syllabus for purposes of display, explication, and practice is an inventory of isolated constructs made available to pedagogy through some form of linguistic analysis. Since grammatical constructs are manipulable items, they can easily be ordered, grouped, combined, tabulated, indexed, etc., for putting a grammatical stamp upon a set of learning materials. Grammatical content in this sense is thus the point of departure for syllabus compilation, as well as its dénouement. Such a syllabus is the very epitome of media for accomplishing what we have referred to as 'the teaching of grammar'.

Where 'communication' is projected as the curricular goal of language learning, there is often some amount of ambivalence and uncertainty as to how and where (or even whether) grammar figures in the content of whatever syllabus is to be conceived. The extreme concepts of a 'communicative syllabus' *vis-à-vis* grammatical content would seem to be represented, on the one hand, by the kind of hierarchy of communicative and semantic 'constituents' with specific grammatical instantiations that was briefly discussed in the introduction to Part 3, and, on the other hand, by the 'graded' communication tasks (in terms of supposed complexity) where grammatical competence is assumed, without explicit teaching, to be the eventual and automatic consequence.[1] Somewhere in between these extremes fall the rest of the proposals for working grammatical material into the communicative syllabus. Yet the authors of all such proposals seem always to be confronting an ever-present dilemma: how does one integrate within the syllabus two aspects of language with fundamentally different organization, range, and dimension – namely, its formal exponents and its functional categories (however one wishes to characterize them)? The nature of the dilemma is no better illustrated than in the various graphic configurations intended to represent one possibility or another for form-function integration in the syllabus. For example, one model would have form and function in separate boxes connected by a directional arrow indicating the earlier focus upon the former. Another model layers the formal elements in a sequential-stage tower-like structure with the functions snaking upwards around it in spiral fashion. Still another model would have separate 'strands' of form and function, together with other strands outside language itself, all woven together into one long syllabus 'braid'. We even find syllabus disposition of form and function as contiguous rectangles, meshing trapezoids, etc.[2] What also contributes to this total lack of agreement as to a possible form-function 'interface', as well as to the proportional representation of each within the syllabus, is the apparent disagreement upon just what it is that language 'function' denotes.

The problems are no less where 'strategies' of language learning are taken to be the organizing principle of syllabus design. The difficulties here would seem to be:

1. that what strategy appears to work for one learner may well not work for another;

2. that the way in which a learner learns – perhaps the over-used learning 'strategy' is the best term we can presently come up with – is not by any means something that would readily suggest how that strategy might be 'teachable';

3. probably most serious of all; that we are as yet very far indeed from knowing anything about how learners go about the business of learning that could be relied upon as an underpinning for the language syllabus.[3]

What sort of driving force in language pedagogy *do* we perceive then? In the last chapter we argued for the centrality of language in the pedagogical curriculum, and it will be necessary for us to carry this argument forward in addressing here the issue of the language syllabus and providing a serious answer to the inevitable question of what is the 'specification' of its grammatical content.

2 The grammatical syllabus

The concept of language and of language learning that we have been steadily developing and elaborating upon through these chapters has very definite implications for the language-teaching syllabus. At this point, however, the reader may be forgiven for possibly having a clearer notion of what the syllabus should *not* be trying to accomplish than of what it should. How, for example, can we label as 'grammatical' a syllabus designed to support the teaching of 'learning' rather than of grammar itself? What sort of content does a syllabus defined as 'grammatical' (in our more sweeping sense of the term) specify?

Given all that we presently know about language, how it is learned, and how it can be taught, the 'grammatical' part of a 'grammatical syllabus' does not entail specification of the language content at all; rather, it specifies *how that language content* (chosen in accordance with a variety of other, non-linguistic criteria) *is to be exploited*.[4] The immediate reasons for *not* assigning a specifying role to grammar are worth reiterating. Grammatical specification in the syllabus has to result in the selection and ordering of grammatical constructs – a necessarily linear and sequential display of language items for learner input. Language acquisition, on the other hand, is *not* a linear progression but a cyclic one, even a metamorphic one. That is, the learner is constantly engaged in reanalysing data, reformulating hypotheses, recasting generalizations, etc. Furthermore, grammatical specification in the syllabus has to assume that encounter with any particular grammatical construct (even if the teaching of 'constructs' could otherwise be justified) will be appropriately timed for all users of that syllabus, whereas we know that the personal learning schedules of individual learners vary a great deal. Finally, grammatical specification in the syllabus presupposes the exposure of the learner to preanalysed grammatical data, whereas the evidence suggests that learning is more effective where the learner is led to work out the analyses for himself.[5]

The kind of relationship of grammar to the language-teaching syllabus being explored here is thus one in which broadly conceived grammatical principles are the real contribution to the pedagogical programme and where the concrete instantiations of these grammatical principles as grammatical phenomena affecting individual learning experience (in whatever way) should not – indeed cannot – be specified in the syllabus.[6]

The 'grammar' side of the grammatical syllabus must therefore meet several criteria: it must be consonant with the 'metamorphic' aspects of language development; it must be such as to accommodate a group of learners who are learning different things, at different times, and in different ways; and it must be conceived in such a way that the learner is enabled progressively to convert his language 'chunks, prefabricated routines, or unopened packages'[7] into analysed language and thereby extend his range of grammatical competence. The kind of grammar that meets these criteria is what this book is all about, and the kind of pedagogical instrument for raising the learner's grammatical consciousness, wherever this is deemed useful, is what we have periodically caught glimpses of throughout the chapters. We need then to look more closely here at such C-R 'instruments', or the means at our disposal for inducing grammatical exploitation by the learner.

3 Instruments of grammatical exploitation[8]

The matter of raising the learner's grammatical consciousness is a multi-faceted one, as we have noted more than once. It can involve anything from mere observation to (for some teachers) the articulation of actual rules. The sort of C-R we will consider is that in which the learner is engaged in an activity consistent with the principles of language, learning, and teaching discussed earlier. The specification of this activity we will term 'instruments' of C-R rather than 'exercises', inasmuch as we are concerned with prototypical examples of the possible means for C-R and not instantiations appropriate to particular learning experiences.

The C-R instruments of learner engagement to be looked at here can be divided into those that ask the learner for a judgement or discrimination of some kind and those that pose a task to be performed or a problem to be solved. These instruments are in no sense claimed to be exhaustive, and no doubt they can be improved upon or even better ones can be devised. They are to be considered as representative of various means for raising learner consciousness to aspects of grammatical system and are not intended as suggestions about how to 'teach' particular grammatical constructs. In many cases the actual language content can, and should, derive from the work of the learners themselves.

3.1 *Judgement, discrimination, and discernment*

At appropriate times in the teaching programme, learners can be led to render judgements on grammaticality, semantic interpretation, lexical choice, presupposition, discourse appropriateness, etc., though great care should be taken to ensure that they understand what is being asked. What the learner labels as 'ungrammatical', for example, might be a bit of language whose propositional content is perceived as semantically anomalous, or even merely unpleasant. In all events, it is obviously best if what is to be judged emanates, as we have said, from learner production itself and is embedded in the original context, though we will relax that stipulation here for the sake of efficiency. Interspersed among the deviant examples would be a few correct ones. Judgement renditions would be plausible, for example, for Spanish-speaking learners grappling with English SVO grammatical-word-order requirements and we might therefore begin to lay this out as in (A), where the learner is asked to identify the 'error' and make the 'correction':

(A) 1. In Lake Maracaibo was discovered the oil.
     2. After a few minutes the guests arrived.
     3. In my country does not appear to exist any constraint on women's rights. etc.

Judgement may also be brought into play for deciding on the appropriateness of conversational responses, as in an instrument such as (B), which of course can be presented in the form of actual dialogue as well as script. The learner, as observer, would be asked merely to signal that something is wrong with B's response:

(B) 1. A Is he leaving now?
       B Yes, he is, because he has an appointment.
     2. A Is he leaving now?
       B Because he has an appointment.
     3. A Why is he leaving now?
       etc.

Discrimination can be induced, here in the realm of semantic interpretation hinging upon the understanding of grammatical relations, merely by displaying a very brief text and asking which among a set of three or four appended propositions is the one (or ones) subsumed in the displayed text. This can be especially effective where the text contains a grammaticized version (e.g. *bitterness among* X) of a proposition in simple-sentence form (X *be bitter*), as in (C):

(C) The passing of the bill has given rise to further bitterness among the various linguistic communities in the province.

1. The various linguistic communities are bitter.
2. Bitterness caused the bill to be passed.
3. The province is bitter at the linguistic community.

The grammatical attributes of the lexicon were discussed in Chapter 8.2, where we looked at a type of C-R instrument for inducing an appropriate lexical choice from among a group of items with shared semantic features but requiring different grammatical context. For a similar example of this we can choose vocabulary sharing the semantic feature of 'denial', as in (D):

(D) Although the Province of Quebec has resisted efforts

| to | ~~avoid~~ ~~deny~~ deprive ~~forbid~~ ~~keep~~ ~~prevent~~ ~~prohibit~~ | it of its French-speaking identity no one can say that he is | ~~avoided~~ ~~denied~~ ~~deprived~~ forbidden ~~kept~~ ~~prevented~~ ~~prohibited~~ |

to speak English. That is, in making French the official language of Quebec, the laws still do not

| ~~avoid~~ ~~deny~~ ~~deprive~~ ~~forbid~~ keep prevent prohibit | anyone |

from speaking whatever language he chooses. Some people speak French and

| avoid ~~deny~~ ~~deprive~~ ~~forbid~~ ~~keep~~ ~~prevent~~ ~~prohibit~~ | speaking English. |

In Canada they don't

| ~~avoid~~ deny ~~deprive~~ ~~forbid~~ ~~keep~~ ~~prevent~~ ~~prohibit~~ | you your rights. |

An additional example of a C-R instrument for effecting learner discrimination was previously discussed in Chapter 6.1, where it is a matter of settling on a text by tracing a path among alternative grammatical versions of single sentences, one of which meets the discourse (given/new) requirements for the proper 'fit'. Although the text displayed here (as (E)) is of technical English, it could in fact have been of many other kinds and of varying degrees of simplicity/complexity.

(E) Weathering and erosion of rock exposed to the atmosphere constantly remove particles from the rock.

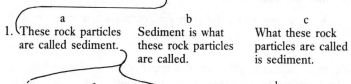

	a	b	c
1.	These rock particles are called sediment.	Sediment is what these rock particles are called.	What these rock particles are called is sediment.

	a	b
2.	The upper layers press down on the lower ones as sediments accumulate.	As sediments accumulate, the upper layers press down on the lower ones.

	a	b
3.	Sediments that stick together form sedimentary rocks.	Sedimentary rocks are formed by sediments that stick together.

	a	b
4.	Such rocks have been able to survive the test of time only in this way.	Only in this way have such rocks been able to survive the test of time.

It is always useful also to direct the learner's attention specifically to *relationships* of certain kinds, and this is what is referred to by the term 'discernment' in the rubric to this section. One very crucial kind of relationship has been discussed at length in several different chapters – namely, all-important grammatical word-order relationships and their effect, through movement rules, upon semantic interpretation. There are many fine examples of possibilities for pedagogical exploitation of this principle and the one we will exemplify is the internal grammatical relations of **infinitival relative clauses** of the sort *the first bus to arrive, the best bus to take*, etc., where the head noun can bear either a (S)ubject or (O)bject relation to the infinitival. One need only indicate this SV or VO relation with, say, a drawn-in arrow, as in (F), and the learner might simply observe these drawn-in relations before being asked to indicate them himself:

(F) 1. That was *a terrible thing to do.*

  2. That was *a terrible thing to happen.*

  etc.

Discernment of such relations becomes more demanding, of course, where longer movement has rendered greater syntactic-semantic **distance** (Chapter 9.1):

  3. ... *a terrible thing* for such a widely respected official *to do*

We will examine other pedagogical devices for raising learner consciousness to grammatical relationships of this kind in the next section.

There are, of course, relationships other than those obtaining between grammatical constituents. The **referential** relations serving **cohesion** (Chapter 7.4), for example, are fairly easy to verify and for these the learner might simply be asked to verbally identify in a given text what the highlighted referent corresponds to, as in (G):

(G) After *they* saved a little money, Howard and Ellen wanted to buy a house. So they *did.* The floor plan was almost exactly the same as *that* of Ellen's parents' home, where *she* was reared. Buying *it* was not easy for *the young couple,* but Ellen was determined to go through with *it. She* could not stand living in their small apartment any longer. She wanted the kind of space *that* she had always lived with. Howard couldn't quite understand *his* wife's insistence on moving to more spacious quarters. *Their* small apartment was big enough for *him.* In fact *it* was almost like *the one* he had lived in as a child. But he could remember *his* mother saying almost daily, 'If only *I* had more room'.[9]

Other C-R exploitation of cohesion through referential relations was laid out in Chapter 8.2.

3.2 *Task completion and problem solving*

The distinction drawn between C-R instruments in this and the preceding section is not a sharp one. The difference essentially is that while 'task completion' and 'problem solving' also involve 'judgement', 'discrimination', and 'discernment', the learner has in addition to *act* upon these intuitions. That is, he is asked to bring these grammatical intuitions to bear in working out their implications for actual language **production** as well as **reflection**.

The first examples of pedagogical exploitation to be taken up here are those bearing upon aspects of the English grammaticization phenomenon. Some of the most pervasive manifestations of grammaticization are bound up with the propositional embedding of sentential elements. Two instances of this – relativization and complementation – are the basis for the C-R instruments modelled in (H) and (I), below, in which what underlies the relative clause and the verb complement appears as a full sentence in brackets.[10] (The use of 'AND' in (H) serves to denote a **non-restrictive relative clause**.) Again, although our examples here make use of fairly advanced English, the procedure is in fact very amenable to task performance at the lowest proficiency levels where relativization and complementation begin to appear. The learner's task of course is to re-create the text in normal English – either verbally, through editing, or by rewriting:

(H) Dear Sir:

I am writing in response to *your company's announcement* [AND *your company's announcement* appeared in last Sunday's edition of the Tampa Herald] of an opening for a systems analyst. [I assume that the position has not already been filled] I enclose *my résumé* [AND one more piece of information should now be added to *my résumé*]. etc.

(I)   *The Norse explorer, Leif Ericson, succeeded in* _____
                                                    The Norse

_____, *but*
explorer reaches the shores of Canada about 1000 A.D.

it is thought _____
                The history of the white man there doesn't

_____. *In 1497 John Cabot, in the service*
begin until much later

of Henry VII, managed   _____
                          John Cabot reaches the shores of Nova

_____ . . . etc.
Scotia

Grammaticization is also brought into play where the learner has to do something about embedded sentential material in major grammatical-category positions. What is required of him is choice of the right complementizer for the embedded material, extraposition to sentence-final position, and use of dummy *it* to mark the extraction site and preserve crucial VO order, as in (J):

(J) 1. Many French Canadians find [They learn English] important.
    2. Quebec makes [Quebec preserves its French-speaking identity] a rule.

3. Quebec takes [French is to be given priority over English] for granted.
4. The government left [Will French be the official language of Quebec?] up to the people to decide.
etc.

A learner task focusing on the preservation of semantic relations through grammatical 'refraction' (i.e. grammaticization) was illustrated earlier in Chapter 8.2 and we will include another example here. The learner rewrites the given sentence using the italicized portion to form the **effected object** construction (Chapter 4.4.3) and whatever other grammatical changes are triggered thereby:

(K) 1. The army finally *located* the crash in a remote area. (*find*)
(. . . finally found the location of . . .)
2. They *immediately inspected* the crash area. (*make*)
3. They didn't *permit* anyone else to visit the area. (*give*)
etc.

Learner ability to handle another effect of grammaticization – attenuated form-meaning relationship – is the principle behind a task in which he or she supplies a natural clause-final verb whose object has been fronted in the course of relativization, as in (L):

(L) 1. [a shelf] higher than I could (reach)
2. [coffee] hotter than I could . . .
3. [a package] larger than I could . . .
4. [a meeting] earlier than I could . . .
etc.

Grammatical realization of broad semantic relations such as cause/effect, reason/result, etc., can also form the basis for meaningful task-performance by the learner. For example, the semantic relationship between *The brakes were faulty* and *The car wasn't safe to drive* can be rendered through a variety of subordinators, prepositions, and conjunctive adverbs (*because, due to, therefore,* etc.) but with different grammatical impact upon the form of the whole. Although the learner task can be laid out as in (D), above, it can also be done in reverse fashion, where the grammatical device remains constant and the surrounding text becomes the variable, as in (M):

(M) I wasn't hurt / I was wearing my seat belt
1. . . . because . . .
2. . . . because of . . .
3. . . . Therefore, . . .
4. . . . As a result, . . .
5. . . . for the simple reason that . . .
etc.

The importance of grammatical choice as a consequence of discourse considerations can translate to a learner problem deriving from the sort of mini-text shown in Activity 1, Chapter 8. In (N), below, the middle sentence of each mini-text is grammatically well formed but ill matched to its context in terms of the arrangement of propositional content. The learner's solution will require rewriting the sentence in question to conform to these discourse requirements:

(N) 1. Air coming up from the lungs causes the vocal cords to vibrate. *Stretching across the larynx are the vocal cords.* The larynx is the upper part of the respiratory tract.
   2. The upper part of the respiratory tract is called the larynx. *The vocal cords stretch across the larynx.* The vocal cords are caused to vibrate by air coming up from the lungs.
   etc.

3.3 *The 'propositional cluster' revisited*

The most significant example of task performance and grammatical problem solving is one that was first introduced in Chapter 5.2, and since recalled a number of times. We refer here of course to the 'propositional cluster' principle and the opportunities therein for sharpening awareness, within a single set of learner-operations, of the effects upon surface form of three interrelated systems – discourse, semantics, and syntax. As a simple demonstration of this, consider (O):

(O) 1a. On stage appeared a man and a child.
    b. sing – child – song
   2a. Last on the programme were a song and a piano piece.
    b. sing – child – song

Notice that although (1b) and (2b) are sketched out in identical fashion, their rendition as normal English will be different. That is, the context of (1b) would lead to *The child sang a song*; that of (2b) would lead to *The song was sung by a child*. Context then has determined the arrangement here of the verb and its arguments (agentive, objective), and these two factors in turn have determined the verb form (passive or active) and the status of the assigned articles (definite or indefinite).

Level of complexity in the propositional cluster may be varied in several different ways: number of arguments assigned by the verb (e.g. *sing* has two, *blame* three, *rain* none, etc.), length of the argument (e.g. with and without premodification), modality (e.g. *would* – [*sing – child – song*]), and of course embedding. For example, all of (O1b) can be embedded as object of the verb *want* (i.e. *The child wanted to sing a song*), sketched here as (O1c):

(O) 1c. want – child – [sing – child – song]

Or *child* in (O2b) can occur as head of a relative clause (e.g. *The child who looked scared sang a song*), sketched here as (O2c):

(O) 2c. sing – child [look scared – child] – song

For the learner's work with verbs having more than two arguments, an appropriate instrument might well include also the 'inverse' of the propositional cluster – that is, laid out separately from the lexical sketch would be a sketch containing only the grammatical case-marking prepositions. This is similar to a notion worked out in Chapter 8.2, example (18), and we illustrate it here as (P):

(P) solve – professor – problem – computer
    1. _____ solved _____ with _____.
    2. _____ was solved by _____ with _____.
    3. _____ solved _____ by the professor.
    4. the _____ of _____ with _____ by _____
    5. _____'s solution by _____
       etc.

There are thus a number of pedagogical values accruing to the propositional-cluster instrument, some of which were touched on earlier, and it is worth recalling them here:

1. The fact that one of the arguments in the cluster must be chosen to serve as subject of the sentence to be crafted by the learner emphasizes the principle of English subject-prominence and the requirement that subject position be filled.
2. The range of possible choice of argument to function as subject reflects the principle that diverse (semantic) predicate-argument relations can be mapped on to (syntactic) subject-verb.
3. Perception of semantic argument relations leads to understanding of the role of the required surface prepositions in marking these relations.
4. That subject-selection determines consequent verb form provides a language-internal motivation for choice of, for example, active versus passive.
5. That choice of subject is not a random but a principled one raises sensitivity to theme/rheme considerations and discourse in general as influences upon the shape of sentences.
6. Necessary syntactic adjustment following from grammatical choice in context makes possible the achievement of text cohesion (e.g.

use of determiners, pronouns) as a natural rather than a contrived feature.

There is still another value to be found in a class of C-R instruments of this sort and it has to do with the learner's target-language lexicon and the grammatical consequences of lexical choice. Vocabulary acquisition is usually perceived by the learner as immensely important, and no doubt rightly so. Certainly an adequate stock of useful vocabulary but little grammatical competence will initially serve some learner needs better than grammatical competence coupled with an impoverished lexicon. The importance of the lexicon derives, however, not only from the usefulness of a store of vocabulary carrying a dictionary 'meaning' in the conventional sense of that term but also from the fact that proper disposition of vocabulary presupposes considerable grammatical knowledge as well. The grammatical properties of a given verb – *like*, for example – include a specification of its (two) possible arguments, its acceptance of a sentential complement (*like to* V . . .), its non-occurrence as a **stative** (**be liking*), etc. Awareness of these and other characteristics can also be sharpened through careful deployment of a propositional-cluster type instrument, which thus serves the function of receptacle for data crucial to the learning process.[11]

4 Grammatical consciousness-raising and the language skills

The instruments of grammatical exploitation that we have just looked at are presented essentially as 'skill-neutral' devices (though pedagogical practicality requires that a number of them appear for the learner in print). Something needs then to be said about the relationship between C-R and the familiar 'four skills' – listening, speaking, reading, and writing. We will consider first the so-called 'receptive skills', listening and reading.

4.1 *The receptive skills and language parsing*

Since spoken language is strung out in time, it can only be attended to in piecemeal fashion, the 'pieces' always being entities smaller than the sentence (Kean 1981). Furthermore, success in the actual 'attending to' (if 'success' can be equated here with 'comprehension') derives not only from the recognition of grammatical signals but also from factors having to do with semantics, pragmatics, the lexicon, etc. All of this knowledge enters into the learner's ability to attend to the language of his input and, more specifically, to successfully parse that input for comprehension (Chapter 9.6).

How then does grammatical C-R enter this picture? One might be tempted, as has often been the case, to 'doctor' the learner's input in such a way that particular grammatical features become more salient and thus more recognizable for learning purposes. Such a procedure would certainly be consistent with the concept of a syllabus that actually specifies grammatical content. Indeed, doctoring of this kind is perhaps the *only* way that 'meaningful' textual material can be rendered usable for the syllabus of grammatical specification, since one has to ensure that the learner attends to precisely what is specified in that meaningful context. In the unlikely event then that the text in question comes naturally 'loaded' with the grammar to be specified, the only recourse for a compiler of a syllabus of this kind is to doctor.

We noted earlier, however, that a grammatical syllabus need not – in fact *should not* – specify grammatical content, and in this concept of a syllabus the question of grammatical doctoring obviously does not enter at all. Rather, entry of grammatical C-R occurs in the form of selective grammatical exploitation of textual material chosen, as we have said, in accord with non-linguistic criteria. What kind of 'exploitation' then are we referring to?

It makes sense to consider where the learner's need to process incoming stretches of language runs into structural difficulty. In other words, what kinds of structural organization make the greatest demands upon the learner's developing ability to parse the target language for comprehension? Certainly the kinds of characteristics that were discussed in Chapter 9 would be one obvious answer to this question. That is, parsing will be more difficult to the following extent:

a) that arguments do not contract semantic relations with their verbs and non-agentive arguments occur in subject position;

b) that grammatical cues to structural organization are often suppressed;

c) that structural discontinuity requires the perception of constituency across stretches of intervening lexical material, etc.

Evidence of any of the factors (a–c) is likely to hinder proper parsing by the learner.[12]

One plausible procedure for better enabling the learner to improve parsing ability for listening comprehension is initially to provide written text to be read simultaneously with what is being heard, the grammatical relationships perhaps typographically highlighted in some way. Mere provision of an accompanying written text for controlled listening comprehension is sufficient, however, to the extent that revealed in the discourse are crucial grammatical signals, or the markers of grammatical relationship. That is, forms such as determiners, prepositions, complementizers, etc. – the very cues that can enable the learner to improve his processing routines – are usually barely audible in speech and thus to be able to *see* them in the accompanying written text would boost the abilities of some learners to become better parsers of their input – to 'learn from listening', as it were.[13]

Another procedure would be to lower the volume (either live or on tape) of those portions of what is being listened to that represent less important propositional content and that can be marked off in terms of constituent breaks.[14] Still another would be to provide the learner with additional comprehension tasks embodying the same structural principle – e.g. parsing of English sentences in which movement rules (i.e. **extraction**) have applied, and where in production of such sentences the learner often leaves pronominal traces (Chapter 9.4.3).[15] In all of this, it should again be noted that the thrust of grammatical C-R is not so much to make the learner a better listener as it is to enhance the learner's ability to learn from listening.

Much of our discussion of listening comprehension will apply in principle to reading comprehension as well, which ought not to be very surprising. The view that we take here is that C-R should be employed to clarify the learner's changing perceptions and reanalyses of the target-language data to which he is exposed, such 'exposure' occurring with him as either listener or reader. This is not to say, however, that there are not noteworthy differences in the role of grammatical C-R for the two kinds of comprehension, e.g. the mere physical setting of the speech event will fill in much of the otherwise missing redundancy that has to be provided for written language.

Perhaps the most important difference, from a learning standpoint, is that of the learner's control over the *quantity* of input data and the *rate* of his exposure to it. In listening comprehension these can be modified (if not through control over tape-playback apparatus) only through the cooperation of the learner's interlocutor, who might be asked to slow down, paraphrase, define, explain, clarify, perhaps even stop, etc., if the learner already has the social, psychological, and linguistic resources to effect that outcome. With reading, however, the learner may exercise a measure of control on his own. He himself can decide to slow down, speed up, skip ahead, skim, re-read as many times as necessary, look up words in the dictionary, consult parallel sources, ask questions of someone else who happens to be present, etc. – in short, he is to a considerably greater extent his own architect of the comprehension format. What then does grammatical C-R have to offer in improving reading comprehension?

Grammatical C-R might improve the learner's ability to thread his way through the structural thicket outlined in points (a–c) above, and thus enhance his capacity to impose a proper structural analysis particularly upon text in which the form-meaning relationships are attenuated. One interesting way in which this can be done is to provide small-print interlinear information in which obscured syntactic relations are clarified. This could be

a) provision of underlying full propositional content that in the surface text is fragmented by the effects of syntactic movement operations;

b) restoration of original constituency for syntactic elements occurring in the text as *discontinuous dependencies*;

c) graphic representation of referential relationship on the order of example (16), Chapter 8.2;

d) display of (optional) grammatical cues that happen not to appear in the text (e.g. *that* as complementizer or relative marker); etc.

Concrete examples of (a–b) might be the following:

(Q)   Text: . . . these errors must be accounted for . . .
        Interlinear: [must – account for these errors]
        Text: . . . such an instrument is difficult to measure with . . .
        Interlinear: [To measure with such an instrument – is difficult]
        Text: . . . look information up that may be valuable . . .
        Interlinear: [look up – information that may be valuable]
        Text: . . . so angered by the reprimand that he quit . . .
            (cf. . . . so angered by the demand that he quit . . .)
        Interlinear: [so angry . . . that he quit]

It is useful once again to stress here that the kinds of possible C-R for reading comprehension that we have called attention to do not require that the actual text be altered in any way. Thus, although an appropriate learner-text may be arrived at through a variety of means, once it is selected there is no attempt to 'simplify' it, as it were, whatever notions of structural simplification one chooses to entertain. This is not to say, however, that with C-R of this kind *some* sort of simplification is not brought into play. 'Simplification' there is – but of the task, not the text. Here, as with listening comprehension, it is again a matter not so much of making the learner a better reader as it is of better enabling the learner *to learn from reading*.

4.2 *The productive skills and comprehensible output*

It is largely with the so-called 'productive skills', speaking and writing, that traditional grammar teaching has long been associated. This would seem to be quite understandable. If the purpose of 'teaching grammar' is to bring it about that the learner 'masters' an inventory of grammatical constructs, then the only real evidence that such teaching has been successful is the appearance of the (correctly formed) constructs in the learner's production, i.e. speech and writing. Moreover, the traditional route by which it has been assumed that this mastery will be achieved is through practice – usually practice in speaking and practice in writing. The relationship of the productive skills to grammar teaching was thus one in which speaking and writing served both as a means to bring about learning of grammatical constructs via practice and as a 'window' for glimpsing the emergence of the grammatical phenomena under conditions of relaxed control. It is a relationship articulated essentially in terms of the teaching, learning, and production of syllabus-specified grammatical *entities* whose limitations we have noted many times in these chapters. What manner of relationship do we see then between the productive skills and the sort of grammar we have been developing here – grammar that is not revealed at all in the specification of syllabus content? More particularly, what kind of grammatical consciousness-raising meshes with this relationship?

Most language classes, no matter what the methodology, provide opportunities for the learner to speak at least to some extent – some more, some less – even if under highly controlled circumstances. What is lacking more often than not, however, is classroom opportunity for the learner to speak in a social context where substantive communication takes place – where the interlocutors have a personal investment in the substance of the conversation and where meaning is 'negotiated' through the give and take of verbal exchange. It has been suggested that this kind of setting, wherein the learner is compelled in a socially natural way to clothe his meaning in as precise a formal expression as possible, leads him to direct his attention to the target-language grammatical resources at his command, and thereby to move forward. It is, in a sense, language acquisition through 'comprehensible output',[16] as it were, or *learning from speaking*.

One of the kinds of learning that come about in such circumstances is that in which the learner, in producing the utterance, must choose from among thematic options that have different grammatical consequences (Chapter 6.3.1). Replay of videotaped exchanges involving particular learners will often reveal where the **argument** chosen for subject of a particular utterance is, in terms of the discourse, a less appropriate **theme** than another available argument but where the second choice would have contracted no semantic relation with its verb and would thus have been conceptually more difficult. We can illustrate this in a fragment of the sort of conversation that might centre on what the learner's real life 'expertise' happens to be (e.g. cooking):

A: What's an easy thing to make?
B: (*It's easy to make*) bread.
A: What about soufflés?
B: I don't usually make them.
A: Why not?
B: *It's hard . . . to turn out every time a good soufflé.*
    (cf. *A good soufflé . . . is hard to turn out every time.*)

It is a matter of capitalizing upon the learner's already raised grammatical consciousness in order to focus attention upon alternative grammatical means of appropriate expression.

It is also known that the degree of formal accuracy in the learner's spoken language can be directly influenced by the nature of the tasks he is asked to perform,[17] one of which such tasks we will discuss here. Common among language-teaching activities is the highly useful story-retelling routine by which the learner demonstrates comprehension of a spoken or written narrative and also the extent of his ability to use the target language. These abilities can be affected by the ways in which the retelling of the story is staged – specifically through manipulation of the operant variables: the type and length of the story, the use of prompts for theme initiation, and the various possible focuses of learner attention (grammatical features, pronunciation, rate of delivery, amount of information detail, etc.). It is above all, however, the 'rehearsal' aspect of these task constraints – another form of 'comprehensible output' – that contributes to improved accuracy in the handling of target-language form.

If the act of meaningful communication produces the 'comprehensible output' that profitably directs the learner's attention toward formal accuracy in speaking, then the learner's act of editing his meaningful written communication can be said to produce the 'comprehensible output' that directs his attention towards formal accuracy in writing. The most graphic demonstration of this is the record of interlanguage development to be noted in learner emendations of written text in which erasure was not possible, as in the composite example from Chapter 3.2. It is not that the learner performs a superficial editorial check upon his written output after the fact, however, but rather that he emends as an integral part of the central composing process. That is, what he wants to express is as much the *consequence* of writing as the reason for it, a characteristic of the activity of writing that has often been noted by others. One of the principal exponents of the concept of grammatical C-R in L2 writing is therefore making the learner aware of what the nature of writing really is – to inculcate in him a disposition toward the emendation of written text as a *necessary*, even enjoyable, part of the writing endeavour. The various paper-and-pencil grammatical problem-solving activities outlined in Section 3 are not inconsistent with these principles, the 'propositional cluster' procedure representing perhaps the best C-R tie-in to writing as a whole.

5 Epilogue

The notion of 'skill' as it is used by language-teaching professionals is one in which the pedagogical demonstration of such 'skill' by the learner will usually be thought of as nothing less than *communicative* ability itself – that is, ability to speak or write. This holds for speaking and writing *per se* as well as for the skills of listening and reading, whose demonstration likewise is usually assumed to be possible through some kind of learner verbalization or writing activity (e.g. comprehension questions). Skill display is thus taken to be the endpoint manifestation of language acquisition by the learner in question, where whatever grammatical accuracy is reached therein is considered the present result of earlier learning and practice. By this reasoning, learning thus enables the learner to demonstrate the skill. While there is certainly some validity to such an assumption, what we have been developing throughout these pages are the implications of exactly the reverse of the assumption – namely, that *demonstration of the skill enables the learner to learn*. It is this concept of 'skill' in relation to 'language learning' that is most compatible with a truly serious approach to grammatical consciousness-raising.

Activities

1. Compare the kinds of pedagogical instrument for grammatical consciousness-raising outlined in Section 3 with others in L2 pedagogy that you happen to be familiar with or have access to. Note as many differences (or similarities) as you can. What criteria would you bring to bear in evaluating these instruments?

2. Devise an exercise for learner testing of grammaticality judgement in **zero-derivation** of causatives (Chapter 7.3.2). Assume that the data you choose to work with have been taken from a passage assigned for reading.

3. Devise an exercise utilizing the concept of instrument (E), p. 163. The text chosen for reworking should be a fairly transparent display of the **given/new** principle.

4. Select a mini-text of about four sentences and lay it out as a series of propositional clusters but with the first sentence intact, as in example (O), p. 167. Disregard for the moment the questions of proficiency level, learning objective, etc.

Notes

1. On this point see, for example, Corder (1981, p. 78), who has this to say:
   > More important, however, is a shift of emphasis away from a preoccupation with the grammar of the target language towards a concern with communication in the target language. The progressive elaboration of the interlanguage system of the learner is a response to his developing need to handle ever more complex communicative tasks. If we can control the level of these correctly, *the grammar will look after itself* [emphasis added]. Instead, then, of grading the linguistic material that we expose the learner to, we should consider grading the communicative demands we make on him, thereby gently leading him to elaborate his approximative system.

2. See Wilkins (1984) for displays of these various configurations.

3. The first two points have been made by Breen (1983, p. 63).

4. Wilkins (1984, p. 87) advances a similar notion.

5. The following passage from Bialystok (1981, p. 19) bears somewhat upon our discussion here: 'Analysed knowledge does not exist as an independent epistemological entity. Rather, it is conceived only as a specialized or marked form of non-analysed knowledge ... Thus, the expectation is that new information enters the system as non-analysed knowledge and, depending on instructional and other factors, may at some point emerge into the analysed regions of the continuum.' It is useful to note that not unrelated to these notions of 'analysed', 'non-analysed' are Widdowson's 'systemic', 'schematic' (Widdowson 1984).

6. It is interesting to note that in this sense then, and admittedly with some stretch of the imagination, the role of grammar in the pedagogical programme is not unlike the role of the United States Constitution in American jurisprudence (if not even, with a deep breath, the role of the Bible in matters of Christian faith). That is, the eighteenth-century architects of the Constitution intended that it should be viewed as a broad, carefully wrought, and comprehensive set of fundamental principles with which the judicial decisions arising from any specific litigation

were not to be inconsistent. This 'loose construction' interpretation of the role of the US Constitution has often been challenged by those who would bend it, in 'strict construction' usage, in support of (or in contravention of) some specific judicial matter under review by the Supreme Court. In a historic decision involving precisely this issue (viz. McCulloch versus the state of Maryland), Chief Justice John Marshall, writing in 1819 for the Court majority, upheld the 'loose construction' interpretation in the following terms:

> The subject is the execution of those great powers on which the welfare of a nation essentially depends. It must have been the intention of those who gave these powers, to insure, as far as human prudence could insure, their beneficial execution. This could not be done by confiding the choice of means to such narrow limits as not to leave it in the power of Congress to adopt any which might be appropriate, and which were conducive to the end. This provision is made in a constitution intended to endure for ages to come, and consequently, to be adapted to the various crises of human affairs. To have prescribed the means by which government should, in all future time, execute its powers, would have been to change, entirely, the character of the instrument, and give it the properties of a legal code. *It would have been an unwise attempt to provide, by immutable rules, for exigencies which if foreseen at all, must have been seen dimly, and which can be best provided for as they occur.* [emphasis added]
> (Taken from P. Smith (1980), *The Constitution: A Documentary and Narrative History*. William Morrow, New York: p. 361.)

If the present author may be excused this bit of anachronism, Justice Marshall could just as well have been writing about the relation between the 'great powers' of grammar broadly conceived and the 'exigencies' of individual learners.

7. See Gleason (1982, p. 355); taken from Widdowson (1984, p. 328), but not included in the references.

8. Many of the examples to follow in this section have been taken from Rutherford (1977).

9. Adapted from 'Apartment vs. House Living: "Need" is Psychological' by Linda Lee Landis, from the *Chicago Tribune*.

10. Note the essential difference between a task of this sort – where the learner gives surface realization to underlying propositions in the course of filling out a *text* – and the well-known 'sentence-combining'. In the latter the learner is usually asked to collapse two well-formed sentences to form a third, more 'complex' one, the ostensible purpose of which is to teach how complex language is 'built up' out of simple language. What is wrong with this, of course, is that language doesn't work that way. As White (1985b, p. 4) puts it, 'the properties of complex sentences are not simply the sum of the properties of simple sentences'. A blatant example of this misconception is to be found in Hunt (1973, p. 170): '[The transformations] take one sentence of a certain sort and another of a certain sort and combine them to produce one new sentence ... The process of combining little sentences into bigger ones can be repeated an

indefinite number of times so that two, three, four, five, and even ten or twenty can be combined into one complicated sentence ... Furthermore the meaning of the complicated sentence is the meaning of all the simple sentences put together.'

11. A passage from a recent work of Chomsky (1982, p. 8) is of relevance here: 'A large part of "language learning" is a matter of determining, from presented data, the elements of the lexicon and their properties. Standard "poverty of stimulus" arguments indicate that the structure of the lexicon itself must be predetermined to quite a substantial extent.'

12. Smith (1975) observes that rarely does it happen that the reader has to choose between two possible semantic interpretations for a given portion of text. Rather, one is much more likely to find *failure* of comprehension (i.e. *no* semantic interpretation).

13. On this notion of learning, Allwright (1984b, p. 205) is worth quoting in full:

> Again there is a distinction worth making between practice opportunities as concerned with target-language phenomena, and as concerned with learning itself. Hearing a native speaker talk offers opportunities for practising listening as a skill, but it also offers opportunities for practising the skill of using listening for the purpose of learning (the distinction may be more clearly captured in the following two questions: How good are you at listening? How good are you at learning from listening?).

Not unrelated to Allwright's distinction in terms of listener *skills* is the distinction made by Sharwood Smith (1983) in terms of input to the *comprehension* system and input to the language acquisition device (see note 6, Chapter 11).

See also Nash-Webber (1975, p. 356), who writes that 'knowledge of the meaningful relations and concepts which different syntactic structures can convey enables the listener to rescue cues to syntactic structure which might otherwise be lost. Among the meaningful relations between two concepts, A and B, that can be communicated syntactically are that B is the location of A, the possessor of A, the agent of A, etc. Other syntactically communicated concepts include set restrictions (via relative clauses), eventhood (via gerund constructions), facthood (via 'that'-complements), etc. Syntactic structure is often indicated by small function words (e.g. prepositions and determiners) which have very imprecise acoustic realizations.'

14. Schank (1975, p. 240) writes that 'knowing what is non-essential or readily inferable from the sentences of a parapraph is crucial in paraphrasing it as well as parsing it.'

15. Successful movement, as Zobl (1985) points out, presupposes learner knowledge of the 'theta principle', since movement of an argument is always, in UG terms, to a non-theta position.

16. The concept, as well as the terminology, is attributable to Swain (1985, p. 249), whose claim is that 'producing the target language may be the trigger that forces the learner to pay attention to the means of expression needed in order to successfully convey his or her own intended meaning.' Also, the role of comprehensible output (p. 252) 'is, at minimum, to provide opportunities for contextualized, meaningful use, to test out

hypotheses about the target language and to move the learner from a purely semantic analysis of the language to a syntactic analysis of it.'

Bialystok (1985) notes that speaking is the skill whose successful utilization depends least upon grammatical knowledge – the skill, one might add, where the learner can get away with less such knowledge. Swain's reference above to 'semantic analysis' is thus like Bialystok's 'unanalysed knowledge': 'In unanalysed representations of language, only the meanings are coded; in analysed representations, both the meanings and the relationship between forms and those meanings are coded. Such analysed representations permit the learner to manipulate those form-meaning relationships to create particular structured uses of language. While conversation may proceed perfectly well from unanalysed representations . . ., other uses of language involved in reading, writing, lecturing, explaining depend on greater analysis of linguistic structure' (Bialystok 1985, p. 257).

17. This observation, as well as the description to follow, are taken from Hulstijn and Hulstijn (1984), who interpret the results of their experimentation as evidence in support of a distinction to be drawn between 'metacognitive knowledge' of the target language and 'executive control' over the realization of that knowledge in actual use. (cf. the Bialystok position quoted earlier.)

Questions to Part Five

1. 'Communication', as we have seen, is a word that figures prominently these days in anything having to do with the teaching and learning of languages. Just how important *is* communication in language pedagogy? Is it a concept that can be talked about in meaningful terms?

2. It was mentioned in Chapter 11.3.1 that a theory of language learning cannot logically be based upon an assumption that the learner will be exposed to each of the language's possible constructions. *Why* can one not logically assume this?

3. What does it mean to say that in a grammar-centred curriculum grammar should not be 'taught'? How would you explain the logic of this to someone else?

4. If grammatical content is not specified in the grammatical syllabus (Chapter 12.2) then where does the material for grammatical C-R come from?

5. How would you explain to someone else the difference between a learner's manifesting a certain language skill and his *learning language* from the manifestation of that skill?

Bibliography

Adjémian, C 1983 The transferability of lexical properties. In Gass, S and Selinker, L (eds.) *Language transfer in language learning*. Newbury House, Rowley, Massachusetts

Allwright, R 1984a The importance of interaction in classroom language learning. *Applied Linguistics* 5: 161–71

Allwright, R 1984b The analysis of discourse in interlanguage studies: the pedagogical evidence. In Davies, Criper, and Howatt (eds.)

Bailey, C J 1982 *On the yin and yang nature of language*. Karoma, Ann Arbor

Bailey, N, Madden, C and Krashen, S 1974 Is there a 'natural sequence' in adult second-language acquisition? *Language Learning* 24: 235–43

Beebe, L 1979 Implications of research on cohesion for ESL teaching. Paper presented at TESOL Convention, Boston

Belasco, S 1985 Toward the identification of a Core Grammar in L2 acquisition. *Studies in Second Language Acquisition* 7: 91–8

Bialystok, E (1981) Psycholinguistic dimensions of second language proficiency. Paper presented at BAAL Conference on Interpretive Strategies in Language Learning, Lancaster.

Bialystok, E 1982 On the relationship between knowing and using linguistic forms. *Applied Linguistics* 3: 181–206

Bialystok, E 1985 The compatibility of teaching and learning strategies. *Applied Linguistics* 6: 255–62

Bobrow, D and Collins, A (eds.) 1975 *Representation and understanding*. Academic Press, New York

Breen, M 1983 Prepared comments on 'Syllabus design: possible future trends' by K Johnson. In Johnson, K and Porter, D (eds.) *Perspectives in communicative language teaching*. Academic Press, New York

Breen, M and Candlin, C N 1980 The essentials of a communicative curriculum in language teaching. *Applied Linguistics* 1: 89–112

Brumfit, C and Johnson, K (eds.) 1979 *The communicative approach to language teaching*. Oxford University Press

Candlin, C N 1983 Syllabus design as a critical process. In Brumfit, C (ed.) *General English syllabus design* (ELT Documents 117) Pergamon Press/ The British Council, Oxford

Candlin, C N and Lotfipour-Saedi, K 1983 Processes of discourse. *Journal of Applied Language Study* 1: 103–33

Capra, F 1982 *The turning point*. Bantam Books, New York

Chafe, W 1972 Discourse structure and human knowledge. In Freedle, R and Carroll, J (eds.) *Language comprehension and the acquisition of knowledge.* Winston, Washington

Chomsky, N 1975 *Reflections on language.* Pantheon Books, New York

Chomsky, N 1981 Principles and parameters in syntactic theory. In Hornstein and Lightfoot (eds.)

Chomsky, N 1982 *Some concepts and consequences of the theory of government and binding* (3rd rev. edn) MIT Press, Cambridge, Massachusetts

Chomsky, N 1984 *Lectures on government and binding.* Foris Publications, Dordrecht

Clark, H and Haviland, S 1977 Comprehension and the given-new contract. In Freedle, R (ed.) *Discourse production and comprehension.* Ablex Publishing Company, Norwood, New Jersey

Comrie, B 1976 *Aspect: an introduction to the study of verbal aspect and related problems.* Cambridge University Press

Comrie, B 1981 *Language universals and linguistic typology.* Basil Blackwell, Oxford

Corder, S P 1973 *Introducing applied linguistics.* Penguin Books, Harmondsworth

Corder, S 1981 *Error analysis and interlanguage.* Oxford University Press

Davies, A 1984 Introduction. In Davies, Criper, and Howatt (eds.)

Davies, A, Criper, C and Howatt, A (eds.) 1984 *Interlanguage.* Edinburgh University Press

Dulay, H and Burt, M 1974 Natural sequences in child second language acquisition. *Language Learning* 24: 137–53

Dulay, H, Burt, M and Krashen, S 1982 *Language two.* Oxford University Press, New York

Eckman, F 1977 On the explanation of some typological facts about raising. In Eckman, F (ed.) *Current themes in linguistics.* Halsted Press, New York

Ellis, R 1984 Can syntax be taught? *Applied Linguistics* 5: 138–55

Emonds, J 1976 *A transformational approach to English syntax.* Academic Press, New York

Firth, J R 1957 *Papers in Linguistics 1934–1951.* Oxford University Press

Flynn, K 1985 *The acquisition of form and function in L2.* Unpublished doctoral dissertation, University of Southern California

Flynn, S 1984 A universal in L2 acquisition based on a PBD typology. In Eckman, F, Bell, L and Nelson, D (eds.) *Universals of second language acquisition.* Newbury House, Rowley, Massachusetts

Frawley, W and Lantolf, J, 1984 Speaking and self-order: a critique of orthodox L2 research. *Studies in Second Language Acquisition* 6: 143–59

Fuller, J and Gundel, J 1985 Topic-prominence in second language acquisition. Unpublished MS, University of Minnesota

Gass, S 1979 Language transfer and universal grammatical relations. *Language Learning* 29: 327–44

Gass, S 1984 A review of interlanguage syntax: language transfer and language universals. *Language Learning* 34: 115–32

Gass, S and Madden, C (eds.) 1983 *Input in second language acquisition.*

Newbury House, Rowley, Massachusetts

Givón, T 1979 *On understanding grammar.* Academic Press, New York

Givón, T 1984 Universals of discourse structure and second language acquisition. In Rutherford, W (ed.) *Language universals and second language acquisition.* John Benjamins, Amsterdam

Gleason, H 1965 *Linguistics and English grammar.* Holt, Rinehart and Winston, New York

Gleason, J 1982 (cited in Widdowson (1984))

Greenberg, J (ed.) 1966 *Universals of language.* MIT Press, Cambridge, Massachusetts

Halliday, M 1967, 1968 Notes on transitivity and theme in English, part 2 (1967) and part 3 (1968). *Journal of Linguistics* 3: 199–244, 4: 179–215

Halliday, M and Hasan, R 1976 *Cohesion in English.* Longman

Harley, B and Swain, M 1984 The interlanguage of immersion students and its implications for second language teaching. In Davies, Criper and Howatt (eds.)

Harries-Delisle, H 1978 Coordination reduction. In Greenberg, J (ed.) *Universals of Human Language* (vol. 4). Stanford University Press

Harris, W H and Levey, J S 1975 *The New Columbia Encyclopedia.* Columbia University Press, New York

Hatch, E 1978 Discourse analysis and second language acquisition. In Hatch, E (ed.) *Second language acquisition.* Newbury House, Rowley, Massachusetts

Hatch, E 1983 *Psycholinguistics: a second language perspective.* Newbury House, Rowley, Massachusetts

Hawkes, N 1983 Prepared comments on 'Curriculum development and English language syllabus design' by R White. In Johnson, K and Porter, D (eds.) *Perspectives in communicative language teaching.* Academic Press, New York

Hawkins, J 1985 *The unity of English-German contrasts.* Croom Helm, London

Hilles, S 1986 Interlanguage and the PRO-drop parameter. *Second Language Research* 2: 33

Hornstein, N and Lightfoot, D (eds.) 1981 *Explanation in linguistics: the logical problem of language acquisition.* Longman

Huebner, T 1983 *A longitudinal analysis: the acquisition of English.* Karoma, Ann Arbor

Hulstijn, J, and Hulstijn, W 1984 Grammatical errors as a function of processing constraints and explicit knowledge. *Language Learning* 34: 23–43

Hunt, K 1973 How little sentences grow into big ones. In Lester, M (ed.) *Readings in applied transformational grammar.* Holt, Rinehart and Winston, New York

Hurford, J, and Heasley, B 1983 *Semantics: a coursebook.* Cambridge University Press

Hurtig, R 1977 Toward a functional theory of discourse. In Freedle, R (ed.) *Discourse production and comprehension.* Ablex Publishing Company, Norwood, New Jersey

Hyams, N 1983 *The acquisition of parameterized grammars.* Unpublished doctoral dissertation, CUNY

Hymes, D 1970 On communicative competence. In Gumperz, J and Hymes, D (eds.) *Directions in sociolinguistics*. Holt, Rhinehart and Winston, New York

Johnson, K and Porter, D (eds.) 1983 *Perspectives in communicative language teaching*. Academic Press, New York

Kean, M-L 1981 Explanation in neurolinguistics. In Hornstein and Lightfoot (eds.)

Kean, M-L 1984 *Second language acquisition and grammatical theory: a matter of projection and marking*. Unpublished paper, Max-Planck Institut, Nijmegen

Kellerman, E 1979 The problem with difficulty. *Interlanguage Studies Bulletin* 4: 27–48

Kellerman, E 1985 If at first you do succeed. In Gass and Madden (eds.)

Kelly, L G 1969 *25 centuries of language teaching*. Newbury House, Rowley, Massachusetts

Krashen, S 1982 *Principles and practice in second language acquisition*. Pergamon, Oxford

Kuno, S 1973 *The structure of the Japanese language*. MIT Press, Cambridge, Massachusetts

Leech, G 1983 *Principles of pragmatics*. Longman

Li, C, and Thompson, S 1976 Subject and topic: a new typology of language. In Li, C (ed.) *Subject and topic*, Academic Press, New York

Lightbown, P 1985 Great expectations: second-language acquisition research and classroom teaching. *Applied Linguistics* 6: 173–89

Mackenzie, J 1981 Pedagogically relevant aspects of case grammar. In James, A, and Westney, P (eds.) *New linguistic impulses in foreign language teaching*. Gunter Narr, Tübingen

McArthur, T 1983 *A foundation course for language teachers*. Cambridge University Press

McLaughlin, B, Rossman, T and McLeod, B 1983 Second language learning: an information processing perspective. *Language Learning* 33: 135–58

Munby, J 1978 *Communicative syllabus design*. Cambridge University Press

Munsell, P and Carr, T 1981 Monitoring the monitor: review of second language acquisition and second language learning. *Language Learning* 31: 493–502

Nash-Webber, B 1975 The role of semantics in automatic speech understanding. In Bobrow and Collins (eds.)

Neuman, R 1977 *An attempt to define through error analysis the intermediate ESL level at UCLA*. Unpublished master's thesis, UCLA.

Newmark, L 1973 How not to interfere with language learning. In Lester, M (ed.) *Readings in applied transformational grammar*. (2nd edn.) Holt, Rinehart and Winston, New York

Newmeyer, F 1983 *Grammatical theory: its limits and its possibilities*. University of Chicago Press

Perlmutter, D and Postal, P 1974 *Relational grammar*. Lecture at summer Institute, Linguistic Society of America

Pica, T 1983 Adult acquisition of English as a second language under different conditions of exposure. *Language Learning* 33: 465–97

Pienemann, M 1985 Learnability and syllabus construction. In Hyltenstam, K and Pienemann, M (eds.) *Modelling and assessing second language acquisition*. Multilingual Matters, Clevedon

Prokop, M, Fearon, D and Rochet, B 1982 Second language learning in *instructional contexts*. Faculty of Education Publication Services, Edmonton

Quirk, R, Greenbaum, S, Leech, G and Svartvik, J 1972 *A grammar of contemporary English*. Longman

Quirk, R, Greenbaum, S, Leech, G and Svartvik, J 1985 *A comprehensive grammar of the English language*. Longman

Reber, A, Kassin, S, Lewis, S and Cantor, G 1980 On the relationship between implicit and explicit modes in the learning of a complex rule structure. *Journal of Experimental Psychology* 6: 492–502

Ritchie, W 1978 The right-roof constraint in an adult-acquired language. In Ritchie, W (ed.) *Second language acquisition research*. Academic Press, New York

Rutherford, W 1977 *Modern English* (vol. 2). Harcourt Brace Jovanovich, New York

Rutherford, W 1982 Functions of grammar in a language teaching syllabus. *Language Learning and Communication* 1: 21–37

Rutherford, W 1983 Language typology and language transfer. In Gass, S, and Selinker, L (eds.) *Language transfer in language learning*. Newbury House, Rowley, Massachusetts

Rutherford, W 1984 Description and explanation in interlanguage syntax: state of the art. *Language Learning* 34: 127–55

Rutherford, W 1986 Grammatical theory and L2 acquisition: a brief overview. *Second Language Research* 2: 1–15

Rutherford, W, and Altman, R 1984 *Discourse competence in L2 acquisition: word order*. Unpublished MS

Rutherford, W and Sharwood Smith, M 1985 Consciousness-raising and universal grammar. *Applied Linguistics* 6: 274–82

Ryle, G 1949 *The concept of mind*. Hutchinson, London

Scarcella, R 1984 *Cohesion in the writing development of native and non-native English speakers*. Unpublished Ph.D dissertation, USC

Schachter, J and Rutherford, W 1979 Discourse function and language transfer. *Working Papers in Bilingualism* 19: 1–12

Schank, R 1975 The structure of episodes in memory. In Bobrow and Collins (eds.)

Schmidt, M 1980 Coordinate structures and language universals in interlanguage. *Language Learning* 30: 397–426

Selinker, L 1972 Interlanguage. *International Review of Applied Linguistics* 10: 209–31

Selinker, L 1985 *Contrastive analysis to interlanguage and back again* (vol. 1). Unpublished MS

Selinker, L, Swain, M and Dumas, G 1975 The interlanguage hypothesis extended to children. *Language Learning* 25: 139–52

Sharwood Smith, M 1981 Consciousness-raising and the second language learner, *Applied Linguistics* 2: 159–68

Sharwood Smith, M 1983 From input to intake: on argumentation in SLA. In Gass and Madden (eds.)

Slobin, D 1979 *Psycholinguistics*. Scott Foresman and Co., Glenview, Illinois

Slobin, D 1983 What the natives have in mind. In Andersen (ed.) *Pidginization and creolization as language acquisition*. Newbury House, Rowley, Massachusetts

Smith, F 1975 *Comprehension and learning*. Holt, Rinehart and Winston, New York

Sorace, A 1985 Metalinguistic knowledge and use of the language in acquisition-poor environments. *Applied Linguistics* 6: 239–54

Spada, N 1986 Some effects of the interaction between type of contact and instruction on the L2 proficiency of adult learners. *Studies in Second Language Acquisition* 8: 181–99

Staal, J 1968 And. *Journal of Linguistics* 4: 79–81

Stevick, E 1980 *Teaching languages: a way and ways*. Newbury House, Rowley, Massachusetts

Swain, M 1985 Communicative competence: some roles of comprehensible input and comprehensible output in its development. In Gass and Madden (eds.)

Thompson, S 1978 Modern English from a typological point of view: some implications of the function of word-order. *Linguistische Berichte* 54: 19–36

Tomlin, R 1985 Interaction of subject, theme, and agent. In Wirth J (ed.) *Beyond the sentence: discourse and sentential form*. Karoma, Ann Arbor

van Baalen, T 1983 Giving learners rules: a study into the effect of grammatical instruction with varying degree of explicitness. *Interlanguage Studies Bulletin* 7: 71–100

van Hest, A-M, Kean, M-L and Kellerman, E 1984 *Some transitives transfer easily*. Paper presented at the 7th AILA Congress, Brussels

van Riemsdijk, H and Williams, E 1986 *Introduction to the theory of grammar*. MIT Press, Cambridge, Massachusetts

Wesche, M 1979 Learning behaviors of successful adult students in intensive language training. *Canadian Modern Language Review* 35: 415–30

White, L 1985a The 'Pro-Drop' parameter in adult second language acquisition. *Language Learning* 35: 47–62

White, L 1985b Is there a logical problem of second language acquisition? *TESL Canada* 2: 29–41

White, L 1985c The acquisition of parameterized grammars: subjacency in second language acquisition. *Second Language Research* 1: 1–17

White, L 1986 Against comprehensible input: the input hypothesis and the development of L2 competence. *Applied Linguistics* 7

Widdowson, H 1978 *Teaching language as communication*. Oxford University Press

Widdowson, H 1979 *Explorations in applied linguistics.* Oxford University Press

Widdowson, H 1983 *Learning purpose and language use.* Oxford University Press

Widdowson, H 1984 Discussant remarks. In Davies, Criper and Howatt (eds.)

Widdowson, H 1986 Grammar, and nonsense, and learning. Unpublished MS

Wilkins, D 1976 *Notional syllabuses.* Oxford University Press

Wilkins, D 1984 Teaching without a language syllabus but with a linguistic focus. *TRANEL* (numéro spécial) 6: 73–91

Ziv, Y 1975 On the relevance of content to the form-function correlation. In Grossman, R, San, L and Vance, T (eds.) *Papers from the parasession on functionalism.* Chicago Linguistics Society

Zobl, H 1980 The formal and developmental selectivity of L1 influences on L2 acquisition. *Language Learning* 30: 43–57

Zobl, H 1982 *An acquisition-centred approach to markedness.* Paper presented at the Second European – North American Workshop on Cross-Linguistic Second Language Acquisition Research, August 22–8, Görde, West Germany

Zobl, H 1983 Markedness and the projection problem. *Language Learning* 33: 293–313

Zobl, H 1986 A functional approach to the attainability of typological targets in L2 acquisition. *Second Language Research* 2: 16–32

Glossary

ablative: the semantic case relation 'direction away from', partially reflected in the use of the English preposition *from*.

accessibility hierarchy: the hierarchical arrangement of syntactic constructs of a single class (e.g. types of relative clause) in terms of their 'accessibility' (i.e. amenability to processing by the user).

adjacency condition: the degree to which a language tolerates the separation of elements bearing a close semantic relation.

adjunct: that part of a constituent attached to its head, e.g. *large* [adjunct] *table* [head].

agent (agentive): the semantic role typically of the initiator of whatever action is represented in the verb.

anaphoric reference (anaphora): reference by repetition or pro-form (pronoun, pro-verb, pro-adverb, etc.).

argument: a semantic role assigned to a noun phrase in close association with a given verb. For example, *hit* (as in *Joe hit the nail with a hammer*) has three arguments: agent (*Joe*), object (*nail*), and instrument (*hammer*).

article, definite/indefinite: see **determiner**.

audio-lingual: a language-teaching methodology rooted in behaviourism and featuring grammar teaching and supervised classroom drill.

auxiliary: the tense-carrying elements of the sentence, e.g. modals, *do, be, have*, etc.

benefactive: the semantic case relation 'for the benefit of'.

branching direction: the structural configuration of a language as determined by the order of its head-adjunct pairs. For example, V(erb)-O(bject) is right-branching, O(bject)-V(erb) left-branching.

canonical word order: a language's most basic arrangement of the elements subject, object, and verb.

causative verb (causation): a verb carrying the meaning of effecting an outcome.

clefting (cleft sentence): a 'focus' construction such as *It's (a book) that (I bought)*.

cohesion: what it is that ties sentences together such that we perceive them as a single text.

collocation (collocate): occurring together.

complementation: see **noun complement**.

complementizer: the word *that* in constructions such as *We believe that . . ./our belief that . . .*

conjunction (conjunctive tie): see **coordination**.

conjunction reduction: collapsing of conjoined constituent structure, e.g. of *John and Mary sang* from *John sang and Mary sang*.

consciousness-raising (C-R): the drawing of the learner's attention to features of the target language.

constituent: that which behaves syntactically as a unit.

coordination: relations of equivalent grammatical rank, as in clauses joined by *and, but, or*, etc. A special case of parataxis. See also **subordination**.

co-reference (co-referential): reference to the same entity.

curriculum: that aspect of the pedagogical programme concerned with what is learned and how it is learned. See also **syllabus**.

dative: the semantic case relation typically reflected in the indirect object, e.g. *(give something) to the poor*.

deixis (deictic): referential terms understood only with relation to the time and place of utterance (e.g. *here, yesterday*).

determiner: a noun modifier of the class that includes articles, demonstratives, possessive adjectives, and a few others.

discontinuity: the breaking of a constituent with intervening material, e.g. *Someone ('s here) who wants you*.

discontinuous dependency: see **discontinuity**.

discourse: verbal expression in speech or writing.

dislocation: movement wherein a pro-form copy of the moved element is retained in the original syntactic position. See also **extraposition**.

distance: see **syntactic-semantic distance**.

effected object: a verb-object construction referring to something that exists only by virtue of the activity of the verb (e.g. *make an attempt*).

ellipsis: omission or deletion of 'understood' elements.

ergative-absolutive: a characteristic of languages in which the object of a transitive verb and the subject of an intransitive verb carry the same morphological coding.

extraction: movement of a constituent to a non-argument position of the sentence. See also **raising**.

extraposition (extrapose): rightward movement of a constituent or subconstituent. See also **dislocation**.

fronting: movement to the front of the sentence.

given-new principle: the discourse principle that (given) knowledge shared between interlocutors (e.g. raised to consciousness) tends to be expressed earlier in the sentence, that later which is not yet shared.

grammar-translation: a language-teaching methodology built upon translation between the mother tongue and the target language.

grammatical word order: the arrangement of canonical constituents in accord with grammatical pressure.

grammaticization: the process of achieving linguistic expression through recourse to grammatical rule.

head: the main part of any constituent. For example, the head of a noun phrase is a noun, of a verb phrase a verb, of a prepositional phrase a preposition, etc.

hyponymy: the relation between a class of things (e.g. *wars*) and a token of that class (*American Revolution*).

interlanguage: the state of the L2 language-learner's competence in terms of knowledge of L2 and control of that knowledge.

instrument (instrumental): the semantic role typically of that by means of which the action represented in the verb is accomplished.

isomorphism: one-to-one correspondence.

language universal: either a constraint upon the form that any language may take or a formal feature observed as common to all known languages.

left-branching: see **branching direction**.

left dislocation: see **dislocation**.

locative: the semantic case relation 'location'. See also **locative adverbial**.

locative adverbial: adverbial of place, e.g. *in the house*.

main clause: the containing (i.e. superordinate) clause of a complex sentence.

notional-functional syllabus: a language-learning syllabus organized on the basis of hierarchically analysed semantic units.

noun complement: a noun-phrase clausal modifier of the kind (*the claim*) *that they proceeded*. See also **relative clause**.

null subject: the principle of optional omission of the (known) subject of the sentence, as in Spanish and Italian.

object (objective): the semantic role typically of the receiver of whatever action is represented in the verb.

object-to-subject raising: see **raising**.

parameter: range of variability of a feature of universal grammar.

parameterized UG: see **parameter**.

parataxis: relations of equivalent grammatical rank; literally 'equal arrangement'.

parse: to analyse (consciously or not) a sentence in terms of its constituent structure.

polysemy: range of meaning in a single word, e.g. *good* as in *good knife*, *good child*, etc.

postposition: the reverse of a preposition, i.e. occurring (as head) at the end rather than the beginning of its phrase and characteristic of left-branching languages.

pragmatic word order: the arrangement of canonical constituents in accord with discourse pressure.

predication: that which is asserted about something.

projection: the learner's positing of grammatical structure not present in his input.

pronominal trace: a pronoun left in the position of an extracted noun phrase, e.g. *it* in *the movie that I saw it*.

propositional cluster: a consciousness-raising device based on verb-argument relations.

pseudo-cleft sentence: a 'focus' construction such as *What (I bought) is (a book)*.

raising: movement of a constituent into an argument position of the sentence. See also **extraction**.

re-analysis: the learner's unconscious submission of holistically learned language 'chunks' to later analytic breakdown.

reference (referential): see **anaphora**.

relative clause: a noun-phrase clausal modifier of the kind (*the claim*) *that they processed*. See also **noun complement**.

relative marker: the relative clause element that is co-referential with the noun phrase modified by the clause.

relativization: the creation of a relative clause.

rheme (rhematic, rhematicity): that information-bearing part of a sentence (i.e. where the new information lies) that 'carries it forward'.

right dislocation: see **dislocation**.

right-branching: see **branching direction**.

stative: the class of verbs and adjectives (e.g. *like, remember, need, tall,* etc.) that denote 'states'. One of their syntactic characteristics is that they do not normally occur in the progressive form (e.g. **I am liking, *He is being tall,* etc.).

structure dependency: the principle that grammatical operations are always necessarily definable with reference to syntactic structure.

structure preservation: the effect of most movement rules in English, where canonical word order is maintained.

subjacency condition: a universal constraint upon movement articulated in terms of the number and kind of constituent boundaries that may be crossed.

subject-predicate: one of two basic sentence-construction types that is found in many languages, as in the English sentence *The elephant's nose* [subject] *is big* [predicate]. See also **topic-comment**.

subject-to-object raising: see **raising**.

subject-to-subject raising: see **raising**.

subordination: clausal relationships of lower-to-higher rank, as in clauses with *because, if, when,* etc. See also **coordination**.

substitution: a 'replacive' grammatical relation between linguistic elements, as with pro-forms.

syllabus: that aspect of the pedagogical programme concerned with the specification of content. See also **curriculum**.

synonymy: equivalence of meaning.

syntactic-semantic distance: the extent to which semantic representation is directly reflected in syntax.

temporal: referring to time.

text: in Hallidayan terms, a passage of discourse manifesting cohesion.

theme (thematic, thematization): the relevance-establishing point of departure of a sentence.

topicalization: the leftward-movement rule that derives constructions like *That I know* from *I know that* in English.

topic-comment: one of two basic sentence-construction types that is found in a number of languages, as in (transliterated) *Elephant* [topic] *nose is big* [comment]. See also **subject-predicate**.

topic-prominence: characteristic of languages with the basic sentence-constituent type topic-comment.

transfer: the influence exerted by one's native language upon the learning of another.

transitive, intransitive: see **transitivity**.

transitivity: characteristic of a verb taking a direct object.

typology: a system of classifying languages by type based on the occurrence of shared characteristics.

universal: see **language universal**.

universal grammar (UG): in the Chomskyan sense, tantamount to the constraints upon the shape of language and its development that are presumed to be programmed in the human species.

verb-argument relation: see **argument**.

zero-derivation: the employment of intransitive verbs as causatives.

Index